CHAMBERS

SUPER-MINI
SPELLING

edited by
Penny Hands

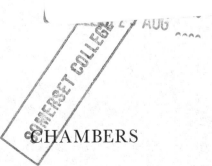

D1460602

CHAMBERS

CHAMBERS

An imprint of Chambers Harrap Publishers Ltd
7 Hopetoun Crescent
Edinburgh EH7 4AY

A CIP catalogue record for this book is available from the British
Library.

ISBN 0-550-14040-9

The publisher would like to acknowledge Catherine Schwarz
for her work on the original text.

Typeset by Chambers Harrap Publishers Ltd, Edinburgh
Printed in Great Britain by Clays Ltd, St Ives plc

Contents

Dewey	Subject headings	
Location DAN	Abstract	
3 week ~~1 week~~ (circled) Reference	Order details 6006D	4.99

Preface

Chambers Super-Mini Spelling has been compiled with a view to providing users with a comprehensive and up-to-date list of words, in a handy-sized format. It has been our concern throughout that words should be easily accessible, since it might be argued that 'if you can't spell a word, you can't look it up in an alphabetical list'. Below are the main features of the dictionary which we hope will make consultation as efficient as possible:

□ A clear, legible typeface is used throughout.

□ Key words and commonly misspelt words are presented in **bold type**.

□ Notes at the beginning of many sections direct the user to other sections where the word they are looking for may be found (eg at 'N' users are reminded that they may need to look under 'PN' or 'KN').

□ Words which may be easily confused (eg *legible/eligible*) are each illustrated by a short example. To give further assistance, these pairs of words are listed at the end of the dictionary.

□ Users who wish to develop their spelling skills will also find a summary of English spelling rules in the appendix. Exceptions to rules regarding parts of verbs and plurals are given in the main text of the dictionary.

Guide to the dictionary

The words in *Chambers Super-Mini Spelling* are listed in straightforward alphabetical order. Plurals and parts of verbs that are liable to cause spelling difficulties are listed under the relevant word.

Plurals

factory	**monkey**	**potato**
pl factories	*pl* monkeys	*pl* potatoes

Parts of verbs

gallop	refer	swim	light
galloped	referred	swam	lit, lighted
galloping	referring	swum	lighting
		swimming	

The part of the verb that is given first under the headword, eg *galloped*, *referred*, *swam*, is the past tense of the verb as in:

    The horse galloped across the field.
    She referred to the subject briefly.
    He swam 20 lengths of the pool before breakfast.

When more than one form is allowable, both have been given, eg *lit*, *lighted* as in:

    She lit (or lighted) the candles.

Where three parts of speech are listed under the headword, the second part listed is the past participle, eg *swum* as in:

    She's swum the Channel three times.

Where only two parts of a verb are listed, the past participle is the same as the past tense, as in:

    The horse has galloped across the field.
    She has already referred to the subject.

The part of the verb given last in every case is the present participle, eg *galloping*, *referring*, *swimming*, *lighting* as in:

    The horse was galloping across the field.
    She is not referring to him.
    He is swimming.
    She is lighting the candles.

Many verbs in English can be spelt with either *-ize* or *-ise*. Which you use is a matter of choice. This guide allows both spellings. Where this is shown in the headword, the alternative is also applicable to the parts of the verb listed below it.

Pronunciation guide

a	as in **hat**	ō	as in **toe**
ä	as in **path**	o͞o	as in **book**
ā	as in **play**	o͞o	as in **moon**
e	as in **leg**	ow	as in **shout**
ē	as in **clean**	u	as in **run**
i	as in **stick**	ū	as in **tune**
ī	as in **side**	ə	as in **infant**
ö	as in **fall**	sh	as in **ship**

A stress mark (') indicates that the syllable following is pronounced with most emphasis.

Abbreviations

pl (s)	plural(s)
compar	comparative
superl	superlative

a

a
a boy: a house: a usual event

aardvark

aback

abacus
pl abacuses

abandon
abandoned
abandoning

abandonment

abase
abased
abasing

abasement

abashed

abate
abated
abating

abatement

abattoir

abbess
pl abbesses

abbey
pl abbeys

abbot

abbreviate
abbreviated
abbreviating

abbreviation

abdicate
abdicated
abdicating

abdication

abdomen

abdominal

abduct

abduction

abductor

abeam

aberrance

aberrancy
pl aberrancies

aberrant

aberration

abet
abetted
abetting

abetter

abeyance

abhor
abhorred
abhorring

abhorrence

abhorrent

abhorrently

abide by
abided by
abode by
abiding by

abiding

ability
pl abilities

abject

abjection

abjectly

abjuration

abjure
abjured
abjuring

ablative

ablaze

able
abler
ablest

able-bodied

ablutions

ably

abnegation

abnormal

abnormality
pl abnormalities

abnormally

aboard
aboard ship

abode

abolish

abolition

abolitionism

abolitionist

A-bomb

abominable

abominably

abominate
abominated
abominating

abomination

aboriginal

aborigine
abort
abortion
abortionist
abortive
abound
about
about-face
about-turn
above
above-board
abracadabra
abrade
 abraded
 abrading
abrasion
abrasive
abrasively
abrasiveness
abreast
abridge
 abridged
 abridging
abridgement,
 abridgment
abroad
 He goes abroad on
 holiday: There's a
 rumour abroad
abrogate
 abrogated
 abrogating
abrogation
abrupt
abruptly
abruptness

abscess
 pl abscesses
abscond
absconder
abseil
 abseiled
 abseiling
absence
absent
absentee
absenteeism
absently
absent-minded
absent-mindedly
absent-mindedness
absinthe
absolute
absolutely
absoluteness
absolution
absolutism
absolutist
absolve
 absolved
 absolving
absorb
absorbed
absorbency
 pl absorbencies
absorbent
absorbing
absorption
abstain
abstainer
abstemious
abstemiously

abstemiousness
abstention
abstinence
abstinent
abstract
abstracted
abstractedly
abstraction
abstruse
abstrusely
absurd
absurdity
 pl absurdities
abulia
abundance
abundant
abundantly
abuse
 abused
 abusing
abusive
abusively
abusiveness
abut
 abutted
 abutting
abutment
abuzz
abysmal
abysmally
abyss
 pl abysses
abyssal
acacia
academe
academic

academically
academy
  pl academies
acanthus
  pl acanthuses
accede
  acceded
  acceding
accelerate
  accelerated
  accelerating
acceleration
accelerator
accent
accentuate
  accentuated
  accentuating
accentuation
accept
  to accept a present: to
  accept his decision
acceptability
acceptable
acceptably
acceptance
access
  access to the
  motorway: He has
  access to his children:
  to access information
  accessed
  accessing
accessibility
accessible
accessibly
accession
accessory
  pl **accessories**

accident
accidental
accidentally
accident-prone
acclaim
acclaimed
acclamation
acclimatization,
  -isation
acclimatize, -ise
  acclimatized
  acclimatizing
acclivity
  pl acclivities
accolade
accommodate
  accommodated
  accommodating
accommodation
accompaniment
accompanist
accompany
  accompanied
  accompanying
accomplice
accomplish
accomplishable
accomplished
accomplishment
accord
accordance
according
accordingly
accordion
accordionist
accost

account
accountability
accountable
accountant
accoutrements
accredit
accreditation
accredited
accrual
accrue
  accrued
  accruing
acculturation
accumulate
  accumulated
  accumulating
accumulation
accumulator
accuracy
accurate
accurately
accursed
accusation
accusative
accuse
  accused
  accusing
accuser
accusingly
accustom
  accustomed
  accustoming
accustomed
ace
acellular
acerbic

acerbity
acetate
acetic
acetic acid
acetone
acetylene
ache
ached
aching
achievable
achieve
achieved
achieving
achievement
achiever
achy
compar achier
superl achiest
acid
acidic
acidity
acidly
ack-ack
acknowledge
acknowledged
acknowledging
**acknowledge-
ment**,
acknowledgment
acme
the acme of perfection
acne
acne on his face
acolyte
acorn
acoustic
acoustically

acoustics
acquaint
acquaintance
acquaintanceship
acquainted
acquiesce
acquiesced
acquiescing
acquiescence
acquiescent
acquiescently
acquire
acquired
acquiring
acquisition
acquisitive
acquit
acquitted
acquitting
acquittal
acre
acreage
acrid
acridly
acrimonious
acrimoniously
acrimony
acrobat
acrobatic
acrobatically
acrobatics
acronym
acropolis
across
acrostic

acrylic
act
acting
action
actionable
action-packed
activate
activated
activating
activation
active
actively
activist
activity
pl activities
actor
actress
pl actresses
actual
actually
actuarial
actuary
pl actuaries
actuate
actuated
actuating
acuity
acumen
acupressure
acupuncture
acupuncturist
acute
acutely
acuteness
ad
an ad in the paper

adage
adagio
adamant
adamantly
Adam's apple
adapt
adaptability
adaptable
adaptation
adapter
the adapter of a play for TV
adaptor
an adaptor for an electrical plug
add
to add two numbers
added
adding
addendum
pl addenda
adder
addict
addicted
addiction
addictive
addition
the addition of the numbers: an addition to the family
additional
additionally
additive
addle
addled
addling
add-on

address
pl addresses
addressed
addressing
addressee
adduce
adduced
adducing
adducible
adenoidal
adenoids
adept
adeptly
adequacy
adequate
adequately
adhere
adhered
adhering
adherence
adherent
adhesion
adhesive
ad hoc
adieu
pl adieus, adieux
ad infinitum
adipose
adjacent
adjectival
adjectivally
adjective
adjoin
adjoined
adjoining
adjoining

adjourn
adjourned
adjournment
adjudge
adjudged
adjudging
adjudgement
adjudicate
adjudicated
adjudicating
adjudication
adjudicator
adjunct
adjust
adjustable
adjustment
adjutant
ad-lib
ad-libbed
ad-libbing
admin
administer
administered
administering
administrate
administrated
administrating
administration
administrative
administratively
administrator
admirable
admirably
admiral
admiralty
admiration
admire

admired
admiring
admirer
admiring
admiringly
admissibility
admissible
admissibly
admission
admit
  admitted
  admitting
admittance
admittedly
admonish
admonishing
admonishingly
admonition
admonitory
ad nauseum
ado
adobe
adolescence
adolescent
adopt
adopted
adoption
adoptive
adorable
adorably
adoration
adore
  adored
  adoring
adorer
adoring

adoringly
adorn
adornment
adrenal
adrenaline
adrift
adroit
adroitly
adroitness
adulate
  adulated
  adulating
adulation
adulatory
adult
adulterate
  adulterated
  adulterating
adulteration
adulterer
adulteress
  pl adulteresses
adultery
adulterous
adulterously
adumbrate
  adumbrated
  adumbrating
adumbration
advance
  advanced
  advancing
advanced
advancement
advantage
advantaged

advantageous
advantageously
advent
adventitious
adventure
adventurer
adventurous
adventurously
adverb
adverbial
adverbially
adversarial
adversary
  pl adversaries
adverse
  in adverse
  circumstances
adversely
adversity
  pl adversities
advert
advertise
  advertised
  advertising
advertisement
advertiser
advertising
advice
  She gave him good
  advice: an advice
  from the bank
advisability
advisable
advise
  to advise him to go
  advised
  advising

advised
advisedly
adviser
advisory
advocaat
*advocaat and
lemonade*
advocacy
advocate
advocated
advocating
adze
aegis
aeolian
aeon, eon
aerate
aerated
aerating
aeration
aerial
aerially
aerie
see eyrie
aerobatics
aerobic
aerobics
aerodrome
aerodynamic
aerodynamically
aerodynamics
aeronautics
aeroplane
aerosol
aesthete

aesthetic
*That colour scheme is
not very aesthetic*
aesthetically
aesthetics
afar
affability
affable
affably
affair
affect
*Will her nervousness
affect her playing?*
affected
affectedly
affectation
affection
affectionate
affectionately
affective
affectively
affidavit
affiliate
affiliated
affiliating
affiliation
affinity
pl affinities
affirm
affirmation
affirmative
affix
afflict
affliction
affluence
affluent

the affluent society
afford
affordable
afforestation
affray
affront
Afghan
aficionado
afield
afloat
afoot
aforementioned
aforesaid
afraid
afresh
aft
after
afterbirth
after-effect
afterlife
aftermath
afternoon
aftershave
aftertaste
afterthought
afterwards
again
against
agape
agar
agate
age
aged
ageing, aging
aged

ageism
ageist
ageless
agency
  pl agencies
agenda
  pl agendas
agent
age-old
agglomeration
agglutinating
agglutination
agglutinative
aggrandize, -ise
aggrandizement,
  -isement
aggravate
  aggravated
  aggravating
aggravatingly
aggravation
aggregate
aggression
aggressive
aggressively
aggressiveness
aggressor
aggrieved
aggro
aghast
agile
agilely
agility
aging
  see ageing
agism

  see ageism
agist
  see ageist
agitate
  agitated
  agitating
agitated
agitatedly
agitation
agitator
agitprop
agnostic
agnosticism
ago
agog
agonize, -ise
agonized, -ised
agonizing, -ising
agonizingly, -isingly
agony
  pl agonies
agoraphobia
agoraphobic
agrarian
agree
  agreed
  agreeing
agreeable
agreeably
agreement
agricultural
agriculturally
agriculture
aground
ague
ahead

aid
  *aid for the poor: come
  to their aid*
aide
  the president's aide
AIDS
ail
  What ails her?
  ailed
  ailing
aileron
ailing
ailment
aim
aimless
aimlessly
air
  fresh air
  aired
  airing
airbag
airborne
airbrush
  pl airbrushes
air-conditioned
air-conditioner
air-conditioning
aircraft
air-drop
  air-dropped
  air-dropping
airfield
airily
airing
airless
airlift
airline

airlock
airmail
airplane
airport
airship
airsick
airspace
airstrip
airtight
airway
airy
aisle
  the aisle in the church
ajar
akimbo
akin
alacrity
alarm
alarming
alarmist
alarmingly
alarmist
alas!
albatross
  pl albatrosses
albeit
albino
  pl albinos
album
alchemist
alchemy
alcohol
alcoholic
alcoholism
alcove

al dente
alder
alderman
ale
  two pints of ale
alert
alertly
alertness
alfalfa
alfresco
algae
algebra
algebraic
algorithm
alias
  pl aliases
alibi
  pl alibis
alien
alienate
  alienated
  alienating
alienation
alight
  alighted
  alighting
align
  aligned
  aligning
alignment
alike
alimentary
alimony
alive
alkali
alkaline

all
  all of you: all in red
Allah
allay
  to allay his fears
  allayed
  allaying
allegation
allege
  alleged
  alleging
alleged
allegedly
allegiance
allegorical
allegorically
allegory
  *Pilgrim's Progress is
  an allegory*
  pl allegories
allegro
alleluia
all-embracing
allergic
allergy
  *an allergy to certain
  foods*
  pl allergies
alleviate
  alleviated
  alleviating
alleviation
alley
  *a bowling alley: He ran
  down the alley*
  pl alleys
alliance

allied
alligator
alliterate
  Sand, sea and sun
  alliterate
  alliterated
  alliterating
alliteration
alliterative
allocate
  allocated
  allocating
allocation
allot
  allotted
  allotting
allotment
all-out
allow
  allowed
  allowing
allowable
allowance
alloy
all-purpose
all right
all-round
all-rounder
allspice
all-time
allude
  He did not allude to the
  matter
  alluded
  alluding
allure
  allured

alluring
allurement
alluring
alluringly
allusion
  He made no allusion to
  the matter
allusive
allusively
alluvial
alluvium
  pl alluvia
ally
  pl allies
  allied
  allying
alma mater
almanac
almighty
almond
almost
alms
alms-house
aloe
aloft
alone
along
alongside
aloof
aloofly
aloofness
alopecia
aloud
alp
alpaca
alpha

alphabet
alphabetical
alphabetically
alphabetize, -ise
  alphabetized
  alphabetizing
alphanumeric
alphanumerical
alphanumerically
alpine
Alps
already
alright
  = all right
alsatian
also
also-ran
altar
  the bridegroom at the
  altar
alter
  to alter your plans: to
  alter a dress
  altered
  altering
alterable
alteration
  alteration to my plans:
  alteration to my dress
altercation
  The altercation ended
  in blows
al'ternate
'alternate
  alternated
  alternating
al'ternately

alternately hot and cold
alternative
alternatively
You could go by bus — alternatively you could go by train
alternator
although
altimeter
altitude
alto
altogether
altruism
altruistic
altruistically
aluminium
alumnus
pl alumni
alveolar
alveolus
pl alveoli
always
alyssum
Alzheimer's (disease)
am
see **be**
amalgam
amalgamate
amalgamated
amalgamating
amalgamation
amaryllis
amass
amateur
an amateur golf player

amateurish
an amateurish attempt at building a shed
amateurishly
amaze
amazed
amazing
amazement
amazingly
ambassador
ambassadress
pl ambassadresses
amber
ambidexterous, ambidextrous
ambience
ambient
ambiguity
pl ambiguities
ambiguous
ambiguously
ambition
ambitious
ambitiously
ambivalence
ambivalent
ambivalently
amble
ambled
ambling
ambrosia
ambulance
ambush
pl ambushes
ameliorate
ameliorated
ameliorating

amelioration
amen
amenable
amend
to amend the law
amendment
amenity
pl amenities
amethyst
amiable
an amiable young man
amiably
amicable
on amicable terms: an amicable separation
amicably
amid, amidst
amiss
amity
ammonia
ammonite
ammunition
amnesia
amnesic
amnesty
pl amnesties
amoeba
amok, amuck
run amok
among, amongst
Divide the chocolate among all four
amoral
She is quite amoral — she doesn't know right from wrong
amorality

amorous
amorously
amorousness
amorphous
amortize, -ise
  amortized
  amortizing
amount
amp
amperage
ampere
ampersand
amphetamine
amphibian
amphibious
amphitheatre
ample
amplification
amplifier
amplify
  amplified
  amplifying
amplitude
amply
amputate
  amputated
  amputating
amputation
amputee
amuck
  see amok
amulet
amuse
  amused
  amusing
amused

amusedly
amusing
amusingly
amusement
an
  an art: an orange: an
  honour
anabolic
anachronism
anachronistic
anachronistically
anaconda
anaemia
anaemic
anaerobic
anaesthetic
anaesthetist
anaesthetize, -ise
  anaesthetized
  anaesthetizing
anagram
anal
analgesic
analogous
analogy
  pl analogies
analysable
analyse
  analysed
  analysing
analysis
  pl analyses
analyst
analytic
analytical
analytically

anarchic
anarchist
anarchistic
anarchy
anathema
anatomical
anatomically
anatomist
anatomy
ancestor
ancestral
ancestry
anchor
  anchored
  anchoring
anchorage
anchorman
  pl anchormen
anchorwoman
  pl anchorwomen
anchovy
  pl anchovies
ancient
ancillary
and
andante
androgen
androgynous
android
anecdotal
anecdote
anemia
  see anaemia
anemometer
anemone
aneroid barometer

anesthesia
see **anaesthesia**
anesthetic
see **anaesthetic**
aneurysm, aneurism
anew
angel
an angel from heaven:
Be an angel and help
me with this
angelfish
angelic
angelica
angelically
anger
angered
angering
angina
angle
an angle of 90°: a new
angle on the story: to
angle for a job: to
angle the camera
angled
angling
angler
Anglican
anglicism
anglicize, -ise
anglicized
anglicizing
angling
anglophile
anglophone
Anglo-Saxon
angora
angrily

angry
compar angrier
superl angriest
angst
anguish
anguished
angular
animal
animate
animated
animating
animated
animatedly
animation
animator
animosity
aniseed
ankle
anklet
annalist
annals
The Annals of the
Parish: in the annals of
crime
an'nex
to annex a country
'annex, annexe
build an annexe to the
house
annihilate
annihilated
annihilating
annihilation
anniversary
pl anniversaries
annotate
annotated

annotating
annotation
announce
announced
announcing
announcement
announcer
annoy
annoyed
annoying
annoyance
annoying
annoyingly
annual
pl annuals
Christmas annuals
annually
annuity
pl annuities
annul
annulled
annulling
annulment
anodyne
anoint
anomalous
anomaly
pl anomalies
anon
anonymity
anonymous
anonymously
anorak
anorexia (nervosa)
anorexic
another

answer
  answered
  answering
answerable
ant
  He was bitten by an ant
antacid
antagonism
antagonist
antagonistic
antagonistically
antagonize, -ise
  antagonized
  antagonizing
Antarctic
anteater
antecedent
antechamber
antediluvian
antelope
  pl antelope,
  antelopes
antenatal
antenna
  pl antennae,
  antennas
anteroom
anthem
anthology
  pl anthologies
anthracite
anthrax
anthropoid
anthropological
anthropologist
anthropology

antibiotic
antibody
  pl antibodies
anticipate
  anticipated
  anticipating
anticipation
anticlimactic
anticlimax
  pl anticlimaxes
anticlockwise
anticoagulant
antics
anticyclone
antidepressant
antidote
antifreeze
antihero
  pl antiheroes
antihistamine
antimatter
antioxidant
antipasto
  pl antipasti,
  antipastos
antipathy
antiperspirant
antipodes
antiquarian
antiquated
  antiquated ideas
antique
  an antique table: a
  valuable antique
anti-semitic
anti-semitism
antiseptic

antisocial
antithesis
  pl antitheses
antler
antonym
anus
  pl anuses
anvil
anxiety
  pl anxieties
anxious
any
anybody
anyhow
anyone
anyplace
anything
anyway
anywhere
aorta
apart
apartheid
apartment
apathetic
apathetically
apathy
ape
  aped
  aping
aperitif
aperture
apex
  pl apexes, apices
aphid
apiary
  pl apiaries

aphasia
aphorism
aphrodisiac
apiary
 pl apiaries
apices
 see apex
apiculture
apiece
aplomb
apocalypse
apocalyptic
apocryphal
apogee
apologetic
apologetically
apologize, -ise
 apologized
 apologizing
apology
 pl apologies
apoplectic
apoplexy
a posteriori
apostle
apostrophe
apothecary
 pl apothecaries
apotheosis
 pl apotheoses
appal
 appalled
 appalling
apparatus
 pl apparatuses,
 apparatus
apparel

apparent
apparently
apparition
appeal
 appealed
 appealing
appear
 appeared
 appearing
appearance
appease
 appeased
 appeasing
appeasement
appellant
appellate
appendage
appendectomy
appendicitis
appendix
 pl appendixes,
 appendices
appertain
 appertained
 appertaining
appetite
appetizer
appetizing, -ising
applaud
applause
apple
appliance
applicable
applicant
application
applicator

appliqué
apply
 applied
 applying
appoint
appointee
appointment
apportion
 apportioned
 apportioning
apposite
appositeness
apposition
appraisal
appraise
 appraised
 appraising
appraiser
appreciable
appreciably
appreciate
 appreciated
 appreciating
appreciation
appreciative
apprehend
apprehension
apprehensive
apprehensively
apprentice
apprenticeship
apprise
 apprised
 apprising
approach
 pl approaches
approachable

approbation
appropriate
 appropriated
 appropriating
appropriately
appropriateness
appropriation
approval
approve
 approved
 approving
approvingly
approximate
 approximated
 approximating
approximately
approximation
après-ski
apricot
April
a priori
apron
apropos of
apse
apt
aptly
aptitude
aptness
aqualung
aquamarine
aquaplane
aquarium
 pl aquaria
Aquarius
aquatic
aqueduct

aquiline
Arab
arabesque
arable
arachnid
arbiter
arbitrarily
arbitrariness
arbitrary
arbitrate
 arbitrated
 arbitrating
arbitration
arbitrator
arboretum
 pl arboreta
arbour
arc
 the arc of a circle: arc
 lamp
arcade
arcane
arch
 pl arches
archaeological
archaeologist
archaeology
archaic
archaically
archangel
archbishop
archdeacon
archduchess
archduke
arched
archeology

 see archaeology
archer
archery
archetypal
archetype
archipelago
 pl archipelagos,
 archipelagoes
architect
architectural
architecturally
architecture
archives
archivist
archway
Arctic
ardent
ardour
arduous
arduousness
are
 see be
area
 pl areas
arena
aren't
 = are not
areola
 pl areolae
argosy
 pl argosies
argot
arguable
arguably
argue
 argued

arguing
argument
argumentative
argumentatively
aria
  pl arias
arid
aridity
Aries
arise
  arose
  A problem arose
  arisen
  A problem has arisen
  arising
aristocracy
aristocrat
aristocratic
aristocratically
arithmetic
arithmetical
arithmetically
arithmetician
ark
  Noah's ark
arm
armada
  pl armadas
armadillo
  pl armadillos
armaments
armband
armchair
armed
armful
armistice

armorial
armour
armoured
armoury
  pl armouries
armpit
army
  pl armies
A-road
aroma
  pl aromas
aromatherapist
aromatherapy
aromatic
arose
  see arise
around
arousal
arouse
  aroused
  arousing
arpeggio
arraign
arraignment
arrange
  arranged
  arranging
arrangement
arras
array
  arrayed
  arraying
arrears
arrest
arresting
arrival

arrive
  arrived
  arriving
arrogance
arrogant
arrogate
  arrogated
  arrogating
arrogation
arrow
arrowroot
arse
arsehole
arsenal
arsenic
arson
arsonist
art
artefact, artifact
arterial
artery
  pl arteries
artesian well
artful
artfully
arthritic
arthritis
arthropod
artichoke
article
articulate
  articulated
  articulating
articulately
articulation
artifact

see **artefact**
artifice
artificial
artificiality
artificially
artillery
artisan
artist
  a portrait artist: a
  concert artist
artiste
  a circus artiste
artistic
artistically
artistry
artless
artwork
arty
as
asbestos
asbestosis
ascend
  ascended
  ascending
ascendancy,
  ascendency
ascendant,
  ascendent
ascension
ascent
  the ascent of the
  mountain: ascent to
  the throne
ascertain
ascertainable
ascetic
  Monks lead ascetic

lives
ascetically
asceticism
ascribable
ascribe
  ascribed
  ascribing
asexual
ash
ashamed
ashamedly
ashen
ashes
ashore
ashtray
aside
asinine
ask
askance
askew
asleep
asp
asparagus
aspartame
aspect
asperity
aspersion
asphalt
asphyxia
asphyxiate
  asphyxiated
  asphyxiating
asphyxiation
aspic
aspidistra

aspirant
aspirate
  aspirated
  aspirating
aspiration
aspire
  aspired
  aspiring
aspirin
aspiring
ass
  pl asses
assail
  assailed
  assailing
assailant
assassin
assassinate
  assassinated
  assassinating
assassination
assault
assay
  an assay of gold
assemblage
assemble
  assembled
  assembling
assembly
  pl assemblies
assent
  The Queen gave her
  assent to the new Bill
assert
assertion
assertive
assertively

assertiveness
assess
assessment
assessor
asset
  pl assets
assiduity
assiduous
assiduousness
assign
  assigned
  assigning
assignation
assignment
assimilable
assimilate
  assimilated
  assimilating
assimilation
assist
assistance
assistant
assizes
associate
  associated
  associating
association
associative
assonance
assuredly
assorted
assortment
assuage
  assuaged
  assuaging
assume

assumed
assuming
assumption
assurance
assure
  assured
  assuring
aster
asterisk
astern
asteroid
asthma
asthmatic
asthmatically
astigmatic
astigmatism
astir
astonish
astonishment
astound
astounded
astounding
astoundingly
astrakhan
astral
astray
astride
astringency
astringent
astrologer
astrological
astrologically
astrology
  Astrology deals with
  the signs of the zodiac
astronaut

astronomer
astronomical
astronomically
astronomy
  He is studying physics
  and astronomy
astrophysicist
astrophysics
astute
astuteness
asunder
asylum
asymmetric
at
atavism
atavistic
ate
  see eat
atelier
atheism
atheist
athlete
athletic
athletically
athletics
atlas
  pl atlases
atmosphere
atmospheric
atmospherically
atmospherics
atoll
atom
atomic
atomize, -ise
  atomized

atomizing
atomizer
atone
  atoned
  atoning
atonement
atrium
  pl atria, atriums
atrocious
atrociousness
atrocity
  pl atrocities
atrophy
  atrophied
  atrophying
attach
  attached
  attaching
attaché
attaché-case
attachment
attack
attacker
attain
attainable
attainment
attempt
attend
attendance
attendant
attention
attentive
attentively
attentiveness
attenuate
  attenuated

attenuating
attenuation
attest
attestation
attic
attire
  attired
  attiring
attitude
attitudinize, -ise
  attitudinized
  attitudinizing
attorney
  pl attorneys
attract
attraction
attractive
attractively
attractiveness
attributable
attribute
  attributed
  attributing
attribution
attributive
attrition
attune
  attuned
  attuning
aubergine
auburn
auction
  auctioned
  auctioning
auctioneer
audacious
audacity

audibility
audible
audibly
audience
audio-typist
audio-visual
audit
  audited
  auditing
audition
auditor
auditorium
  pl auditoriums,
  auditoria
auditory
au fait
augment
augmentation
augur
  His behaviour did not
  augur well for the
  future.
  augured
  auguring
'August
au'gust
auk
aunt
  her aunt and uncle
auntie
au pair
aura
  pl auras, aurae
aural
  = of hearing
  Her aural facilities
  were impaired

aurally
aurora
  pl auroras, aurorae
auspices
auspicious
austere
austerely
austerity
authentic
authentically
authenticate
  authenticated
  authenticating
authentication
authenticity
author
authoritarian
authoritative
authority
  pl authorities
authorization,
  -isation
authorize, -ise
  authorized
  authorizing
autism
autistic
autobiographical
autobiography
  pl autobiographies
autocracy
  autocracies
autocrat
autocratic
autocue
autograph

automat
automate
  automated
  automating
automatic
automatically
automation
automaton
  pl automatons,
  automata
automobile
automotive
autonomous
autonomy
autopilot
autopsy
  pl autopsies
auto-reverse
autumn
autumnal
auxiliary
  pl auxiliaries
avail
  availed
  availing
availability
available
avalanche
avant-garde
avarice
avaricious
avatar
avenge
  avenged
  avenging
avenger

avenue
aver
  averred
  averring
average
  averaged
  averaging
averse
  I'm not averse to work
aversion
avert
aviary
  pl aviaries
aviation
aviator
avid
avidity
avocado
avocet
avoid
avoidable
avoidably
avoidance
avoirdupois
avow
avowal
avowed
avowedly
avuncular
await
awake
  awoke
  awaking
  awoken
awaken
  awakened
  awakening

award
aware
awareness
awash
away
awe
awe-inspiring
awesome
awestruck
awful
awfully
awfulness

awhile
awkward
awkwardly
awkwardness
awl
  the cobbler's awl
awning
awoke
awry
axe
  an axe for chopping wood

  pl axes
axed
axing
axiom
axiomatic
axis
  pl axes
  turning on an axis
axle
aye
azalea
azure

b

babble
  babbled
  babbling
baboon
baby
  pl babies
  babied
  babying
babyhood
babyish
babysit
  babysat
  babysitting
babysitter
bachelor
bachelorhood

bacillus
  pl bacilli
back
backache
backbench
backbencher
backbiting
backbone
backbreaking
backcloth
backcomb
backdate
  backdated
  backdating
backdrop

backer
backfire
  backfired
  backfiring
backgammon
background
backhand
backhanded
backing
backlash
backlog
backpack
backpacker
backpacking
back-pedal

back-pedalled
back-pedalling
backside
backslide
backslid
backsliding
backspace
backspaced
backspacing
backstage
backstroke
backtrack
backup
backward
backwards
backwater
bacon
bacteria
bacterial
bacteriologist
bacteriology
bacterium
pl bacteria
bad
a bad boy
compar worse
superl worst
bade
see **bid**
badge
badger
badgered
badgering
badly
compar worse
superl worst
badminton

bad-tempered
baffle
baffled
baffling
bag
bagged
bagging
bagatelle
bagel
baggage
bagginess
baggy
compar baggier
superl baggiest
Baghdad
baguette
bagpipes
Bahamas
bail
to pay bail: to bail him
out of prison
bailed
bailing
bailiff
bait
baited
He baited his line
baiting
baize
bake
baked
baking
baker
bakery
pl bakeries
balaclava
balalaika

balance
balanced
balancing
balcony
pl balconies
bald
balderdash
baldness
bale
a bale of cotton
baleful
balefully
bale out
to bale out of an
aircraft: to bale out
water
baled out
baling out
balk, baulk
balked, baulked
balking, baulking
ball
a ball of wool: a tennis
ball: a formal ball
ballad
ballast
ballcock
ballerina
ballet
balletic
ballet shoes
ballistic
balloon
ballot
to vote in a secret
ballot
balloted
balloting

ballpark
ballpoint
ballroom
balm
balmy
balsa (wood)
balti
balustrade
bamboo
bamboozle
  bamboozled
  bamboozling
ban
  pl bans
  government bans on
  smoking
  banned
  banning
banal
banality
  pl banalities
banana
band
bandage
  bandaged
  bandaging
bandana
bandeau
  pl bandeaux
bandit
bandstand
bandwagon
bandy
  bandied
  bandying
bandy(-legged)
bane

bang
banger
bangle
banish
banishment
banister
banjo
  pl banjos, banjoes
bank
banker
banknote
bankrupt
bankruptcy
banner
banns
  marriage banns
banquet
  banqueted
  banqueting
banshee
bantam
banter
bantering
baptism
baptismal
baptist
baptize, -ise
  baptized
  baptizing
bar
  barred
  barring
barb
barbarian
barbaric
barbarically

barbarity
  pl barbarities
barbecue
  barbecued
  barbecuing
barbed
barber
barbershop
barbiturate
bard
bare
  to bare one's teeth
  bared
  baring
bare
  bare legs
bareback
barefaced
barefoot
barely
bareness
bargain
  bargained
  bargaining
barge
  barged
  barging
bargepole
baritone
barium
bark
barley
barmaid
barman
  pl barmen
bar mitzvah
barmy

barn
hay in the barn
barnacle
barnyard
barometer
baron
He has the title of baron: Baron Smith of Baberton
baroness
pl baronesses
baronet
baronetcy
baroque
barracks
barracuda
barrage
barrel
barren
barren fields: a barren woman
barrenness
barricade
barricaded
barricading
barrier
barring
barrister
barrow
bartender
barter
bartered
bartering
basal
basalt
base
This paint has an oil

base: the base of his spine: to use the office as a base: to base an argument on facts
based
basing
baseball
baseline
basement
bash
bashful
bashfully
basic
basically
basil
basilica
basilisk
basin
basis
pl bases
bask
basket
basket-ball
bas-relief
bass [bās]
the bass singer
pl basses
the basses in the choir
bass [bas]
pl bass
The fisherman caught several bass
bassist
bassoon
bastard
bastardize
bastardized

bastardizing
baste
basted
basting
bastion
bat
batted
batting
batch
pl batches
bated
with bated breath
bath
to bath the baby
bathed
bathing
bathe
to bathe in the sea: to bathe a wound
bathed
bathing
bather
bathos
bathrobe
bathroom
bathtub
bathysphere
batik
batman
baton
a policeman's baton
batsman
battalion
batten
The joiner put up a batten
batter
battered

battering

battery
pl batteries

battle
battled
battling

battle-axe

battledress

battlement

battleship

batty

bauble

baulk
see **balk**

bauxite

bawdiness

bawdy

bawl
The child began to bawl

bay
bayed
baying

bayonet

bazaar, bazar
an Eastern bazaar: a church bazaar

bazooka

be
to be helpful
am, is, are
was, were
been
he has been: they have been
being
He is being funny: a human being

beach
a sandy beach
pl beaches

beachcomber

beachcombing

beacon

bead

beadle

beady

beagle

beak

beaker

beam

bean
a French bean

beansprout

beanshoot

beanstalk

bear
a brown bear: I can't bear the noise: to bear the strain: to bear children
bore
He bore it
borne
I have borne it
bearing

bearable

beard

bearded

beardless

bearer

bearing

bearskin

beast

beastliness

beastly

beat
to beat someone at tennis
beat
He beat her
beaten
He has beaten her

beatific

beatifically

beatify
beatified

beatifying

beatitude

beatnik

beau [*bō*]
Her latest beau is very handsome

beautiful

beautifully

beauteous

beautician

beautify
beautified
beautifying

beauty
pl beauties

beaver

beaver away
beavered away
beavering away

becalmed

became
see **become**

because

beck

beckon

beckoned
beckoning

become
became
He became a doctor
become
He has become a doctor
becoming

becoming

bed
bedded
bedding

bedazzle
bedazzled
bedazzling

bedbug

bedclothes

bedding

bedeck

bedevil
bedevilled
bedevilling

bedevilment

bedlam

bedpan

bedraggled

bedridden

bedrock

bedroom

bedsit

bedsitter

bedspread

bed-wetting

bee
a honey bee

beech

pl beeches
a beech tree

beef

beefburger

beefeater

beefy

beehive

beekeeper

beeline

been
see **be**

beep

beeper

beer
a pint of beer

beeswax

beet
sugar beet

beetle

beetling

beetroot

befall
befell
What befell him?
befallen
What has befallen you?
befalling

befit
befitted
befitting

befittingly

before

beforehand

befriend

befuddle
befuddled

befuddling

beg
begged
begging

began
see **begin**

beget
begot
begotten

beggar

beggarly

begin
began
It began to rain
begun
It has begun to rain
beginning

begonia

begrudge
begrudged
begrudging

beguile
beguiled
beguiling

begun
see **begin**

behalf

behave
behaved
behaving

behaviour

behavioural

behaviourism

behead

behest

behind

behold
beheld

beholding
beholden
beholder
beige
being
see **be**
bejewelled
belabour
belaboured
belabouring
belated
belatedly
belch
beleaguer
beleaguered
beleaguering
belfry
pl belfries
belie
belied
belying
belief
to show his belief in God
believable
believe
to believe in God
believed
believing
belittle
belittled
belittling
bell
a church bell
belladonna
bell-bottoms
bell-boy

belle
the belle of the ball
belles-lettres
bellicose
belligerence
belligerent
bellow
Bulls bellow
bellows
bell-ringer
belly
pl bellies
bellyache
belly-dance
belly-danced
belly-dancing
belly-dancer
belly-flop
bellyful
belong
belonged
belonging
belongings
beloved
below
below the level
belt
beluga
belying
see **belie**
bemoan
bemoaned
bemoaning
bemuse
bemused
bemusing
bench

pl benches
benchmark
bend
bent
bending
bendy
beneath
benediction
benefactor
benefice
beneficial
beneficially
beneficiary
pl beneficiaries
benefit
benefited
benefiting
benevolence
benevolent
benign
benignly
bent
see **bend**
benzine
bequeath
bequeathed
bequeathing
bequest
berate
berated
berating
bereaved
bereavement
bereft
beret
She wore a blue beret
bergamot

beriberi

berk

berry
a holly berry
pl berries

berserk

berth
a berth on a ship
berthed
berthing

beryl

beseech
beseeched,
besought
beseeching

beseechingly

beset
beset
besetting

beside
beside the tree

besides
*Others, besides him,
will come*

besiege
besieged
besieging

besmirch

besom

besotted

bespoke

best
see **good**

bestial

bestiality

bestially

bestiary

pl bestiaries

bestir
bestirred
bestirring

bestow

bestowal

best-seller

best-selling

bet
bet, (*rare*) betted
betting

beta

beta-blocker

betel

bête noire
pl bêtes noires

betray
betrayed
betraying

betrayal

betroth

betrothal

betrothed

better
bettered
bettering

better
see **good**

betterment

betting
see **bet**

between
*Divide the chocolate
between you and your
sister: between
London and New York*

bevel
bevelled

bevelling

beverage

bevy
pl bevies

bewail
bewailed
bewailing

beware

bewilder
bewildered
bewildering

bewitch

beyond

bhangra

biannual

bias
biased, biassed
biasing, biassing

bib

bible

biblical

bibliographer

bibliographic

bibliography
pl bibliographies

bibliophile

bicameral

bicarbonate

bicentenary

bicentennial

biceps

bicker
bickered
bickering

bicycle

bid
bid, bade [*bad*]

He bid 10: He bade him farewell
bidding
biddable
bidder
bide
bided, bode
biding
bidet
biennial
biennially
bier
a funeral bier
bifocal
bifocals
bifurcate
bifurcated
bifurcating
big
compar bigger
superl biggest
bigamist
bigamous
bigamy
bigger, biggest
see **big**
bighead
big-headed
bight
= a bay
the Great Australian Bight
bigot
bigoted
bigotry
bigwig
bijou

bike
biker
bikini
pl bikinis
bilateral
bilberry
pl bilberries
bile
bilge
bilingual
bilingualism
bilious
biliousness
bill
billboard
billet
billeted
billeting
billet doux
pl billets-doux
billiards
billion
billionaire
billionairess
pl billionairesses
billionth
billow
billposter
bimbo
bin
binary
bind
bound
books bound in leather: to be bound to lose
binding

binder
bindweed
binge
binged
binging
bingo
binoculars
biochemical
biodegradable
biographer
biographical
biography
pl biographies
biological
biologically
biologist
biology
bionic
biopsy
pl biopsies
biorhythm
biplane
birch
pl birches
bird
birdie
bird-watcher
Biro®
birth
the birth of her child
birthday
birthmark
birthplace
birthright
biscuit
bisect

bisexual
bishop
bishopric
bison
bistro
bit
  see **bite**
bitch
  pl bitches
bitchiness
bitchy
bite
  Did the dog bite the man?
  bit
  The dog bit me
  bitten
  The dog has bitten me
bitter
bittern
bitterness
bittersweet
bitty
bitumen
bivouac
  bivouacked
  bivouacking
bi-weekly
bizarre
  clowns wearing bizarre costumes: We met in bizarre circumstances
blab
  blabbed
  blabbing
blabber
black

blackberry
  pl blackberries
blackbird
blackboard
blackcurrant
blacken
  blackened
  blackening
blackguard
blackhead
blackjack
blackleg
blacklist
blackmail
  blackmailed
  blackmailing
blackmailer
blackness
blackout
blacksmith
bladder
blade
blame
  blamed
  blaming
blameless
blanch
blancmange
bland
blandishments
blank
blanket
  blanketed
  blanketing
blare
  blared
  blaring

blarney
blasé
blaspheme
  blasphemed
  blaspheming
blasphemous
blasphemy
blast
blast-off
blatant
blaze
  blazed
  blazing
blazer
blazon
  blazoned
  blazoning
bleach
  pl bleaches
bleak
bleakness
blearily
bleary
bleat
bleed
  bled
  bleeding
bleep
bleeper
blemish
  pl blemishes
blend
blender
bless
  blessed
  blessing
blew

see blow

blether

blight

blimey

blimp

blind

blindfold

blinding

blindness

blink

blinkered

blinkers

blip

bliss

blissful

blissfully

blister
  blistered
  blistering

blithe

blithely

blitz

blizzard

bloated

bloater

blob

bloc
  the Eastern bloc of nations

block
  a block of wood: a block of flats: to block a pipe

blockade
  blockaded
  blockading

blockage

blockbuster

blockhead

bloke

blond
  blond hair

blonde
  She's a beautiful blonde

blood

bloodbath

bloodcurdling

bloodhound

bloodshed

bloodstained

bloodsucker

bloodthirsty

bloody

bloom
  bloomed
  blooming

blossom
  blossomed
  blossoming

blot
  blotted
  blotting

blotch
  pl blotches

blotchy

blotter

blotting-paper

blouse

blow
  blew
  He blew the trumpet
  blown

He has blown the trumpet
  blowing

blow-by-blow

blow-dry
  blow-dried
  blow-drying

blower

blowhole

blowlamp

blowtorch
  pl blowtorches

blowy

blowzy

blubber
  blubbered
  blubbering

bludgeon
  bludgeoned
  bludgeoning

blue
  a blue sky

bluebell

blueberry
  pl blueberries

bluebird

bluebottle

blue-chip

blue-collar

blueprint

blues

bluff

blunder
  blundered
  blundering

blunderbuss
  pl blunderbusses

blunt

blur
 blurred
 blurring

blurb

blurt out

blush
 pl blushes

bluster
 blustered
 blustering

boa

boa constrictor

boar
 a wild boar

board
 a board of directors: a wooden board: to board a ship: to board up a window: to board at a guest house

boarder

boarding

boarding-card

boarding-pass

boardroom

boast
 to boast about his achievements

boastful

boastfully

boat

boater

boathook

boathouse

boating

boatswain, bosun

bob
 bobbed
 bobbing

bobbin

bobsleigh

bobtail

bode
 boded
 boding

bodge
 bodged
 bodging

bodice

bodily

bodkin

body
 pl bodies

body-building

bodyguard

bodysuit

bodywork

boffin

bog down
 bogged down
 bogging down

bogey
 pl bogeys

boggle
 boggled
 boggling

boggy

bogie

bogus

bohemian

boil
 boiled
 boiling

boiler

boisterous

bold

bolero

bollard

bollocks

bolshie, bolshy

bolster up
 bolstered up
 bolstering up

bolt

bomb
 bombed
 bombing

bombard

bombardment

bombastic

bomber

bombshell

bombsite

bonanza

bond

bondage

bonding

bone

bonehead

bonfire

bong

bongo

bonhomie

bonk

bonkers

bonnet

bonny
 a plump, bonny baby

bonsai

bonus
pl bonuses

bony
bony elbows: bony fist

boo
booed
booing

booby

boogie

book

bookable

bookcase

bookie
to bet with a bookie

bookish

book-keeping

booklet

bookmaker

bookmark

bookseller

bookshelf
pl bookshelves

bookshop

boom
boomed
booming

boomerang

boon

boor
an ill-mannered boor

boorish

boost
*to boost his
self-confidence: to
boost his resistance to
polio*

booster

boot

bootee
a baby's bootee

booth
pl booths

bootleg

booty
*booty from the
wrecked ship*

booze
boozed
boozing

booze-up

borage

borax

border
bordered
bordering

borderline

bore
see **bear**

bore
*He's a tiresome bore:
to bore a hole: to bore
him with a long
speech*
bored
a bored listener
boring

boredom

born
*His mother died when
he was born*

borne
see **bear**

borough
*Boroughs have royal
charters*

borrow

borstal

borzoi

bosom

boss
pl bosses

bossa nova

bossy

bosun
see **boatswain**

botanical

botanically

botanist

botany

botch

both

bother
bothered
bothering

bothersome

bothy
pl bothies

bottle
bottled
bottling

bottleneck

bottom
bottomed
bottoming

bottomless

botulism

boudoir

bouffant

**bougainvillaea,
bougainvillea**

bough
the bough of a tree

bought
 see **buy**
bouillabaisse
bouillon
boulder
boulevard
bounce
 bounced
 bouncing
bouncer
bouncy
bound
 see **bind**
bound
 bounded
 The dog bounded
 over to us
 bounding
boundary
 pl boundaries
boundless
bounteous
bountiful
bounty
 pl bounties
bouquet
 a bouquet of flowers
bouquet garni
bourgeois
bourgeoisie
bout
boutique
bovine
bow [*bow*]
 to bow one's head
 bowed
 bowing

bow [*bō*]
 a bow in her hair
bowdlerize
 bowdlerized
 bowdlerizing
bowels
bower
bowl
bow-legged
bowler
bowling
bowls
box
 pl boxes
boxer
boxing-glove
boxwood
boy
 a fair-haired boy
boycott
 boycotted
 boycotting
boyfriend
boyhood
boyish
boyishness
bra
brace
 braced
 bracing
bracelet
braces
bracing
bracken
bracket
 bracketed
 bracketing

brackish
bradawl
brae (*Scots*)
 a steep brae
brag
 bragged
 bragging
braggart
braid
braille
brain
 brained
 braining
brainchild
 pl brainchildren
brainless
brainstorm
brainstorming
brainteaser
brainwash
brainwashing
brainwave
brainy
braise
 braised
 braising
brake
 to put on the car
 brake: to brake going
 round a corner
 braked
 braking
braless
bramble
bran
branch
 pl branches

brand

brandish

brand-new

brandy
pl brandies

brash

brass
pl brasses

brasserie

brassière
What size of brassière?

brassily

brassy

brat

bravado

brave

bravely
braved
braving

bravery

bravo

bravura

brawl

brawn

brawny

bray
The ass began to bray
brayed
braying

brazen

brazen it out
brazened it out
brazening it out

brazier
a brazier of burning coal

brazil-nut

breach
a breach of the peace: a breach in the defences: to breach their defence
pl breaches

bread
a loaf of bread

breaded

breadfruit

breadline

breadth

breadwinner

break
to break a leg
broke
He broke a cup
broken
He has broken a cup
breaking

breakable

breakage

breakaway

breakdancing

breakdown

breaker

breakfast

break-in

breaking-point

breakneck

breakout

breakthrough

break-up

breakwater

bream

breast

breastbone

breastfeed
breastfed
breastfeeding

breaststroke

breath
a breath of air: take a breath

breathalyse
breathalysed
breathalysing

breathalyser

breathe
to breathe in
breathed
breathing

breather

breathing

breathless

breathtaking

breathy

bred
see **breed**

breech
the breech of a gun: a breech delivery of a child

breeches

breed
bred
He bred cocker spaniels
breeding

breeze

breezily

breezy

brethren

breve

breviary
  pl breviaries
brevity
brew
brewery
  pl breweries
brewing
briar, brier
bribe
  bribed
  bribing
bribery
bric-à-brac
brick
bricklayer
bridal
  bridal party
bride
bridegroom
bridesmaid
bridge
  bridged
  bridging
bridle
  a horse's bridle: to
  bridle in anger
  bridled
  bridling
brief
briefcase
briefing
briefly
briefs
brier
  see briar
brigade
brigadier

brigand
bright
brighten
  brightened
  brightening
brill
brilliance
brilliant
brim
  brimmed
  brimming
brimful
brimless
brimstone
brine
bring
  brought
  bringing
brink
briny
brioche
briquette
brisk
brisket
bristle
  bristled
  bristling
bristly
brittle
broach
  to broach the subject
  broached
  broaching
broad
broadcast
  broadcast
  broadcasting

broadcaster
broaden
  broadened
  broadening
broad-minded
broadness
broadsheet
brocade
broccoli
brochure
brogue
broil
broiler
broke, broken
  see break
broken-hearted
broker
brokerage
bromide
bronchial
bronchitic
bronchitis
brontosaurus
bronze
bronzed
brooch
  a silver brooch
  pl brooches
brood
broody
brook
broom
broomstick
broth
brothel
brother

brotherhood
brother-in-law
  pl brothers-in-law
brotherly
brougham
brought
  see bring
brouhaha
brow
browbeat
  browbeat
  browbeating
brown
brownie
  pl brownies
browning
browse
  browsed
  browsing
bruise
  bruised
  bruising
brunch
brunette
brunt
brush
  pl brushes
brush-off
brush-up
brusque
brusquely
brusqueness
brussels sprout
brutal
brutality
brutalize
  brutalized

brutalizing
brutally
brute
brutish
bubble
  bubbled
  bubbling
bubbly
buccal
buccaneer
buccaneering
buck
bucket
  bucketed
  bucketing
bucketful
buckle
  buckled
  buckling
buckler
buckram
buckshot
buckskin
buckwheat
bucolic
bud
  budded
  budding
Buddhism
Buddhist
buddleia
buddy
budge
  budged
  budging
budgerigar

budget
  budgeted
  budgeting
budgetary
budgie
buff
buffalo
  pl buffaloes
buffer
buffet ['bŏōfā]
  the station buffet: a
  buffet supper
buffet ['bufit]
  Heavy waves buffet
  the boat
  buffeted
  buffeting
buffoon
buffoonery
bug
  bugged
  bugging
bugbear
bug-eyed
bugger
buggery
buggy
  pl buggies
bugle
bugler
build
  built
  building
builder
build-up
built-up
bulb

bulbous
bulge
 bulged
 bulging
bulghar wheat
bulgy
bulimia
bulk
bulkhead
bulkily
bulky
bull
bulldog
bulldoze
 bulldozed
 bulldozing
bulldozer
bullet
bulletin
bullet-proof
bullfight
bullfighter
bullfinch
bullfrog
bullion
bullish
bullock
bullring
bull's-eye
bullshit
 bullshitted
 bullshitting
bully
 pl bullies
 bullied
 bullying

bulrush
 pl bulrushes
bulwark
bum
bumbag
bumble
 bumbled
 bumbling
bumble-bee
bumf, bumph
bump
bumper
bumpkin
bumptious
bumptiousness
bumpy
bun
bunch
 pl bunches
bundle
 bundled
 bundling
bung
bungalow
 pl bungalows
bungee
bungle
 bungled
 bungling
bunion
bunk
bunk-bed
bunker
bunkum
bunny
 pl bunnies

bunsen burner
bunting
buoy
 a mooring buoy
buoyancy
buoyant
bur
 see burr
burble
 burbled
 burbling
burden
 burdened
 burdening
burdensome
burdock
bureau
 pl bureaux, bureaus
bureaucracy
 pl bureaucracies
bureaucrat
bureaucratic
bureau de change
burgeon
 burgeoned
 burgeoning
burger
burgh
 Burgh is a Scots form
 of 'borough'
burglar
burglary
 pl burglaries
burgle
 burgled
 burgling
burial

buried
  see bury
burlesque
burly
burn
  burnt, burned
  burning
burner
burnish
burp
burr, bur
burrow
bursar
bursary
  pl bursaries
burst
  burst
  bursting
bury
  to bury the corpse
  buried
  burying
bus
  pl buses
bush
  pl bushes
bushed
bushel
bushman
bushy
busier, busiest
  see busy
busily
business
  pl businesses

businesslike
businessman
  pl businessmen
businesswoman
  pl businesswomen
busk
busker
bust
bustard
bustle
  bustled
  bustling
bust-up
busty
busy
  compar busier
  superl busiest
but
  no-one but her: But I
  didn't know
butane
butch
butcher
butchery
butler
butt
  to butt in
butter
buttercup
butterfingers
butterfly
  pl butterflies
buttermilk
butterscotch

buttocks
button
  buttoned
  buttoning
buttonhole
buttress
  pl buttresses
buxom
buy
  to buy a new car
  bought
  buying
buyer
buyout
buzz
buzzard
buzzer
by
  written by him: Stand
  by me!
bye
  a bye in cricket
bye-bye
by-election
bygone
by-law, bye-law
bypass
  bypassed
  bypassing
by-product
bystander
byte
byword

C

If the word you're looking for sounds as if it begins *ch* but you can't find it there, remember that **C** on its own can sometimes be pronounced *ch* (as in *cello, cellist*), as can **CZ** (*Czech*).

cab
cabaret
cabbage
caber
cabin
cabinet
cable
  cabled
  cabling
cabriolet
cacao
cache
  a cache of jewels
cachet
cack-handed
cackle
  cackled
  cackling
cacophonous
cacophony
cactus
  pl cacti, cactuses
cad
cadaver
cadaverous
caddie
  a golf caddie
  pl caddies
caddish

caddy
  a tea caddy
  pl caddies
cadence
cadenza
cadet
cadge
  cadged
  cadging
cadger
cadre
caesarean
café
cafeteria
  pl cafeterias
cafetière
caffeine
caftan
  see **kaftan**
cage
  caged
  caging
cagey, cagy
cagily
cagoule
cahoots
cairn
cairngorm
Cairo

cajole
  cajoled
  cajoling
cajolery
Cajun
cake
  caked
  caking
calabash
calabrese
calamine
calamitous
calamity
  pl calamities
calciferous
calcify
  calcified
  calcified
calcium
calculable
calculate
  calculated
  calculating
calculation
calculator
calculus
caldera
calendar
calf
  a cow and her calf: the

calf of his leg
pl calves
calibrate
  calibrated
  calibrating
calibration
calibre
calico
call
caller
calligrapher
calligraphy
calling-card
callipers, calipers
callisthenic
callisthenics
callosity
callous
  hard-hearted and
  callous
callow
callus
  a callus on the skin
  pl calluses
calm
calmness
calorie
calorific
calorimeter
calque
calumnious
calumny
  pl calumnies
calvary
calve
  When will the cow
  calve?

calved
calving
calypso
  pl calypsos
cam
camaraderie
camber
came
  see come
camel
camellia
cameo
  pl cameos
camera
  pl cameras
camiknickers
camisole
camomile,
chamomile
camouflage
  camouflaged
  camouflaging
camp
campaign
  campaigned
  campaigning
campaigner
campanologist
campanology
camper
camphor
camping
campion
campsite
campus
  pl campuses

camshaft
can
  could
  He could go now
can
  canned
  They canned the
  tomatoes
  canning
canal
canary
  pl canaries
canasta
cancan
cancel
  cancelled
  cancelling
cancer
cancerous
candelabrum
  pl candelabra,
  candelabrums
candid
candidacy
candidate
candidature
candied
candle
candlelight
candlelit
candlestick
candlewick
candour
candy
  pl candies
candyfloss
cane

caned
caning
canine
caning
canister
canker
cankerous
cannabis
canned
  see **can**
cannelloni
cannery
  pl canneries
cannibal
cannibalism
cannibalistic
cannibalize
cannily
cannon
  a cannon in battle
cannonball
cannon into
  cannoned into
  cannoning into
cannot
canoe
  pl canoes
  canoed
  canoeing
canon
  a deacon and a
  canon: a canon of the
  saints: a law or canon
canonization,
  -isation
canonize, -ise
  canonized

canonizing
canoodle
  canoodled
  canoodling
can-opener
canopy
  pl canopies
cant
  jargon and cant: a
  cant or slope: Did the
  boat cant?
  canted
  canting
can't
  = cannot
  I can't go
cantankerous
cantata
  pl cantatas
canteen
canter
  cantered
  cantering
canticle
cantilever bridge
canto
canton
canvas
  canvas for painting: a
  canvas tent
  pl canvases
canvass
  to canvass for votes
  canvassed
  canvassing
canvasser
canyon
cap

capped
capping
capability
  pl capabilities
capable
capably
capacious
capacitor
capacity
  pl capacities
cape
caper
  capered
  capering
capercaillie,
  capercailzie
capillary
  pl capillaries
capita
capital
capitalism
capitalist
capitalistic
capitalization
capitalize, -ise
  capitalized
  capitalizing
capitation
capitulation
capitulate
  capitulated
  capitulating
capitulation
capon
capped
  see **cap**
cappuccino

caprice
capricious
Capricorn
capsicum
capsize
  capsized
  capsizing
capstan
capsule
captain
  captained
  captaining
captaincy
  pl captaincies
caption
captious
captivate
  captivated
  captivating
captivation
captive
captivity
captor
capture
  captured
  capturing
car
carafe
caramel
caramelization,
  -isation
caramelize, -ise
  caramelized
  caramelizing
carapace
carat
  18 carat gold

caravan
caravanette
caravanning
caravanserai
caraway
carbine
carbohydrate
carbolic
carbon
carbonaceous
carbonate
carbonated
carboniferous
carbuncle
carburettor,
  carburetter
carcase, carcass
carcinogen
carcinogenic
card
cardamom
cardboard
cardiac
cardigan
cardinal
cardiogram
cardiologist
cardiology
cardiovascular
cardphone
care
  cared
  caring
career
careerism

carefree
careful
carefully
carefulness
careless
carelessness
career
  careered
  careering
carer
caress
  pl caresses
  caressed
  caressing
caretaker
careworn
cargo
  pl cargoes
Caribbean
caribou
caricature
caricaturist
caries
carillon
caring
carmine
carnage
carnal
carnation
carnival
carnivore
carnivorous
carob
carol
  carolled
  carolling

carotene
carousal
carouse
  caroused
  carousing
carousel
carp
carpal
  a carpal in the hand
carpel
  the carpel of a plant
carpenter
carpentry
carpet
  carpeted
  carpeting
carpetbagger
carriage
carriageway
carried
  see **carry**
carrier
carrion
carrot
  grated carrot
carry
  carried
  carrying
carrycot
carry-on
carry-out
cart
  a horse and cart
carte blanche
cartel
carthorse
cartilage

  cartilage in the knee
cartilaginous
cartographer
cartography
carton
  a carton of milk
cartoon
  a Walt Disney cartoon
cartoonist
cartouche
cartridge
  a cartridge for a gun:
  film cartridge
cartwheel
carve
  carved
  carving
carvery
  pl carveries
carving-knife
  pl carving-knives
cascade
  cascaded
  cascading
case
  cased
  casing
casement
cash
  to cash a cheque:
  ready cash
cashew
cashier
  cashiered
  cashiering
cashmere
casing

casino
  pl casinos
cask
casket
cassava
casserole
cassette
cassock
cassowary
  pl cassowaries
cast
  the cast of a play: a
  cast in his eye: to cast
  a play: to cast a glance
  cast
  casting
castanets
castaway
caste
  a social caste
caster
  see **castor**
castigate
  castigated
  castigating
castigation
cast-iron
castle
cast-off
castor, caster
castor-oil
castor, caster sugar
castrate
  castrated
  castrating
castration
castrato

pl castrati, castratos

casual

casually

casualty
  pl casualties

cat

cataclysm

cataclysmic

catacomb

catalepsy

catalogue
  catalogued
  cataloguing

catalyst

catamaran

cataplexy

catapult

cataract

catarrh

catastrophe

catastrophic

catastrophically

catatonia

catatonic

catcall

catch
  caught
  catching

catch-all

catching

catchment

catchpenny

catchphrase

catchword

catchy

catechism

catechize
  catechized
  catechizing

categorical

categorically

categorize
  categorized
  categorizing

category
  pl categories

cater
  catered
  catering

caterer

catering

caterpillar

caterwauling

catfish

catgut

catharsis
  pl catharses

cathartic

cathedral

catherine-wheel

catheter

cathode ray tube

catholic

Catholic

catkin

catnap

cat-o'-nine-tails

cattery
  pl catteries

cattle

catty

catwalk

caucus

caught
  see catch

cauldron

cauliflower

causal

causality

causative

cause
  caused
  causing

causeway

caustic

caustically

cauterize, -ise
  cauterized
  cauterizing

caution
  cautioned
  cautioning

cautionary

cautious

cavalcade

cavalier
  Cavaliers and Roundheads: a cavalier attitude

cavalry
  infantry and cavalry

cave

caveat

cave in
  caved in
  caving in

caveman
  pl cavemen

cavern
cavernous
caviare, caviar
cavil
  cavilled
  cavilling
caving
cavity
  pl cavities
cavort
cavy
  pl cavies
caw
cayenne
cayman
CD-player
cease
  ceased
  ceasing
ceasefire
ceaseless
cedar
cede
  ceded
  ceding
cedilla
Ceefax®
ceilidh
ceiling
  He painted the ceiling white
celandine
celebrate
  celebrated
  celebrating
celebration
celebratory

celebrity
  pl celebrities
celeriac
celery
celestial
celibacy
celibate
cell
  a prison cell: a battery cell: a living cell: a monk's cell
cellist
cello
cellophane®
cellular
  cellular blankets
cellulite
celluloid
cellulose
  cellulose paint
cement
cemetery
  pl cemeteries
cenotaph
censor
  a film censor: to censor letters
  censored
  censoring
censorial
censorious
censorship
censure
  to censure a naughty child
  censured
  censuring

census
  pl censuses
cent
  a dollar and a cent
centaur
centenarian
  She is a centenarian
centenary
  She celebrated her centenary
  pl centenaries
centennial
centigrade
centigramme
centilitre
centimetre
centipede
central
centrality
centralization, -isation
centralize, -ise
  centralized
  centralizing
centrally
centrally-heated
centre
centrefold
centre-forward
centre-half
centrepiece
centrifugal
centrifuge
centurion
century
  pl centuries

ceramic
cereal
breakfast cereal: barley and other cereals
cerebral
ceremonial
ceremonious
ceremony
pl ceremonies
cerise
ceroc
certain
certainly
certainty
pl certainties
certifiable
certificate
certify
certified
certifying
certitude
cervical
cervix
pl cervices
cessation
cession
cesspit
cesspool
chador
chafe
My shoes chafe my heels: to chafe at the delay
chafed
chafing
chaff

to chaff each other good-naturedly
chaffed
chaffing
chaffinch
pl chaffinches
chagrin
chain
chained
chaining
chainmail
chainsaw
chain-smoker
chair
chaired
chairing
chairlift
chairman
pl chairmen
chairperson
chairwoman
pl chairwomen
chaise longue
pl chaises longues
chalet
chalice
chalk
chalky
challenge
challenged
challenging
chamber
chamberlain
chambermaid
chamberpot
chameleon
chamois, shammy

champ
champagne
champion
championed
championing
championship
chance
chanced
chancing
chancel
chancellery
pl chancelleries
chancellor
chancer
chancery
pl chanceries
chancy
chandelier
chandler
change
changed
changing
changeable
changeless
changeling
change-over
channel
channelled
channelling
chant
chanter
chanterelle
chantry
pl chantries
chanty
see shanty
chaos

chaotic
chaotically
chap
chapati, chapatti
chapel
chaperone
  chaperoned
  chaperoning
chaplain
chaplaincy
  pl chaplaincies
chapped
chapter
char
  charred
  charring
charabanc
character
characteristic
characteristically
characterization,
  -isation
characterize, -ise
  characterized
  characterizing
characterless
charade
charcoal
charge
  charged
  charging
chargeable
charger
chariot
charioteer
charisma

charismatic
charitable
charitably
charity
  pl charities
charlatan
charm
charmer
charming
charmless
charnel-house
chart
  charted
  *They have charted the
  coastline*
  charting
charter
  chartered
  We chartered a plane
  chartering
charwoman
chary
chase
  chased
  *The dog chased the
  cat*
  chasing
chasm
chassis
chaste
  a chaste woman
chasten
  chastened
  chastening
chastise
  chastised
  chastising
chastisement

chastity
chat
  chatted
  chatting
château
  pl châteaux
chattels
chatter
  chattered
  chattering
chatterbox
chattily
chattiness
chatty
chauffeur
chauffeuse
chauvinism
chauvinist
chauvinistic
cheap
  at a cheap price
cheapen
  cheapened
  cheapening
cheapskate
cheat
check
  *a police check on
  cars: to check the oil:
  to check a sum*
checked
  a checked dress
check-in
checklist
checkmate
check-out
checkpoint

check-up

cheek

cheekbone

cheekily

cheeky

cheep
*the cheep of a bird: to
cheep merrily*
cheeped
cheeping

cheer
cheered
cheering

cheerful

cheerfully

cheerily

cheerio

cheerleader

cheerless

cheers

cheery

cheese

cheeseburger

cheesecake

cheesecloth

cheeseparing

cheesy

cheetah

chef

chef d'œuvre
pl chefs d'œuvre

chemical

chemically

chemist

chemistry

chemotherapy

chenille

cheque
a bank cheque

chequebook

chequered
a chequered career

cherish

cheroot

cherry
pl cherries

cherub
pl cherubs, cherubim

chervil

chessboard

chess

chest

chesterfield

chestnut

chesty

chevron

chew

chewing-gum

chewy

chic [*shēk*]

chicane

chicanery

chick

chicken

chicken out
chickened out
chickening out

chickenfeed

chickenpox

chickpea

chickweed

chicory

chide
chided
chiding

chief

chiefly

chieftain

chiffon

chignon

chihuahua

chilblain

child
pl children

childbearing

childbirth

childhood

childish

childless

childlike

childminder

childproof

children
see child

Chile

chill

chilli, chili
*chilli pepper: chili con
carne*
pl chillies, chilies

chilling

chilly
a chilly wind

chime
chimed
chiming

chimerical

chimney
pl chimneys

chimneypot
chimney-sweep
chimpanzee
chin
china
chinchilla
chink
chinless
chintz
chintzy
chip
  chipped
  chipping
chipboard
chipmunk
chipolata
chiromancy
chiropodist
chiropody
chiropractic
chiropractor
chirp
chirpily
chirpy
chirrup
  chirruped
  chirruping
chisel
  chiselled
  chiselling
chit
chit-chat
chitterlings
chivalrous
chivalry
chive

chivvy
  chivvied
  chivvying
chlorinate
  chlorinated
  chlorinating
chlorine
chloroform
chlorophyll
chock-a-block
chock-full
chocolate
choice
choir
  a church choir: a
  children's choir
choirboy
choirgirl
choke
  choked
  choking
choker
cholera
cholesterol
chomp
choose
  to choose a book
  chose
  He chose a book
  chosen
  He has chosen a book
  choosing
choosy
chop
  chopped
  chopping
chopper

chopping-board
choppy
chopsticks
choral
chorale
chord
  a musical chord: the
  chord of a circle
chore
choreograph
choreographer
choreography
chorister
chortle
  chortled
  chortling
chorus
  pl choruses
chose, chosen
  see choose
chough
choux
chow
chowder
christen
  christened
  christening
Christian
Christianity
Christmas
Christmassy
chromatic
chrome
chromium
chromosome
chronic

chronically
chronicle
chronicler
chronological
chronologically
chronology
chronometer
chrysalis
chrysanthemum
chub
chubby
chuck
chuckle
 chuckled
 chuckling
chuffed
chum
chummy
chunk
chunky
church
 pl churches
churchgoer
churchwarden
churchyard
churlish
churlishness
churn
chute
 a rubbish chute: The
 child slid down the
 chute
chutney
 pl chutneys
cicada
cider

cigar
cigarette
cigarette-lighter
cinch
cinder
cinema
cinematic
cinematographer
cinematography
cinnamon
cipher
circa
circle
 circled
 circling
circuit
circuitous
circular
circularity
circulate
 circulated
 circulating
circulation
circulatory
circumcise
 circumcised
 circumcising
circumcision
circumference
circumflex
circumlocution
circumnavigate
 circumnavigated
 circumnavigating
circumscribe
 circumscribed

circumscribing
circumspect
circumstances
circumstantial
circumstantiate
 circumstantiated
 circumstantiating
circumvent
circus
 pl circuses
cirrus clouds
cissy
 pl cissies
cistern
citadel
citation
cite
 *to cite as proof: to cite
 as a divorce co-
 respondent*
 cited
 citing
citizen
citizenship
citizenry
citric acid
citrus fruit
cittern
city
 pl cities
civet
civic
civics
civil
civilian
civility
 pl civilities

civilization, -isation
civilize, -ise
  civilized
  civilizing
civilly
civvies
clack
  clacked
  clacking
clad
cladding
claim
  claimed
  claiming
claimant
clairvoyance
clairvoyant
clam
clamber
  clambered
  clambering
clammy
clamorous
clamour
clamp
clam up
  clammed up
  clamming up
clampdown
clan
clandestine
clandestinely
clang
clanger
clank
clannish
clansman

pl clansmen
clanswoman
  pl clanswomen
clap
  clapped
  clapping
clapper
clapperboard
claptrap
claret
clarification
clarify
  clarified
  clarifying
clarinet
clarinettist
clarion
clarity
clash
  pl clashes
clasp
class
  pl classes
classic
classically
classical
classicism
classicist
classics
classifiable
classification
classify
  classified
  classifying
classless
classmate

classroom
classy
clatter
  clattered
  clattering
clause
claustrophobia
claustrophobic
clavichord
clavicle
claw
clay
clayey
claymore
clean
  cleaned
  cleaning
cleaner
cleanliness
cleanness
cleanse
  cleansed
  cleansing
cleanser
clean-shaven
clear
  cleared
  clearing
clearance
clear-cut
clearly
clearness
clearway
cleavage
cleave
cleaver

clef

cleft

clematis

clemency

clement

clementine

clench

clergy

clergyman

cleric

clerical

clerk

clever

cleverness

cliché

click

client

clientele

cliff

cliffhanger

climactic

climate

climatic

climatological

climax
  pl climaxes

climb

climbable

climb-down

climber

clime

clinch
  pl clinches

cling
  clung
  clinging

clinger

clingfilm

clingy

clinic

clinical

clinically

clinician

clink

clip
  clipped
  clipping

clipboard

clipper

clique

cliquey

clitoris
  pl clitorises

cloak

cloakroom

clobber

cloche

clock

clockwatcher

clockwise

clockwork

clod

clodhopper

clog
  clogged
  clogging

cloister

cloistered

clone

cloned

cloning

clonk

close [*klōs*]

closely

close [*klōz*]
  closed
  closing

closeness

closet

closet with
  closeted with
  closeting with

close-up

closure

clot
  clotted
  clotting

cloth
  pl cloths
  dish cloths

clothe
  clothed
  clothing

clothes
  bedclothes: children's
  clothes

clothing

cloud

cloudburst

cloudless

cloudy

clove

cloven-hoofed

clover

clown

cloy
  cloyed
  cloying

club

clubbed
clubbing
clubhouse
cluck
clue
 pl clues
clueless
clump
clumsily
clumsiness
clumsy
clung
 see cling
cluster
 clustered
 clustering
clutch
 pl clutches
clutter
 cluttered
 cluttering
coach
 pl coaches
coagulant
coagulate
 coagulated
 coagulating
coagulation
coal
coalesce
 coalesced
 coalescing
coalescence
coalface
coalfield
coalition
coarse

coarse sand: *a coarse
sense of humour*
coarsely
coarsen
 coarsened
 coarsening
coarseness
coast
coastal
coaster
coastguard
coastline
coat
 coated
 coating
coat-hanger
co-author
coax
cob
cobalt
cobble
 cobbled
 cobbling
cobbler
cobra
cobweb
cocaine
coccyx
 pl coccyxes,
 coccyges
cochineal
cochlea
 pl cochleae
cock
cockade
cockatoo
cockatrice

cockerel
cocker spaniel
cockfighting
cockily
cockle
cockleshell
cockney
cockpit
cockroach
 pl cockroaches
cockscomb
cocksure
cocktail
cocky
cocoa
coconut
cocoon
 cocooned
 cocooning
cod
coda
coddle
 coddled
 coddling
code
codeine
codger
codicil
codification
codify
 codified
 codifying
co-driver
codswallop
coeducation
co-educational

coefficient
coerce
 coerced
 coercing
coercion
coercive
coeval
coexist
coexistence
co-existent
coffee
coffer
coffin
cog
cogency
cogent
cogitate
 cogitated
 cogitating
cogitative
cognac
cognate
cognition
cognitive
cognizance, -isance
cogwheel
cohabit
 cohabited
 cohabiting
cohabitation
cohere
 cohered
 cohering
coherence
coherent
cohesion

cohesive
cohort
coiffeuse
coiffure
coil
 coiled
 coiling
coin
 coined
 coining
coinage
coincide
 coincided
 coinciding
coincidence
coincidental
coke
coital
coitus
coke
cola
colander
cold
cold-blooded
cold-hearted
coldness
cole
coleslaw
colic
colicky
coliseum
colitis
collaborate
 collaborated
 collaborating
collaboration

collaborator
collaborative
collaboratively
collaborator
collage
 *The children made a
 collage*
collagen
collapse
 collapsed
 collapsing
collapsible
collar
 collared
 collaring
collarbone
collarless
collate
 collated
 collating
collateral
collation
collator
colleague
collect
collectable
collection
collective
collectively
collectivism
collector
college
 college and university
collegiate
collide
 collided
 colliding

collie

collier

colliery
 pl collieries

collision

collocate
 collocated
 collocating

collocation

colloquial

colloquialism

colloquially

colloquium
 pl colloquia

colloquy
 pl colloquies

collusion

collusive

collywobbles

cologne

colon

colonel

colonial

colonialism

colonialist

colonially

colonic

colonist

colonization,
 -isation

colonize, -ise
 colonized
 colonizing

colonnade

colony
 pl colonies

colophon

colorant

colossal

colostomy

colour
 coloured
 colouring

colourful

colourfully

colourless

colt

coltish

coltsfoot

columbine

column

columnist

coma
 in a deep coma

comatose

comb

combat
 combated
 combating

combatant

combination

combine
 combined
 combining

combine harvester

combustible

combustion

come
 came
 He came today
 come
 He has come
 coming

comeback

comedian

comedienne

comedown

comedy
 pl comedies

comeliness

comely

comestible

comet

come-uppance

comfit

comfort

comfortable

comfortably

comforter

comfrey

comic

comical

comically

coming
 see come

comity

comma
 a comma or a full stop

command

commandant

commandeer
 commandeered
 commandeering

commander

commandment

commando
 pl commandoes

commemorate
commemorated
commemorating
commemoration
commemorative
commence
commenced
commencing
commencement
commend
commendable
commendation
commensurable
commensurate
comment
commentary
pl commentaries
commentate
commentated
commentating
commentator
commerce
commercial
commercialism
commercialization
commercialize
commercialized
commercializing
commercially
commis
commiserate
commiserated
commiserating
commiseration
commissar
commissarial

commissariat
commissary
pl commissaries
commission
commissionaire
commissioned
commissioning
commissionaire
a cinema commissio-
naire
commissioner
the High
Commissioner
commit
committed
committing
commitment
committal
committee
commode
commodious
commodity
pl commodities
commodore
common
commoner
common-law
commonplace
Commonwealth
commotion
communal
commune
communed
communing
communicable

communicate
communicated
communicating
communication
communicative
communion
communiqué
communism
communist
community
pl communities
commutable
commutative
commute
commuted
commuting
commuter
compact
compactness
companion
companionable
companionably
companionship
company
pl companies
comparable
comparably
comparative
comparatively
compare
compared
comparing
comparison
compartment
compass
a compass to find the

direction
pl compasses
The climbers carried compasses

compasses
Use compasses to draw a circle

compassion
compassionate
compassionately
compatibility
compatible
compatibly
compatriot
compel
compelled
compelling
compendious
compendium
pl compendiums, compendia
compensate
compensated
compensating
compensation
compensatory
compère
compete
competed
competing
competence
competent
competition
competitive
competitor
compilation
compile

compiled
compiling
compiler
complacency
complacent
complain
complained
complaining
complainant
complaint
complaisant
complement
the complement of a verb: the complement of an angle: make up a full complement
complementary
complementary angles: a complementary amount
complete
completely
completed
completing
completeness
completion
complex
pl complexes
complexion
complexity
pl complexities
compliance
compliant
complicate
complicated
complicating
complication
complicity

complied
see **comply**
compliment
a compliment to a beautiful woman
complimentary
complimentary remark: complimentary ticket
comply
complied
complying
component
comport
comportment
compose
composed
composing
composer
composite
composition
compositor
compos mentis
compost
composure
compound
comprehend
comprehensibility
comprehensible
comprehension
comprehensive
comprehensively
comprehensiveness
compress
compression
compressor
comprise

comprised
comprising
compromise
compromised
compromising
compulsion
compulsive
compulsively
compulsorily
compulsory
compunction
computation
compute
computed
computing
computer
computerization,
-isation
computerize, -ise
computerized
computerizing
comrade
comradeship
con
conned
conning
concatenate
concatenated
concatenating
concatenation
concave
concavity
conceal
concealed
concealing
concealment
concede

conceded
conceding
conceit
conceited
conceivable
conceivably
conceive
conceived
conceiving
concentrate
concentrated
concentrating
concentration
concentric
concept
conceptual
conception
conceptualism
conceptualize, -ise
conceptualized
conceptualizing
conceptually
concern
concernedly
concernedness
concerning
concert
a musical concert
concerted
concertina
concerto
pl concertos
concession
concessionary
conciliate
conciliated

conciliating
conciliation
conciliatory
concise
conciseness
conclave
conclude
concluded
concluding
conclusion
conclusive
conclusively
concoct
concoction
concomitant
concord
concordance
concordat
concourse
concrete
concubine
concur
concurred
concurring
concurrence
concurrent
concuss
concussion
condemn
condemned
condemning
condemnation
condemnatory
condensation
condense
condensed

condensing
condenser
condescend
condescending
condescension
condiment
condition
  conditioned
  conditioning
conditional
conditionally
condole
  condoled
  condoling
condolences
condom
condominium
condone
  condoned
  condoning
condor
conducive
conduct
conduction
conductor
conductress
  pl conductresses
conduit
cone
coney
  see cony
confabulate
  confabulated
  confabulating
confabulation
confection
confectioner

confectionery
confederacy
confederate
confederation
confer
  conferred
  conferring
conference
conferencing
conferment
confess
confession
confessional
confessor
confetti
confidant
  the king's trusted
  confidant
confidante
  She was the queen's
  confidante
confide
  confided
  confiding
confidence
confident
  confident of success
confidential
confidentiality
confidentially
configuration
confine
  confined
  confining
confinement
confines
confirm

confirmation
confirmatory
confiscate
  confiscated
  confiscating
confiscation
conflagration
conflate
conflated
conflating
conflation
conflict
confluence
confluent
conform
conformation
conformist
conformity
confound
confounded
confront
confrontation
confuse
  confused
  confusing
confusion
confute
  confuted
  confuting
conga
congeal
  congealed
  congealing
congenial
congenially
congenital

conger eel
congested
congestion
conglomerate
  conglomerated
  conglomerating
conglomeration
congratulate
  congratulated
congratulating
congratulations
congratulatory
congregate
  congregated
  congregating
congregation
congregational
congress
  pl congresses
congressional
congressman
  pl congressmen
congresswoman
  pl congresswomen
congruence
congruent
congruity
congruous
conical
conifer
coniferous
conjectural
conjecture
  conjectured
  conjecturing
conjoin
conjoint

conjugal
conjugate
  conjugated
  conjugating
conjugation
conjunction
conjunctivitis
conjuncture
conjure
  conjured
  conjuring
conjuror
conker
conman
connect
connectable
connection
connector
conned
  see con
connivance
connive at
  connived at
  conniving at
connoisseur
connotation
connotative
connote
  connoted
  connoting
conquer
  conquered
  conquering
conqueror
conquest
conscience
  a bad conscience

conscientious
  a conscientious
  worker
conscientiousness
conscious
  Is the patient con-
  scious now?: *a con-*
  scious decision:
  conscious of his
  disability
consciousness
conscript
conscription
consecrate
  consecrated
  consecrating
consecration
consecutive
consecutively
consensus
consent
consequence
consequent
consequential
consequently
conservable
conservancy
conservation
conservationist
conservatism
conservative
conservatoire
conservatory
  pl conservatories
conserve
  conserved

conserving
consider
 considered
 considering
considerable
considerably
considerate
considerately
consideration
consign
consignment
consist
consistency
consistent
consistory
consolable
consolation
consolatory
console
 consoled
 consoling
consolidate
 consolidated
 consolidating
consolidation
consolidator
consonance
consonant
consonantal
'consort
 the Queen's consort
con'sort
 to consort with
 criminals
consortium
 pl consortia,
 consortiums

conspicuous
conspicuousness
conspiracy
 pl conspiracies
conspirator
conspiratorial
conspire
 conspired
 conspiring
constable
constabulary
constancy
constant
constellation
consternation
constipate
 constipated
 constipating
constipation
constituency
 pl constituencies
constituent
constitute
 constituted
 constituting
constitution
constitutional
constitutionally
constrain
constraint
constrict
constriction
construct
construction
constructive
constructively

construe
 construed
 construing
consul
 He is British consul in
 Spain
consular
consulate
consult
consultancy
consultant
consultation
consultative
consumable
consume
 consumed
 consuming
consumer
consumerism
consummate
 consummated
 consummating
consummation
consumption
consumptive
contact
contactable
contagion
contagious
contain
 contained
 containing
containable
container
containerize, -ise
 containerized
 containerizing

containment
contaminant
contaminate
  contaminated
  contaminating
contamination
contemplate
  contemplated
  contemplating
contemplation
contemplative
contemporaneous
contemporary
contempt
contemptible
contemptibly
contemptuous
contend
contender
content
contented
contention
contentious
contentment
contents
contest
contestable
contestant
context
contextual
contiguity
contiguous
continence
continent
continental
contingency

pl contingencies
contingent
continual
  in continual pain:
  There have been
  continual attacks on
  his life
continually
continuance
continuation
continue
  continued
  continuing
continuity
continuous
  a continuous line of
  cars
continuously
continuum
  pl continua,Z
  continuums
contort
contortion
contortionist
contour
contraband
contrabass
contraception
contraceptive
contract
contractable
contraction
contractor
contractual
contradict
contradiction

contradictory
contralto
  pl contraltos
contraption
contrariness
contrary
contrast
contravene
  contravened
  contravening
contravention
contretemps
contribute
  contributed
  contributing
contribution
contributor
contributory
contrite
contritely
contrition
contrivance
contrive
  contrived
  contriving
control
  controlled
  controlling
controllable
controller
controls
controversial
controversially
controversy
  pl controversies
conundrum

conurbation
convalesce
  convalesced
  convalescing
convalescence
convalescent
convection
convector
convene
  convened
  convening
convener
convenience
convenient
convent
convention
conventional
conventionally
converge
  converged
  converging
convergence
convergent
conversant
conversation
conversational
conversationalist
conversationally
converse
  conversed
  conversing
conversely
conversion
convert
converter
convertible

convex
convexity
convey
  conveyed
  conveying
conveyance
conveyancer
conveyancing
conveyor belt
convict
conviction
convince
  convinced
  convincing
convivial
convivially
conviviality
convocation
convoke
  convoked
  convoking
convoluted
convolvulus
convoy
  convoyed
  convoying
convulse
  convulsed
  convulsing
convulsion
convulsive
convulsively
cony, coney
coo
  cooed
  cooing
cook

cookbook
cooker
cookery
cookie
cooking
cool
coolant
cooler
coolie
coolly
coolness
coop
  a chicken coop
cooper
co-operate
  co-operated
  co-operating
co-operation
co-operative
co-operatively
co-opt
  co-opted
  co-opting
co-optive
coop up
  cooped up
  cooping up
co-ordinate
  co-ordinated
  co-ordinating
co-ordination
co-ordinator
coot
cop
  copped
  copping
cope

coped
coping
copier
co-pilot
coping-stone
copious
cop-out
copper
copper-bottomed
copperplate
coppice
copra
copse
copula
copulate
  copulated
  copulating
copulation
copy
  pl copies
  copied
  copying
copybook
copycat
copyright
copywriter
coquetry
coquette
coquettish
coquettishness
coracle
coral
  a coral reef: a
  necklace of coral
cor anglais
  pl cors anglais

cord
  the cord of a
  dressing-gown:
  spinal cord: vocal
  cords
cordial
cordiality
cordially
cordite
cordless
cordon
  cordoned
  cordoning
cordon bleu
cordon off
  cordoned off
  cordoning off
corduroy
core
  cored
  coring
corer
co-respondent
  the co-respondent in
  a divorce case
corgi
  pl corgis
coriander
cork
corkage
corker
corkscrew
corm
cormorant
corn
cornea
  pl corneas

corner
  cornered
  cornering
corner-stone
cornet
  He plays the cornet:
  ice-cream cornet
cornflakes
cornflour
  to thicken the sauce
  with cornflour
cornflower
  a pretty blue
  cornflower
cornice
cornucopia
cornucopian
corny
corolla
corollary
  pl corollaries
corona
  pl coronae, coronas
coronary
  pl coronaries
coronation
coroner
coronet
  a baron's coronet
corpora
corporal
corporate
corporation
corporeal
corps [*kör*]
  corps of an army:
  corps de ballet

pl corps

corpse
dead as a corpse
pl corpses

corpulence

corpulent

corpuscle

corral
cattle in the corral: a corral of wagons

correct

correction

corrective

correctness

corrector

correlate
correlated
correlating

correlation

correlative

correspond

correspondence

correspondent
a letter from a regular corespondent

corridor

corrigendum
pl corrigenda

corroborate
corroborated
corroborating

corroboration

corroborative

corroborator

corrode
corroded
corroding

corrosion

corrosive

corrugated

corrupt

corruptible

corruption

corset

cortège

cortex
pl cortices

cortical

cortisone

cosh
pl coshes

cosily

cosiness

cosmetic

cosmic

cosmological

cosmologist

cosmology

cosmonaut

cosmopolitan

cosmos

cosset
cosseted
cosseting

cost
cost
*That coat cost £30:
That has cost him his life*
costed
Have you costed the research project?
costing

co-star

co-starred
co-starring

cost-effective

costermonger

costliness

costly

costume

costumier

cosy

cot

cote

coterie

cottage

cottager

cotton

cottongrass

cottonwool

couch
pl couches

couch grass

couchette

cougar

cough

could
see can

couldn't
= could not

coulomb

council
the town council

councillor
a town councillor

counsel
He was her counsel in the divorce case

counsel

to counsel him to stay
counselled
counselling
counsellor
a marriage guidance counsellor
count
countable
countdown
countenance
countenanced
countenancing
counter
countered
countering
counteract
counteractive
counter-attack
counterbalance
counterfeit
counterfoil
countermand
counterpane
counterpart
counterpoint
counter-revolution
counter-revolutionary
countersign
counter-signature
counter-tenor
counterweight
countess
pl countesses
countless
country
pl countries

countryman
pl countrymen
countryside
countrywide
county
pl counties
coup
the president was killed in the coup
couple
coupled
coupling
couplet
coupling
coupon
courage
courageous
courgette
courier
course
the course of the river: in the course of time: in due course
coursebook
courser
coursing
court
courteous
courtesan
courtesy
He behaved with politeness and courtesy
courthouse
courtier
courtly
court-martial

pl courts-martial
court-martialled
court-martialling
courtroom
courtship
courtyard
couscous
cousin
couture
couturier
cove
coven
covenant
covenanter
cover
covered
covering
coverage
coverall
covering
coverlet
covert
cover-up
covet
coveted
coveting
covetous
covetousness
covey
pl coveys
cow
coward
cowardice
cowardly
cowbell
cowboy

cowed
cower
  cowered
  cowering
cowherd
cowl
co-worker
cowpat
cowpox
cowshed
cowslip
cox
coxless
coxcomb
coxswain
coy
coyness
coyote
coypu
  pl coypu, coypus
crab
crabbed
crabby
crack
crackdown
cracker
crackers
crackle
  crackled
  crackling
cracknel
crackpot
cradle
  cradled
  cradling
cradle-snatcher

craft
craftsman
craftily
craftiness
craftsman
  pl craftsmen
craftswoman
  pl craftswomen
crafty
crag
craggy
cram
  crammed
  cramming
crammer
cramp
  cramped
  crampon
cranberry
  pl cranberries
crane
cranefly
  pl craneflies
cranesbill
cranial
crank
crankshaft
cranky
cranny
  pl crannies
crape
  see **crêpe**
crapulence
crapulent
crapulous
crash

  pl crashes
crash-land
  crash-landed
  crash-landing
crass
crassness
crate
crater
cravat
crave
  craved
  craving
craven
crawl
crawler
crayfish
crayon
craze
crazily
crazy
creak
  the creak of the stairs:
  The beams began to
  creak
creaky
cream
  creamed
  creaming
creamer
creamery
creamy
crease
  creased
  creasing
create
  created
  creating

creation
creative
creativity
creator
creature
crèche
credence
credentials
credibility
credible
credibly
credit
  credited
  crediting
creditable
creditor
creditworthy
credo
credulity
credulous
creed
creek
  fishing-boats in the creek: canoeing in the creek
creel
creep
  crept
  creeping
creeper
creepy-crawly
  pl creepy-crawlies
cremate
  cremated
  cremating
cremation

crematorium
crème caramel
crème de la crème
crème fraîche
crenellated
Creole
creosote
crêpe, crape
crept
  see **creep**
crepuscular
crescendo
crescent
cress
crest
crestfallen
cretin
cretinous
crevasse
  a crevasse in the ice
crevice
  a crevice in the rock
crew
crewcut
crib
  cribbed
  cribbing
cribbage
crick
cricket
cricketer
cried
  see **cry**
crier
cries
  see **cry**

crikey
crime
criminal
criminality
criminally
criminologist
criminology
crimson
cringe
  cringed
  cringing
crinkle
  crinkled
  crinkling
crinkly
crinoline
cripple
  crippled
  crippling
crisis
  pl crises
crisp
crispbread
crispy
criss-cross
criterion
  pl criteria
critic
critical
critically
criticism
criticize, -ise
  criticized
  criticizing
critique
croak

croaky
crochet ['krōshā]
  to crochet a shawl
  crocheted
  crocheting
crock
crockery
crocodile
crocus
  pl crocuses
croft
crofter
croissant
crone
crony
  pl cronies
crook
crooked
crookedness
croon
  crooned
  crooning
crooner
crop
  cropped
  cropping
cropper
croquet
croquette
cross
  pl crosses
  crossed
  crossing
crossbar
crossbow
cross-check
cross-country

cross-examine
  cross-examined
  cross-examining
cross-eyed
cross-fertilize
  cross-fertilized
  cross-fertilizing
crossfire
crossing
crossness
crosspatch
cross-question
  cross-questioned
  cross-questioning
cross-refer
  cross-referred
  cross-referring
cross-reference
crossroads
cross-section
cross-stitch
crosswind
crosswise
crossword
crotch
crotchet
  a musical crotchet
crotchety
crouch
croup
croupier
croupy
crow
  crowed,
  (old) crew
  The baby crowed: The
  cock crew

crowing
crowbar
crowd
crowded
crown
crucial
crucially
crucible
crucifix
  pl crucifixes
crucifixion
crucify
  crucified
  crucifying
cruciform
crude
crudely
crudeness
crudity
cruel
cruelly
cruelty
cruet
cruise
  cruised
  cruising
cruiser
crumb
crumble
  crumbled
  crumbling
crumbly
crumby
crumpet
crumple
  crumpled

crumpling
crunch
crunchy
crusade
crusader
crush
crusher
crust
crustacean
crusty
crutch
 pl crutches
crux
cry
 pl cries
 cried
 crying
crybaby
 pl crybabies
cryogenics
crypt
cryptic
cryptically
cryptogram
cryptography
crystal
crystalline
crystallization, -isation
crystallize, -ise
 crystallized
 crystallizing
cub
cubbyhole
cube
cubic

cubicle
cuckold
 cuckolded
 cuckolding
cuckoldry
cuckoo
 pl cuckoos
cucumber
cud
cuddle
 cuddled
 cuddling
cuddly
cudgel
cue
 a cue in billiards: The actor missed his cue
cuff
 pl cuffs
cufflinks
cuisine
cul-de-sac
culinary
cull
culminate
 culminated
 culminating
culmination
culottes
culpability
culpable
culprit
cult
cultivate
 cultivated
 cultivating
cultivation

cultivator
cultural
culture
cultured
cumbersome
cumin
cummerbund
cumulative
cumulus
cuneiform
cunning
cup
 cupped
 cupping
cupboard
cupful
 pl cupfuls
Cupid
cupidity
cupola
cup-tie
cur
curable
curacy
curate
curator
curb
 to act as a curb on his extravagances: Curb your desires!
curd
curdle
 curdled
 curdling
cure
 cured

curing
cure-all
curettage
curette
curfew
curio
  pl curios
curiosity
  pl curiosities
curious
curl
curler
curlew
curlicue
curling
curly
curmudgeon
curmudgeonly
currant
  currants and sultanas:
  black and red currants
currency
  pl currencies
current
  a current of air: an
  electric current: the
  current financial year:
  a current account:
  That rumour is current
curriculum
  pl curricula, curri-
  culums
curriculum vitae
  pl curricula vitae
curry
  pl curries
  curried

currying
curse
  cursed
  cursing
cursive
cursor
cursorily
cursory
curt
curtail
  curtailed
  curtailing
curtailment
curtain
curtain-raiser
curtness
curtsy
  She made a curtsy to
  the queen
  pl curtsies
  curtsied
  curtsying
curvaceous
curvature
curve
  curved
  curving
curvy
cushion
  cushioned
  cushioning
cushy
cusp
cuss
cussed
cussedness
custard

custodial
custodian
custody
custom
customarily
customary
customer
customs
cut
  cut
  cutting
cutaway
cutback
cute
cutely
cuteness
cuticle
cutlass
  pl cutlasses
cutlery
cutlet
cut-off
cutter
cut-throat
cutting
cuttlefish
cut-up
cyanide
cybernetics
cyberspace
cyclamen
cycle
  cycled
  cycling
cyclic
cyclical

cyclist
cyclone
cygnet
  *a swan and her
  cygnet*
cylinder
cylindrical
cylindrically
cymbal
  He plays the cymbals

cynic
cynical
cynically
cynicism
cynosure
cypress
  pl cypresses
Cyprus
Cyrillic

cyst
cystic
cystitis
cytological
cytology
cytoplasm
czar
  see tsar
Czech

d

dab
  dabbed
  dabbing
dabble
  dabbled
  dabbling
dabbler
dachshund
dactyl
dad
daddy
  pl daddies
dado
  pl dadoes, dados
daffodil
daft
dagger
daguerreotype

dahlia
daily
  pl dailies
daintily
daintiness
dainty
daiquiri
dairy
  milk from the dairy
  pl dairies
dais
  pl daises
daisy
  pl daisies
daisy-wheel
dale
dalliance
dally

dallied
dallying
dam
  to dam a river
  dammed
  *He dammed up the
  river*
  damming
damage
  damaged
  damaging
damask
dame
dammed
  see dam
damn
  to damn a soul: *Damn!
  I've dropped it*
  damned

a damned soul: that
damned dog
damning
damnable
damnation
damned
  see **damn**
damp
damp-course
dampen
  dampened
  dampening
dampener
damper
dampness
damp-proof
damsel
damselfly
  pl damselflies
damson
dan
dance
  danced
  dancing
dancer
dandelion
dandruff
dandy
danger
dangerous
dangle
  dangled
  dangling
Danish
dank
dankness
dapper

dappled
dare
  dared
  daring
daredevil
dark
darken
  darkened
  darkening
darkness
darkroom
darling
darn
dart
dartboard
darter
darts
dash
  pl dashes
dashboard
dashing
dastardly
data
  sing datum
databank
database
date
  dated
  dating
dateline
date-stamp
dative
datum
  see **data**
daub
  daubed
  daubing

daughter
daughter-in-law
  pl daughters-in-law
daughterly
daunt
daunting
dauntless
davit
dawdle
  dawdled
  dawdling
dawdler
dawn
day
daybreak
daydream
daydreamer
daylight
daytime
daze
  dazed
  dazing
dazzle
  dazzled
  dazzling
deacon
deaconess
  pl deaconesses
deactivate
  deactivated
  deactivating
deactivation
dead
deaden
  deadened
  deadening
deadline

deadliness
deadlock
deadly
deadness
deadpan
deadweight
deaf
deafen
 deafened
 deafening
deafness
deal
 dealt
 dealing
dealer
dealings
dean
deanery
 pl deaneries
dear
 *a dear friend: The
 shoes are too dear*
dearly
dearness
dearth
death
death-bed
deathly
death-rate
deathtrap
deb
debacle
debar
 debarred
 debarring
debarment

debase
 debased
 debasing
debasement
debatable
debate
 debated
 debating
debauched
debauchery
debenture
debilitate
 debilitated
 debilitating
debilitation
debility
debit
 debited
 debiting
debonair
debrief
debriefing
débris, debris
debt
debtor
debug
 debugged
 debugging
debunk
début, debut
debutante
decade
decadence
decadent
decaff
decaffeinate
 decaffeinated

decaffeinating
decagon
decagonal
decahedral
decahedron
decamp
decant
decanter
decapitate
 decapitated
 decapitating
decapitation
decathlete
decathlon
decay
 decayed
 decaying
decease
deceased
deceit
deceitful
deceitfully
deceive
 deceived
 deceiving
deceiver
decelerate
 decelerated
 decelerating
deceleration
December
decency
decent
decentralization,
 -isation
decentralize, -ise

decentralized
decentralizing
deception
deceptive
deceptively
decibel
decide
decided
deciding
decidedly
decider
deciduous
decilitre
decimal
**decimalization,
-isation**
decimalize, -ise
decimalized
decimalizing
decimate
decimated
decimating
decipher
deciphered
deciphering
decipherable
decision
decisive
decisively
decisiveness
deck
deck-chair
declaim
declaimed
declaiming
declamation
declamatory

declaration
declarative
declare
declared
declaring
declassification
declassify
declassified
declassifying
declension
decline
declined
declining
declivity
pl declivities
decode
decoded
decoding
decoder
décolleté
decommission
decommissioned
decommissioning
decompose
decomposed
decomposing
decomposition
decompress
decompression
decongestant
deconstruction
decontaminate
decontaminated
decontaminating
decontamination
décor, decor
decorate
decorated

decorating
decoration
decorative
decoratively
decorator
decorous
decorum
decoy
decoyed
decoying
decrease
decreased
decreasing
decree
decreed
decreeing
decrepit
decry
to decry modern youth
decried
decrying
dedicate
dedicated
dedicating
dedication
dedicatory
deduce
deduced
deducing
deducible
deduct
deductible
deduction
deductive
deed
deem
deep

deepen
  deepened
  deepening
deep-freeze
deep-fry
  deep-fried
  deep-frying
deeply
deep-rooted
deep-seated
deep-set
deer
  He shot a deer
  pl deer
deerstalker
deface
  defaced
  defacing
defacement
defamation
defamatory
defame
  defamed
  defaming
default
defaulter
defeat
  defeated
  defeating
defeatism
defeatist
defecate
  defecated
  defecating
defecation
defect
defection

defective
defector
defence
defenceless
defend
defendant
defender
defensible
defensive
defensively
defensiveness
defer
  deferred
  deferring
deference
deferential
deferentially
deferment
deferral
defiance
defiant
deficiency
  pl deficiencies
deficient
deficit
defied
  see defy
defile
  defiled
  defiling
defilement
definable
define
  defined
  defining
definite

definitely
definition
definitive
definitively
deflate
  deflated
  deflating
deflation
deflationary
deflect
deflection
deflower
deforest
deforestation
deform
deformed
deformity
  pl deformities
defraud
defray
  defrayed
  defraying
defrayal
defrock
defrost
deft
deftness
defunct
defuse
  defused
  defusing
defy
  defied
  defying
degenerate
  degenerated
  degenerating

degeneration
degenerative
degradable
degradation
degrade
  degraded
  degrading
degree
dehumanize, -ise
  dehumanized
  dehumanizing
dehydrate
  dehydrated
  dehydrating
dehydration
de-ice
de-icer
deification
deify
  deified
  deifying
deign
  deigned
  deigning
deism
deist
deity
  pl deities
déjà vu
dejected
dejection
delay
  delayed
  delaying
delectable
delectably
delectation

delegate
  delegated
  delegating
delegation
delete
  deleted
  deleting
deleterious
deletion
Delhi
deliberate
  deliberated
  deliberating
deliberately
deliberation
delicacy
  pl delicacies
delicate
delicately
delicatessen
delicious
delight
delighted
delightedly
delightful
delightfully
delimit
  delimited
  delimiting
delimitation
delineate
  delineated
  delineating
delineation
delinquency
delinquent

delirious
delirium
deliver
  delivered
  delivering
deliverance
delivery
  pl deliveries
dell
delphinium
delta
delude
  deluded
  deluding
deluge
  deluged
  deluging
delusion
  He's under the
  delusion that he's
  Napoleon
delusive
delusory
de luxe
delve
  delved
  delving
demagogic
demagogue
demagogy
demand
demarcate
  demarcated
  demarcating
demarcation
demean
  demeaned

demeaning
demeanour
demented
dementia
demerara
demerit
demigod
demijohn
demise
demist
demo
demob
  demobbed
  demobbing
demobilization,
  -isation
demobilize, -ise
  demobilized
  demobilizing
democracy
  pl democracies
democrat
democratic
democratically
demographic
demography
demolish
demolition
demon
demonic
demonstrable
demonstrably
demonstrate
  demonstrated
  demonstrating
demonstration

demonstrative
demonstrator
demoralization
demoralize, -ise
  demoralized
  demoralizing
demote
  demoted
  demoting
demotic
demotion
demur
  demurred
  demurring
demure
demurely
demureness
demurral
demystification
demystify
  demystified
  demystifying
den
denationalization,
  -isation
denationalize, -ise
  denationalized
  denationalizing
dendrite
dendrologist
dendron
denial
denied
  see deny
denier
denigrate
  denigrated

denigrating
denim
denizen
denominate
  denominated
  denominating
denomination
denominational
denominator
denotation
denote
  denoted
  denoting
dénouement
denounce
  denounced
  denouncing
dense
densely
denseness
density
  pl densities
dent
dental
dentine
dentist
dentistry
denture
denudation
denude
  denuded
  denuding
denunciation
deny
  denied
  denying
deodorant

deodorize, -ise
  deodorized
  deodorizing
depart
department
departmental
departure
depend
dependable
dependant
  His wife and children
  are his dependants
dependence
dependent
  His wife is dependent
  on him
depersonalize, -ise
  depersonalized
  depersonalizing
depict
depiction
depilatory
deplete
  depleted
  depleting
depletion
deplorable
deplorably
deplore
  deplored
  deploring
deploy
  deployed
  deploying
deployment
depopulate
deport

deportation
deportee
deportment
depose
  deposed
  deposing
deposit
  deposited
  depositing
deposition
depositor
depository
  pl depositories
depot, depôt
depraved
depravity
deprecate
  to deprecate her
  behaviour
  deprecated
  deprecating
deprecation
deprecatory
depreciate
  The pound will
  depreciate
  depreciated
  depreciating
depreciation
depredation
depress
depressant
depressed
depressing
depression
deprivation
deprive

deprived
depriving
depth
deputation
deputize, -ise
  deputized
  deputizing
deputy
  pl deputies
derail
  derailed
  derailing
derailment
deranged
derangement
derby
deregulate
  deregulated
  deregulating
deregulation
derelict
dereliction
deride
  derided
  deriding
de rigueur
derision
derisive
derisively
derisory
derivation
derivative
derive
  derived
  deriving
dermatitis
dermatologist

dermatology
dermis
derogatorily
derogatory
derrick
derring-do
desalinate
desalination
descant
descend
descended
descending
descendant
He is a descendant of Queen Victoria
descendent
a descendent slope
descent
describe
described
describing
description
descriptive
descry
to descry a ship at sea
descried
descrying
desecrate
desecrated
desecrating
desecration
deselect
deselection
desensitize
desensitized
desensitizing
de'sert

to desert from the army: to desert one's family
'desert
a desert island
deserter
desertion
deserts
deserve
deserved
deserving
deservedly
desiccate
desiccated
desiccating
desiccation
desiccator
desideratum
desiderata
design
designed
designing
designate
designated
designating
designation
designer
desirability
desirable
desirably
desire
desired
desiring
desirous
desist
desk
desk-top

desolate
desolated
desolation
despair
despaired
despairing
despatch
see **dispatch**
desperado
pl desperadoes, desperados
desperate
desperately
desperation
despicable
despicably
despise
despised
despising
despite
despoil
despoiled
despoiling
despoliation
despondency
despondent
despot
despotic
despotically
despotism
dessert
the dessert course
dessertspoon
destabilize, -ise
destabilized
destabilizing
destination

destined
destiny
destitute
destroy
  destroyed
  destroying
destroyer
destructible
destruction
destructive
desultorily
desultory
detach
  detached
  detaching
detachable
detachment
detail
  detailed
  detailing
detain
  detained
  detaining
detainee
detect
detectable
detection
detective
detector
détente
detention
deter
  deterred
  deterring
detergent
deteriorate

deteriorated
deteriorating
deterioration
determinant
determination
determine
  determined
  determining
determiner
determinism
deterrent
detest
detestable
detestably
detestation
dethrone
  dethroned
  dethroning
detonate
  detonated
  detonating
detonator
detour
detoxification
detract
detraction
detriment
detrimental
detritus
de trop
deuce
Deutschmark
devaluation
devalue
  devalued
  devaluing

devastate
  devastated
  devastating
devastation
develop
  developed
  developing
developer
development
developmental
deviant
deviate
  deviated
  deviating
deviation
device
  a device for boring
  holes
devil
devilish
devilry
devious
deviousness
devise
  to devise a plan
  devised
  devising
devoid
devolution
  the devolution of
  power from central
  government
devolutionist
devolve
  devolved
  devolving
devote

devoted
devoting
devotedly
devotee
devotion
devour
devout
devoutness
dew
  the morning dew
dewclaw
dewdrop
dewy
dexterity
dexterous, dextrous
dextrose
dhoti
diabetes
diabetic
diabolic
diabolical
diabolically
diachronic
diadem
diagnose
  diagnosed
  diagnosing
diagnosis
  pl diagnoses
diagnostic
diagonal
diagonally
diagram
diagrammatic
dial
  dialled

dialling
dialect
dialectal
dialogue
dialysis
diamanté
diameter
diametric
diametrically
diamond
diaper
diaphanous
diaphragm
diarist
diarrhoea
diary
  *Make a note in your
  diary*
  pl diaries
diatribe
dibble
dice
dicey
dichotomous
dichotomy
  pl dichotomies
dick
dicky
dictate
  dictated
  dictating
dictation
dictator
dictatorial
dictatorially
dictatorship

diction
dictionary
  pl dictionaries
dictum
  pl dictums, dicta
did
  see do
didactic
didactically
diddle
  diddled
  diddling
didgeridoo
didn't
die
  to die young
  died
  He died young
  dying
  dying young
diehard
diesel
diet
  dieted
  dieting
dietary
dietetic
dietician
differ
  differed
  differing
difference
different
differential
differentiate
  differentiated
  differentiating

differentiation
difficult
difficulty
  pl difficulties
diffidence
diffident
diffract
diffraction
diffuse
  diffused
  diffusing
diffusion
dig
  dug
  digging
digest
digestible
digestion
digestive
digger
digit
digital
digitalis
dignified
dignitary
  pl dignitaries
dignity
digress
digression
digs
dike, dyke
dilapidated
dilapidation
dilatation
dilate
  dilated

dilating
dilatory
dildo
dilemma
dilettante
diligence
diligent
dill
dilly-dally
  dilly-dallied
  dilly-dallying
diluent
dilute
  diluted
  diluting
dilution
diluvial
dim
  dimmed
  dimming
dime
dimension
dimensional
diminish
diminuendo
diminution
diminutive
dimmer
dimness
dimple
dimpled
dimwit
din
  dinned
  dinning
dinar

dine
  dined
  dining
diner
ding
ding-dong
dinghy
  a sailing dinghy
  pl dinghies
dinginess
dingo
  pl dingoes
dingy
  dark and dingy
dining-room
dinky
dinner
dinner-jacket
dinosaur
dint
diocesan
diocese
diode
dioxide
dip
  dipped
  dipping
diphtheria
diphthong
diploma
  pl diplomas
diplomacy
diplomat
diplomatic
diplomatically
dipper

dipsomania
dipsomaniac
dipstick
dire
direct
 directed
 directing
direction
directive
directly
directness
director
directorship
directory
 pl directories
dirge
dirigible
dirk
dirndl
dirt
dirtiness
dirty
dirtily
 dirtied
 dirtying
disability
 pl disabilities
disable
 disabled
 disabling
disablement
disabuse
 disabused
 disabusing
disadvantage
disadvantaged
disadvantageous

disaffected
disaffection
disagree
 disagreed
 disagreeing
disagreeable
disagreeably
disagreement
disallow
disappear
 disappeared
 disappearing
disappearance
disappoint
disappointed
disappointment
disapprobation
disapproval
disapprove
 disapproved
 disapproving
disarm
disarming
disarrange
 disarranged
 disarranging
disarrangement
disarray
disassociate
 disassociated
 disassociating
disaster
disastrous
disavow
disavowal
disband

disbandment
disbelief
 He looked at me in
 disbelief
disbelieve
 to disbelieve a story
 disbelieved
 disbelieving
disburse
disbursement
disc, disk
discard
discern
discernible
discernibly
discerning
discernment
discharge
 discharged
 discharging
disciple
disciplinarian
disciplinary
discipline
disclaim
disclaimer
disclose
 disclosed
 disclosing
disclosure
disco
discoloration,
 discolouration
discolour
 discoloured
 discolouring

discomfiture
discomfort
disconcert
disconcerting
disconnect
disconnection
disconsolate
disconsolately
discontent
discontented
discontentment
discontinue
  discontinued
  discontinuing
discord
discordant
discothèque
discount
discourage
  discouraged
  discouraging
discouragement
discourse
  discoursed
  discoursing
discourteous
discourtesy
discover
  discovered
  discovering
discoverer
discovery
  pl discoveries
discredit
  discredited
  discrediting
discreditable

discreet
  asking discreet
  questions
discrepancy
  pl discrepancies
discrete
  split up into three
  discrete groups
discreteness
discretion
discretionary
discriminate
  discriminated
  discriminating
discrimination
discursive
discus
  He throws the discus
  pl discuses
discuss
  to discuss a problem
discussion
disdain
  disdained
  disdaining
disdainful
disdainfully
disease
diseased
disembark
disembarkation
disembodied
disembowel
  disembowelled
  disembowelling
disembowelment
disenchant

disenchanted
disenchantment
disenfranchise
  disenfranchised
  disenfranchising
disenfranchisement
disengage
  disengaged
  disengaging
disengagement
disentangle
  disentangled
  disentangling
disestablish
disestablishment
disfavour
disfigure
  disfigured
  disfiguring
disfigurement
disgorge
  disgorged
  disgorging
disgrace
  disgraced
  disgracing
disgraceful
disgracefully
disgruntled
disguise
  disguised
  disguising
disgust
disgusted
disgusting
dish
  pl dishes

disharmonious
disharmony
dishearten
  disheartened
  disheartening
dishevelled
dishevelment
dishonest
dishonesty
dishonour
dishonourable
dishonourably
dishwasher
dishwater
dishy
disillusion
  disillusioned
  disillusioning
disillusionment
disincentive
disinclined
disinfect
disinfectant
disinformation
disingenuous
disinherit
  disinherited
  disinheriting
disintegrate
  disintegrated
  disintegrating
disintegration
disinter
  disinterred
  disinterring
disinterest

disinterested
disinterestedness
disinterment
disjointed
disk
diskette
dislike
  disliked
  disliking
dislocate
  dislocated
  dislocating
dislocation
dislodge
  dislodged
  dislodging
disloyal
disloyally
disloyalty
dismal
dismally
dismantle
  dismantled
  dismantling
dismay
  dismayed
  dismaying
dismember
  dismembered
  dismembering
dismemberment
dismiss
dismissal
dismissive
dismount
disobedience
disobedient

disobey
  disobeyed
  disobeying
disobliging
disorder
disordered
disorderliness
disorderly
disorganized, -ised
disorient
disorientate
disorientation
disown
disparage
  disparaged
  disparaging
disparagement
disparate
disparity
  pl disparities
dispassionate
dispassionately
dispatch, despatch
  pls dispatches,
  despatches
dispel
  dispelled
  dispelling
dispensable
dispensary
  pl dispensaries
dispensation
dispense
  dispensed
  dispensing
dispenser
dispersal

disperse
 dispersed
 dispersing
dispersion
dispirit
dispirited
dispiriting
displace
 displaced
 displacing
displacement
display
 displayed
 displaying
displease
 displeased
 displeasing
displeasure
disposable
disposal
dispose
 disposed
 disposing
disposition
dispossess
dispossession
disproportionate
disproportionately
disprove
 disproved
 disproving
disputable
disputation
dispute
 disputed
 disputing
disqualification

disqualify
 disqualified
 disqualifying
disquiet
disquieting
disquietude
disregard
disrepair
disreputable
disreputably
disrepute
disrespect
disrespectful
disrespectfully
disrobe
 disrobed
 disrobing
disrupt
disruption
disruptive
dissatisfaction
dissatisfy
 dissatisfied
 dissatisfying
dissect
dissection
dissemble
 dissembled
 dissembling
disseminate
 disseminated
 disseminating
dissemination
dissension

dissent
 dissented
 dissenting
dissenter
dissertation
disservice
dissidence
dissident
dissimilar
dissimilarity
 pl dissimilarities
dissimulate
 dissimulated
 dissimulating
dissimulation
dissipate
 dissipated
 dissipating
dissipation
dissociate
 dissociated
 dissociating
dissociation
dissoluble
dissolute
dissolution
dissolve
 dissolved
 dissolving
dissonance
dissonant
dissuade
 dissuaded
 dissuading
dissuasion
distaff

distance
distanced
distancing
distant
distaste
distasteful
distastefully
distemper
distend
distensible
distension
distil
distilled
distilling
distillation
distiller
distillery
  pl distilleries
distinct
distinction
distinctive
distinctiveness
distinguish
distinguishable
distinguished
distinguishing
distort
distorted
distortion
distract
distracted
distracting
distraction
distraught
distress
distressing

distribute
distributed
distributing
distribution
distributive
distributor
district
distrust
distrustful
distrustfully
disturb
disturbance
disturbed
disturbing
disunite
disunited
disuniting
disunity
disuse
disused
disyllabic
ditch
  pl ditches
dither
dithered
dithering
ditherer
ditto
ditty
  pl ditties
diuretic
diurnal
diva
Divali
divan
dive

dived
diving
dive-bomb
dive-bomber
dive-bombing
diver
diverge
diverged
diverging
divergence
divergent
diverse
diversification
diversify
diversified
diversifying
diversion
diversity
divert
divest
divide
divided
dividing
dividend
dividers
divination
divine
divined
divining
diving-board
diving-suit
divining-rod
divinity
  pl divinities
divisibility
divisible
division

divisional

divisive

divisiveness

divisor

divorce
  divorced
  divorcing

divorcee

divorced

divot

divulge
  divulged
  divulging

divvy

dizziness

dizzy

do
  does, do
  did
  He did it
  done
  He has done it
  doing

docile

docilely

docility

dock

docker

docket

dockyard

doctor
  doctored
  doctoring

doctoral

doctorate

doctrinaire

doctrinal

doctrine

document

documentary
  pl documentaries

documentation

dodder

dodderer

doddery

doddle

dodecagon

dodecahedron

dodge
  dodged
  dodging

dodger

dodgy

dodo
  pl dodos, dodoes

doe
  a buck and a doe

doer

does
  see do

doesn't
  = does not

doff

dog
  dogged
  dogging

dog-collar

dog-eared

dog-end

dogfish

dogged

doggedly

doggerel

doggy
  pl doggies

doggy-bag

doggy-paddle

doghouse

dogma

dogmatic

dogmatically

dogmatism

dogmatize, -ise
  dogmatized
  dogmatizing

do-gooder

dogsbody

dogwood

doh

doily, doyley
  a doily for a cake

doing
  see do

do-it-yourself

doldrums

dole

doleful

dolefully

dolefulness

dole out
  doled out
  doling out

dollar

dollop

dolly
  a child's dolly
  pl dollies

dolmen

dolorous

dolphin
dolphinarium
dolt
domain
dome
domed
domestic
domestically
domesticated
domestication
domesticity
domicile
dominance
dominant
dominate
　dominated
　dominating
domination
domineer
　domineered
　domineering
dominion
domino
　pl dominoes
don
　donned
　donning
donate
　donated
　donating
donation
done
　see do
donkey
　pl donkeys
donnish
donor

don't
　= do not
doodle
　doodled
　doodling
doom
doomed
doomsday
door
doorbell
doorman
　pl doormen
doormat
doorstep
doorstop
doorway
dope
　doped
　doping
dopey
dormant
dormer window
dormitory
　pl dormitories
dormouse
　pl dormice
dorsal
dosage
dose
　dosed
　dosing
dosh
doss down
dosser
doss-house
dossier
dot

dotage
dote on
　doted on
　doting on
doth
dotted
dotty
double
　doubled
　doubling
double-barrelled
double-breasted
double-check
double-cross
double-decker
double-edged
double-glazed
double-glazing
double-jointed
doubles
doublethink
doublet
doubly
doubt
　doubted
　doubting
doubter
doubtful
doubtfully
doubtless
douche
dough
　dough for bread
doughnut
doughnutting
doughy

dour
douse
  doused
  dousing
dove
dovecote
dovetail
  dovetailed
  dovetailing
dowager
dowdily
dowdy
dowel
down
down-and-out
down-at-heel
downcast
downer
downfall
downgrade
  downgraded
  downgrading
downhearted
downhill
download
down-market
downpour
downright
downside
downsizing
downstairs
downstream
down-to-earth
downtown
downtrodden
downturn

downward
downwards
dowry
  pl dowries
dowse
dowser
doyley
  see **doily**
doze
  dozed
  dozing
dozen
drab
drachma
draconian
draft
  a rough draft: to draft a
  plan
drag
  dragged
  dragging
dragnet
dragon
  St George and the
  dragon
dragonfly
  pl dragonflies
dragoon
  the dragoon guards:
  Did he dragoon you
  into going?
  dragooned
  dragooning
drain
drainage
drainpipe
drake
drama

  pl dramas
dramatic
dramatically
dramatics
dramatist
dramatization,
  -isation
dramatize, -ise
  dramatized
  dramatizing
drank
  see **drink**
drape
  draped
  draping
draper
drapery
drapes
drastic
drastically
draught
  a cold draught: a
  draught of ale
draughtsman
draughtsmanship
draughty
draw
  drew
  He drew a sketch
  drawn
  He has drawn a sketch
  drawing
drawback
drawbridge
drawer
drawing-pin
drawl

drawn
 see **draw**

drawstring

dread

dreaded

dreadful

dreadfully

dreadfulness

dreadlocks

dreadnought

dream
 dreamed, dreamt
 dreaming

dreamer

dreamily

dreamy

drearily

dreary

dredge
 dredged
 dredging

dredger

dregs

drench

dress
 pl dresses
 dressed
 dressing

dressage

dresser

dressing

dressing-down

dressing-gown

dressing-table

dressmaker

dressmaking

dressy

drew
 see **draw**

drey
 pl dreys

dribble
 dribbled
 dribbling

dried
 see **dry**

drift

driftwood

drill

drily
 see **dry**

drink
 drank
 He drank some water
 drunk
 *He has drunk some
 water*
 drinking

drinkable

drink-driving

drinker

drip
 dripped
 dripping

drip-dry
 drip-dried
 drip-drying

drip-feed
 drip-fed
 drip-feeding

dripping

drive
 drove
 He drove her car

driven
 He has driven her car
 driving

drive-in

drivel
 drivelled
 drivelling

driven
 see **drive**

driver

drizzle
 drizzled
 drizzling

drizzly

droll

dromedary
 pl dromedaries

drone
 droned
 droning

drool
 drooled
 drooling

droop
 drooped
 drooping

droopy

drop
 dropped
 dropping

droplet

dropout

droppings

dross

drought

drove
 see **drive**

drove

drover

drown

drowsily

drowsiness

drowsy

drudge
  drudged
  drudging

drudgery

drug
  drugged
  drugging

druggist

drugstore

druid

drum
  drummed
  drumming

drummer

drumstick

drunk
  see drink

drunkard

drunken

drunkenness

dry
  dried
  drying

dryad

dry-clean
  dry-cleaned
  dry-cleaning

dry-cleaner

dryer

dryly, drily

dryness

dual

a dual purpose: a dual carriageway

duality

dub
  dubbed
  dubbing

Dubai

dubiety

dubious

dubiousness

ducal

ducat

duchess
  pl duchesses

duchy
  pl duchies

duck
  ducked
  ducking

duck
  ducks and drakes

duckboard

duckling

duct

dud

dude

dudgeon
  in high dudgeon

due
  Your account is due: Go due south: death due to starvation

duel
  They fought a duel

duellist

dues

duet

duettist

duff

duffel-coat,
  duffle-coat

duffer

dug
  see dig

dugout

duke

dukedom

dulcet

dulcimer

dull

dullard

dullness

dully
  He spoke dully and boringly

duly
  He duly arrived

dumb

dumbbell

dumbfound

dumbly

dumbness

dumbstruck

dumbwaiter

dummy
  pl dummies

dump

dumpling

dumpy

dun
  dunned
  dunning

dunce

dunderhead
dune
dung
dungarees
dung-beetle
dungeon
 jailed in a dungeon
dunk
duodecimal
duodenal
dupe
 duped
 duping
duplex
 pl duplexes
duplicate
 duplicated
 duplicating
duplication
duplicitous
duplicity
durability
durable
durably
duration
duress
during
dusk
dusky

dust
dustbin
dustcart
duster
dustman
 pl dustmen
dustpan
dusty
Dutch
duteous
dutiable
dutiful
dutifully
duty
 pl duties
duty-bound
duty-free
duvet
dwarf
 pl dwarfs, dwarves
 dwarfed
 dwarfing
dweeb
dwell
 dwelled, dwelt
 dwelling
dwindle
 dwindled
 dwindling

dye
 to dye a dress red
dyed
 She dyed her dress
dyeing
 dyeing a dress red

dying
 see die

dyke
 see dike

dynamic
dynamically
dynamics
dynamism
dynamite
dynamo
 pl dynamos
dynastic
dynasty
 pl dynasties
dysentery
dysgraphia
dyslexia
dysmenorrhoea
dyspepsia
dyspeptic
dystrophy

e

If the word you're looking for sounds as if it begins *ee* but you can't find it there, try looking under **AE** for words like *aesthetic*, and **OE** for words like *oestrogen*.

each
eager
eagerness
eagle
eagle-eyed
ear
earache
eardrum
earful
earl
earldom
earliness
early
   compar earlier
   superl earliest
early
earmark
earmuff
earn
earner
earnest
earnings
earphone
earpiece
ear-piercing
earplug
earring
earshot

ear-splitting
earth
earthbound
earthenware
earthling
earthly
   in this earthly life: no earthly use
earthquake
earth-shattering
earthworm
earwig
earthy
   an earthy sense of humour. These potatoes are very earthy
earwig
ease
   eased
   easing
easel
easier, easiest
   see **easy**
easily
east
eastbound
Easter
easterly
   an easterly wind

eastern
   eastern customs
eastward
eastwards
easy
   compar easier
   superl easiest
easy-going
eat
   ate
   He ate a cake
   eaten
   He has eaten a cake
   eating
eatable
eaten
   see **eat**
eatery
eau-de-cologne
eaves
eavesdrop
   eavesdropped
   eavesdropping
eavesdropper
ebb
ebony
ebullience
ebullient
eccentric
eccentricity

pl eccentricities

ecclesiastic

ecclesiastical

echelon

echidna

echo
pl echoes

eclectic

eclecticism

eclipse
an eclipse of the sun:
to eclipse his glory
eclipsed
eclipsing

eco-friendly

ecological

ecologically

ecologist

ecology

economic
the country's
economic future:
an economic rent

economical
economical use of
supplies: He is
extravagant; she is
economical

economically

economics

economist

economize, -ise
economized
economizing

economy
pl economies

ecosphere

ecosystem

ecotourism

ecstasy
pl ecstasies

ecstatic

ecstatically

ectopic

ectoplasm

ecu

ecumenical

eczema

eddy
pl eddies

edelweiss

edge
edged
edging

edgeways

edgily

edgy

edible

edict

edification

edifice

edify
edified
edifying

edit
edited
editing

edition
a new edition of his
book: the evening
edition of the
newspaper

editor

editorial

editorially

educable

educatable

educate
educated
educating

education

educational

educationally

educationalist

educationist

educator

edutainment

eel

eerie
an eerie silence: a
dark eerie house

eerily

eeriness

efface
effaced
effacing

effacement

effect
the effect of the drug:
the effect of the new
lighting: The new law
is not yet in effect:
goods and effects: to
effect a reconciliation
effected
effecting

effective

effectively

effectiveness

effectual

effectually

effectuate
  effectuated
  effectuating
effeminate
effeminately
effervesce
  effervesced
  effervescing
effervescence
effervescent
effete
effeteness
efficacious
efficacy
efficiency
efficient
effigy
  pl effigies
effluent
  *The factory's effluent
  caused disease*
efflux
effort
effortless
effrontery
effulgence
effulgent
effusion
effusive
effusively
egalitarian
egalitarianism
egg
egg on
  egged on
  egging on

egg-cup
egghead
egg-nog
eggplant
eggshell
egg-timer
ego
egocentric
egocentricity
egoism
egoist
egoistic
egoistically
egotism
egotist
egotistic
egotistically
egress
egret
Egypt
eider
eiderdown
eider duck
eight
eighteen
eighteenth
eightfold
eighth
eighties
eightieth
eighty
Einstein
Eire
either
ejaculate

ejaculated
ejaculating
ejaculation
ejaculatory
eject
ejection
ejector
eke out
  eked out
  eking out
elaborate
  elaborated
  elaborating
elaboration
élan
elapse
  elapsed
  elapsing
elastic
elasticated
elasticity
elated
elation
elbow
  pl elbows
  elbowed
  elbowing
elbow-grease
elbow-room
elder
  *the elder of the (two)
  brothers*
elderberry
  pl elderberries
elderly
eldest
  the eldest of four

brothers
elect
electable
election
electioneer
 electioneered
 electioneering
elective
elector
electoral
electorate
electric
electrical
electrically
electrician
electricity
electrification
electrify
 electrified
 electrifying
electrocardiogram
electro-convulsive
electrocute
 electrocuted
 electrocuting
electrocution
electrode
electrolysis
electron
electronic
electronically
electronics
electroplate
 electroplated
 electroplating
elegance

elegant
elegiac
elegize, -ise
 elegized
 elegizing
elegy
 pl elegies
element
elementary
elephant
elephantiasis
elephantine
elevate
 elevated
 elevating
elevation
elevator
eleven
elevenses
eleventh
elf
 pl elves
elfin
elfish
elicit
 to elicit information
 elicited
 eliciting
elicitation
elide
 elided
 eliding
eligibility
eligible
 an eligible bachelor:
 eligible for the job
eliminate

eliminated
eliminating
elimination
eliminator
elision
élite, elite
elitism
elitist
elixir
elk
ellipse
 a geometrical ellipse
 pl ellipses
ellipsis
 pl ellipses
elliptical
elliptically
elm
elocution
elocutionary
elocutionist
elongate
 elongated
 elongating
elongation
elope
 eloped
 eloping
elopement
eloquence
eloquent
else
elsewhere
elucidate
 elucidated
 elucidating

elude
He tried to elude his pursuers
eluded
eluding

elusive

elusiveness

elver

elves
see **elf**

emaciated

emaciation

e-mail, email

emanate
emanated
emanating

emanation

emancipate
emancipated
emancipating

emancipation

emasculate
emasculated
emasculating

emasculation

embalm

embalmment

embankment

embargo
pl embargoes

embark

embarkation

embarrass
embarrassed
embarrassing

embarrassment

embassy

pl embassies

embed
embedded
embedding

embellish

embellishment

ember

embezzle
embezzled
embezzling

embezzlement

embezzler

embitter

emblazon
emblazoned
emblazoning

emblem

emblematic

embodiment

embody
embodied
embodying

embolden

embolism

emboss

embrace
embraced
embracing

embrasure

embrocation

embroider
embroidered
embroidering

embroidery

embroil
embroiled
embroiling

embryo
pl embryos

embryologist

embryonic

emend
to emend the manuscript

emendation

emerald

emerge
emerged
emerging

emergence

emergency
pl emergencies

emergent

emeritus

emery

emetic

emigrant
an emigrant to America from Britain

emigrate

emigration
emigration from Britain

eminence

eminent

eminently

emir

emirate

emissary
pl emissaries

emission
the emission of gases

emissive

emit

emitted
emitting
emollient
emolument
emote
emoted
emoting
emotion
emotional
emotionally
emotive
empathetic
empathize, -ise
empathized
empathizing
empathy
emperor
emphasis
The emphasis must be on hygiene: The emphasis is on the first syllable
emphasize, -ise
to emphasize its value: to emphasize the word 'new'
emphasized
emphasizing
emphatic
emphatically
emphysema
empire
empirical
empirically
empiricism
empiricist
emplacement

employ
employed
employing
employable
employee
He sacked his young employee
employer
His employer gave him a rise
employment
emporium
pl emporiums, emporia
empower
empress
pl empresses
emptiness
empty
emptied
emptying
empty-handed
emu
emulate
emulated
emulating
emulation
emulsifier
emulsify
emulsified
emulsifying
emulsion
enable
enabled
enabling
enact
enactment

enamel
enamelled
enamelling
enamoured of
en bloc
encampment
encapsulate
encapsulated
encapsulating
encapsulation
encase
encasement
encephalitis
enchant
enchanter
enchantment
enchantress
pl enchantresses
enchilada
encircle
enclave
enclose
enclosed
enclosing
enclosure
encode
encompass
encore
encounter
encountered
encountering
encourage
encouraged
encouraging
encouragement
encroach
encroachment

encrust
encumber
encumbrance
**encyclopaedia,
encyclopedia**
encyclopaedic,
encyclopedic
end
endanger
endangered
endangering
endear
endeared
endearing
endearment
endeavour
endemic
ending
endive
endless
endmost
endocrine
endogamy
endometriosis
endorphin
endorse
endorsed
endorsing
endorsement
endoscope
endoscopy
endow
endowment
endurance
endure
endured

enduring
enema
enemy
pl enemies
energetic
energetically
energize, -ise
energized
energizing
energy
pl energies
enervate
enervated
enervating
enfold
enforce
enforced
enforcing
enforceable
enforcement
enfranchise
enfranchised
enfranchising
enfranchisement
engage
engaged
engaging
engagement
engender
engine
engineer
engineered
engineering
engorged
engrave
engraved
engraving

engraver
engross
engrossed
engulf
enhance
enhanced
enhancing
enhancement
enigma
enigmatic
enigmatically
enjoin
enjoy
enjoyed
enjoying
enjoyable
enjoyment
enlarge
enlarged
enlarging
enlargement
enlighten
enlightened
enlightening
enlightenment
enlist
enliven
enlivened
enlivening
en masse
enmesh
enmity
ennoble
ennoblement
ennui
enormity
enormous

enough

enquire
 see **inquire**

enrage
 enraged
 enraging

enrapt

enrich

enrichment

enrol
 enrolled
 enrolling

enrolment

en route

ensconce
 ensconced
 ensconcing

ensemble

enshrine

enshroud

ensign

enslave

enslavement

ensnare

ensue
 ensued
 ensuing

en suite

ensure
 Great effort will ensure
 success
 ensured
 ensuring

entail
 entailed
 entailing

entangle

entangled
 entangling

entanglement

enter
 entered
 entering

enterprise

enterprising

entertain
 entertained
 entertaining

entertainer

entertainment

enthral
 enthralled
 enthralling

enthralment

enthrone

enthuse
 enthused
 enthusing

enthusiasm

enthusiast

enthusiastic

enthusiastically

entice
 enticed
 enticing

enticement

entire

entirely

entirety

entitle
 entitled
 entitling

entitlement

entity

entomb

entomologist
 The entomologist
 studied the insects

entomology

entourage

entr'acte

entrails

'entrance

en'trance
 entranced
 entrancing

entrant

entrap

entrapment

entreat
 entreated
 entreating

entreaty
 pl entreaties

entrée

entrenched

entrepreneur

entrepreneurial

entrust

entry
 pl entries

entwine

entwined

entwining

E-number

enumerate
 enumerated
 enumerating

enumeration

enunciate
 enunciated

enunciating
enunciation
en'velop
The mist began to envelop the hills
enveloped
enveloping
'**envelope**
a brown envelope
enviable
enviably
envious
environment
environmental
environmentally
environmentalist
environs
envisage
envisaged
envisaging
envoy
envy
envied
envying
enzyme
eon
see aeon
epaulet, epaulette
ephemera
ephemeral
ephemerally
epic
epicentre
epicure
epicurean
epidemic

epidermis
epidural
epiglottis
epigram
a witty epigram
epigrammatic
epilepsy
epileptic
epilogue
epiphany
episcopacy
episcopal
episcopalian
episiotomy
episode
episodic
epistemology
epistle
epitaph
an epitaph on his grave
epithet
'Great' was the epithet given to King Alfred
epitome
epitomize, -ise
epitomized
epitomizing
epoch
eponym
eponymous
equable
equably
equal
equalled
equalling

equality
equalize, -ise
equalized
equalizing
equalizer, -iser
equally
equanimity
equate
equated
equating
equation
equator
equatorial
equerry
pl equerries
equestrian
equidistance
equidistant
equilateral
equilibrium
equine
equinoctial
equinox
equip
equipped
equipping
equipment
equitable
equitably
equity
equivalent
equivocal
equivocally
equivocate
equivocated
equivocating

era
 pl eras
eradicate
 eradicated
 eradicating
eradication
erase
 erased
 erasing
eraser
erasure
ere
 ere dawn
erect
erection
erectness
ergo
ergonomic
ergonomically
ergonomics
ermine
erode
 eroded
 eroding
erogenous
erosion
erosive
erotic
 erotic pictures of nudes
erotically
erotica
eroticism
err
 to err is human
 erred
 erring

errand
errant
erratic
 an erratic driver
erratically
erratum
 pl errata
erroneous
error
ersatz
erstwhile
eructation
erudite
eruditely
erudition
erupt
eruption
escalate
 escalated
 escalating
escalation
escalator
escapade
escape
 escaped
 escaping
escapement
 the escapement of a watch
escapism
escapist
escapologist
escapology
escarpment
 a rocky escarpment
eschew

eschewal
escort
escritoire
escudo
escutcheon
Eskimo
 pl Eskimos
esoteric
espadrille
esparto
especial
especially
espionage
esplanade
espousal
espouse
 espoused
 espousing
espresso
esprit
espy
 espied
 espying
Esq
 = Esquire
 John Brown Esq
essay
 He wrote an essay on Shakespeare
essayist
essence
essential
essentially
establish
establishment
estate

esteem
  esteemed
  esteeming
esthetic
  see aesthetic
estimable
estimate
  estimated
  estimating
estimation
estimator
estranged
estuary
  pl estuaries
etc
  = et cetera
etch
etching
eternal
eternally
eternity
ethanol
ether
ethereal
ethereally
ethical
ethically
ethics
ethnic
ethnicity
ethnocentric
ethnocentricity
ethnography
ethnologist
ethnology
ethology

ethos
etiquette
etymological
etymologically
etymologist
  An etymologist is
  interested in words
etymology
  pl etymologies
eucalyptus
  pl eucalypti,
  eucalyptuses
eugenic
eugenics
eulogistic
eulogize, -ise
  eulogized
  eulogizing
eulogy
  pl eulogies
eunuch
euphemism
euphemistic
euphemistically
euphonious
euphonium
euphony
euphoria
euphoric
euphorically
eureka
eurhythmics
European
euthanasia
evacuate
  evacuated

evacuating
evacuation
evacuee
evade
  evaded
  evading
evaluate
  evaluated
  evaluating
evaluation
evanesce
  evanesced
  evanescing
evanescence
evanescent
evangelical
evangelist
evangelistic
evangelize, -ise
  evangelized
  evangelizing
evaporate
  evaporated
  evaporating
evaporation
evasion
evasive
evasively
evasiveness
eve
even
evening
evenness
evensong
event
eventful
eventfully

eventide
eventual
eventuality
  pl eventualities
eventually
ever
everglade
evergreen
everlasting
evermore
every
everybody
everyone
everything
everywhere
evict
eviction
evidence
evident
evidently
evil
evildoer
evilly
evince
  evinced
  evincing
evocation
evocative
evocatively
evoke
  evoked
  evoking
evolution
  the evolution of the
  species: Darwin's
  theory of evolution

evolutionary
evolutionist
evolve
  evolved
  evolving
ewe
  a ram and a ewe
ewer
ex
  pl ex's, exes
exacerbate
  exacerbated
  exacerbating
exacerbation
exact
exacting
exactitude
exactness
exaggerate
  exaggerated
  exaggerating
exaggeration
exalt
exaltation
exalted
exam
examination
examine
  examined
  examining
examinee
examiner
example
exasperate
  exasperated
  exasperating
exasperation

excavate
  excavated
  excavating
excavation
excavator
exceed
exceedingly
excel
  excelled
  excelling
excellence
excellency
excellent
except
  Nobody except John
  went: We enjoyed it
  except for the rain
excepting
exception
exceptional
exceptionally
excerpt
excess
  an excess of alcohol
  pl excesses
excessive
excessively
exchange
  exchanged
  exchanging
exchangeable
exchequer
ex'cise
  excise a passage from
  a book
  excised
  excising

'excise
customs and excise

excision

excitable

excitably

excitation

excite
excited
exciting

excited

excitement

exciting

exclaim
exclaimed
exclaiming

exclamation

exclamatory

exclude
excluded
excluding

exclusion

exclusive

exclusively

excommunicate

excommunication

excrement

excrescence

excreta

excrete
excreted
excreting

excretion

excretory

excruciating

exculpate
exculpated
exculpating

exculpation

excursion

excusable

excuse
excused
excusing

execrable

execrably

execrate
execrated
execrating

execration

execute
executed
executing

execution

executioner
He was put to death by the executioner

executive

executor
executor of his will

exegesis
pl exegeses

exemplar

exemplary

exemplification

exemplify
exemplified
exemplifying

exempt

exemption

exercise
ballet exercises: *exercises in spelling*: *to exercise your body*
exercised

exercising

exert

exertion

exeunt

exhalation

exhale
exhaled
exhaling

exhaust
exhausted
exhausting

exhaustible

exhausting

exhaustion

exhaustive

exhibit
exhibited
exhibiting

exhibition

exhibitioner

exhibitionism

exhibitionist

exhibitor

exhilarate
exhilarated
exhilarating

exhort

exhortation

exhumation

exhume
exhumed
exhuming

exigency
pl exigencies

exigent

exiguous

exile
 exiled
 exiling
exist
existence
existential
existentialism
existentialist
exit
 exited
 exiting
exodus
 pl exoduses
exogamy
exogenous
exonerate
 exonerated
 exonerating
exoneration
exorbitance
exorbitant
exorcism
exorcist
exorcize, -ise
 to exorcize the house
 of spirits
 exorcized
 exorcizing
exotic
exotica
exotically
expand
 Metals expand when
 heated
expandable
expanse
expansion

expansionism
expansionist
expansive
 a talkative and
 expansive person
expat
expatiate
 to expatiate about an
 experience
 expatiated
 expatiating
expatriate
expect
 expected
 expecting
expectancy
expectant
expectation
expectorant
expectorate
 expectorated
 expectorating
expedience
expediency
expedient
expedite
 expedited
 expediting
expedition
expeditious
expel
 expelled
 expelling
expend
 to expend energy
expendable
expenditure

expense
expensive
 expensive clothes
expensively
experience
 experienced
 experiencing
experiment
experimental
experimentally
experimentation
expert
expertise
expiate
 to expiate a crime
 expiated
 expiating
expire
 expired
 expiring
expiry
explain
 explained
 explaining
explanation
explanatory
expletive
explicable
explicably
explicit
explode
 exploded
 exploding
exploit
 exploited
 exploiting
exploitation

exploration
explore
 explored
 exploring
explorer
explosion
explosive
exponent
expo
exponent
exponential
export
exportation
exporter
expose
 exposed
 exposing
exposition
exposure
expound
express
expressible
expression
expressionless
expressive
expressively
expressly
expropriate
 expropriated
 expropriating
expropriation
expulsion
expulsive
expunge
 expunged
 expunging

expurgate
 expurgated
 expurgating
exquisite
 exquisitely
extant
 Cannibalism is still extant in a few areas
extemporary
extempore
extemporization, -isation
extemporize, -ise
 extemporized
 extemporizing
extend
extendable
extensible
extension
extensive
extensively
extent
extenuate
 extenuated
 extenuating
extenuation
exterior
exterminate
 exterminated
 exterminating
extermination
exterminator
external
externalize, -ise
externally
extinct
 The dodo is extinct:

 That volcano is now extinct
extinction
extinguish
extinguisher
extirpate
extirpation
extol
 extolled
 extolling
extolment
extort
extortion
extortionate
extortionately
extortionist
extra
extract
extraction
extractor
extra-curricular
extradite
 extradited
 extraditing
extradition
extramarital
extramural
extraneous
extraordinarily
extraordinary
extrapolate
 extrapolated
 extrapolating
extrapolation
extrasensory
extraterrestrial

extravagance
extravagant
extravaganza
extravert
  see **extrovert**
extreme
extremely
extremism
extremist
extremity
  pl extremities
extricable
extricate
  extricated
  extricating

extrovert, extravert
exuberance
exuberant
exude
  exuded
  exuding
exult
exultant
exultation
eye
  eyed
  eyeing
eyeball
eyebright
eyebrow

eye-catching
eyeful
eyeglass
eyelash
eyelet
eyelid
eye-opener
eyesight
eyesore
eyewash
eyewitness
eyrie, eyry, aerie
  an eagle's eyrie

f

If you can't find the word you're looking for under **F**, it could
be that it starts with a different letter. Try looking under **PH** for
words like *pharmacy*, *photograph* and *physical*.

fa
fable
fabric
fabricate
  fabricated
  fabricating
fabrication
fabulous
façade
face

faced
facing
faceless
facelift
face-saving
facet
facetious
facetiousness
facia
  see **fascia**

facial
facially
facile
facilely
facilitate
  facilitated
  facilitating
facility
  pl facilities
facsimile

fact
faction
factional
factious
factor
factory
  pl factories
factotum
factual
facultative
faculty
  pl faculties
fad
faddish
faddy
fade
  faded
  fading
faecal
faeces
faerie, faery
  *Spencer wrote the
  Faerie Queen: the
  magical land of faerie*
faff
fag
faggot
fah
Fahrenheit
fail
  failed
  failing
fail-safe
failure
fain
  *Fain would he die for
  love*

faint
  *She felt faint and
  collapsed: a faint
  noise: to faint in the
  heat*
faint-hearted
faintness
fair
  *Children enjoy a fair:
  She has fair hair: a
  fair attempt*
fairground
fairing
fairness
fairway
fairy
  *the fairy on the
  Christmas tree: fairy
  stories*
  pl fairies
fairyland
fait accompli
  pl faits accomplis
faith
faithful
faithfully
faithfulness
faithless
faithlessness
fake
  faked
  faking
falcon
falconer
falconry
fall
  fell
  He fell off the wall

fallen
  *He has fallen off the
  wall*
  falling
fallacious
fallacy
  pl fallacies
fallen
  see **fall**
fallibility
fallible
fallopian
fallout
fallow
false
falsely
falsehood
falseness
falsetto
falsification
falsify
  falsified
  falsifying
falsity
falter
  faltered
  faltering
fame
familial
familiar
familiarity
familiarize, -ise
  familiarized
  familiarizing
family
  pl families
famine

famished
famous
fan
 fanned
 fanning
fanatic
fanatical
fanatically
fanaticism
fancier
fanciful
fancy
 pl fancies
 fancied
 fancying
fancy-free
fandango
fanfare
fang
fanlight
fantail
fantasize, -ise
 fantasized
 fantasizing
fantastic
fantastically
fantasy
 pl fantasies
fanzine
far
 compar farther
 superl farthest
faraday
faraway
farce
farcical

fare
 bus fare: How did you
 fare?
 fared
 faring
farewell
far-fetched
far-flung
farinaceous
farm
farmer
farmhouse
farming
farmstead
farmyard
far-off
far-out
far-reaching
farrier
farrow
far-sighted
far-sightedness
fart
farther, farthest
 see far
farthing
fascia, facia
fascinate
fascinated
fascinating
fascination
fascism
fascist
fashion
 fashioned
 fashioning

fashionable
fashionably
fast
fasten
 fastened
 fastening
fastener
fast-forward
fastidious
fastidiousness
fastness
fast-track
fat
 compar fatter
 superl fattest
fatal
fatally
fatalism
fatalist
fatalistic
fatality
 pl fatalities
fate
 a fate worse than
 death
fated
fateful
fatefully
father
fatherhood
father-in-law
 pl fathers-in-law
fatherland
fatherless
fatherly
fathom

fathomed
fathoming
fathomless
fatigue
fatness
fatten
fattened
fattening
fattiness
fatty
fatuous
fatuousness
fatwa
faucet
fault
faultless
faulty
faun
A faun is an imaginary creature
fauna
faux pas
pl faux pas
favour
favoured
favouring
favourable
favourably
favourite
favouritism
fawn
fawn in colour: a deer and its fawn: Courtiers fawn on the king
fawning
fax
faxed

faxing
fear
fearful
fearfully
fearless
fearlessly
fearlessness
fearsome
feasibility
feasible
feasibly
feast
feat
a difficult feat
feather
feathered
featherweight
feathery
feature
featured
featuring
featureless
febrile
February
feckless
fecund
fecundity
fed
see feed
federal
federalism
federalist
federate
federated
federating
federated

federation
fee
feeble
feeble-minded
feeble-mindedness
feebleness
feebly
feed
fed
feeding
feedback
feeder
feel
felt
feeling
feeler
feelgood
feeling
feet
see foot
feign
Did she feign sleep?
feigned
feigning
feint
a feint in fencing
feisty
felicitate
felicitation
felicitous
felicity
pl felicities
feline
fell
see fall
fell
felled

He felled the tree
felling
fellatio
fellow
fellowship
felon
felonious
felony
 pl felonies
felt
 see **feel**
felt
female
feminine
femininely
femininity
feminism
feminist
femme fatale
 pl femmes fatales
femoral
femur
fen
fence
 fenced
 fencing
fencer
fend
fender
feng shui
fennel
fenugreek
feral
ferment
 to ferment beer: in a
 ferment of excitement

fermentation
fern
ferocious
ferociousness
ferocity
ferret
 ferreted
 ferreting
ferric
ferrous
ferrule
ferry
 pl ferries
 ferried
 ferrying
fertile
fertility
fertilization, -isation
fertilize, -ise
 fertilized
 fertilizing
fertilizer, -iser
fervent
fervid
fervour
fester
 festered
 festering
festival
festive
festively
festivity
 pl festivities
festoon
 festooned
 festooning
feta

fetal, foetal
fetch
fetching
fête
 a stall at the summer
 fête
fetid, foetid
fetish
 pl fetishes
fetishist
fetlock
fetters
fettle
fettuccine
fetus, foetus
 pl fetuses, foetuses
feud
feudal
feudalism
fever
fevered
feverfew
feverish
few
fey
fez
 pl fezzes
fiancé
 He is her fiancé
fiancée
 She is his fiancée
fiasco
 pl fiascos
fib
 fibbed
 fibbing

fibber
fibre
fibreboard
fibreglass
fibre-optic
fibre optics
fibril
fibrillate
  fibrillated
  fibrillating
fibrillation
fibroid
fibrosis
fibrous
fibula
  pl fibulae, fibulas
fickle
fickleness
fiction
fictional
fictitious
fiddle
  fiddled
  fiddling
fiddler
fiddlesticks
fidelity
fidget
  fidgeted
  fidgeting
fidgety
fiduciary
fief
field
fielder
field-marshal

fieldmouse
  pl fieldmice
fieldwork
fiend
fiendish
fierce
fiercely
fierceness
fiery
fiesta
fife
fifteen
fifteenth
fifth
fifties
fiftieth
fifty
fifty-fifty
fig
fight
  fought
  fighting
fighter
figment
figurative
figuratively
figure
figured
figurehead
figurine
filament
filch
file
  filed
  She filed the letter.
  She filed her nails

filing
filial
filibuster
filigree
fill
  filled
  We filled the bucket
  filling
filler
fillet
  filleted
  filleting
fillip
filly
  pl fillies
film
filo
Filofax®
filter
  filtered
  filtering
filth
filthy
filtrate
filtration
fin
final
  a final separation
finally
finale
  the finale at the end of
  the concert
finalist
finality
finalization, -isation
finalize, -ise
  finalized

finalizing

finance
financed
financing

financial

financially

financier

finch
pl finches

find
found
He found the ball
finding

finder

findings

fine
fined
fining

finery

finesse

fine-tune
fine-tuned
fine-tuning

finger
fingered
fingering

fingerboard

fingerbowl

fingermark

fingernail

fingerprint

fingerstall

fingertip

finicky

finish

finished

finite

Finnish

fiord, fjord

fir
a fir tree: a fir cone

fire
fired
firing

firearm

fireball

fire-bomb

firebrand

firecracker

fire-eater

fire-extinguisher

fire-fighter

fire-fighting

fireguard

firelighter

fireman
pl firemen

fireplace

fireside

fireworks

firm

firmament

firmness

first

first aid

first-class

first-hand

firstly

first-rate

firth

fiscal

fish
pl fish

fishcake

fisherman
pl fishermen

fishery
pl fisheries

fishing-rod

fishmonger

fishy

fission
nuclear fission

fissure
a fissure in the rock

fist

fistful

fisticuffs

fit
compar fitter
superl fittest
fitted
fitting

fitful

fitfully

fitment

fitness

fitting

five

fiver

fix

fixedly

fixation

fixative

fixer

fixture

fizz

fizzle out
fizzled out
fizzling out

fizzy

fjord
  see fiord

flab

flabbergasted

flabbiness

flabby

flaccid

flag
  flagged
  flagging

flagellation

flageolet

flagon

flagpole

flagrancy

flagrant

flagship

flagstaff

flagstone

flail
  flailed
  flailing

flair
  a flair for dressmaking

flak

flake
  flaked
  flaking

flaky

flamboyance

flamboyant

flame
  flamed
  flaming

flamenco

flamingo
  pl flamingos,
  flamingoes

flammable
  *Flammable material
  burns easily*

flan

flange

flank

flannel

flannelette

flap
  flapped
  flapping

flapjack

flapper

flare
  *a flare as a signal: Did
  the fire flare up?*
  flared
  flaring

flare-up

flash
  pl flashes

flashback

flashbulb

flasher

flashgun

flashily

flashlight

flashpoint

flashy

flask

flat
  compar flatter
  superl flattest

flatfish

flatness

flatten
  flattened
  flattening

flatter
  flattered
  flattering

flatterer

flattery

flatulence

flatulent

flatworm

flaunt

flautist

flavour
  flavoured
  flavouring

flavoursome

flaw

flawed

flawless

flax

flaxen

flay
  flayed
  flaying

flea
  bitten by a flea

fleck

flecked

fled
  see flee

fledged

fledgling

flee
  to flee from the enemy
  fled

fleeing

fleece
fleeced
fleecing

fleecy

fleet

fleeting

flesh

fleshy

flew
see fly

flex

flexibility

flexible

flexitime

flick

flicker
flickered
flickering

flier

flight

flightiness

flighty

flimsy

flinch

fling
flung
flinging

flint

flip
flipped
flipping

flip-flop

flippancy

flippant

flipper

flirt

flirtation

flirtatious

flit
flitted
flitting

float
floated
floating

flock
flocks of sheep

floe
an ice floe

flog
flogged
flogging

flood
flooded
flooding

floodgate

floodlighting

floodlit

floor
floored
flooring

floorboard

flop
flopped
flopping

floppy

flora

floral

floret

florid

florin

florist

floss

flotation

flotilla

flotsam

flounce
flounced
flouncing

flounder
floundered
floundering

flour
Bread is made with flour

flourish
pl flourishes
flourished
flourishing

floury
floury potatoes: My hands are floury

flout
flouted
flouting

flow
a flow of blood: to flow smoothly
flowed
flowing

flower
a beautiful flower: Will that bush flower this year?
flowered
flowering

flowerpot

flowery
a flowery material: flowery language

flown
see fly

flu
a flu epidemic

fluctuate
fluctuated
fluctuating

fluctuation

flue
The sweep cleaned the flue

fluency

fluent

fluff

fluffy

flugelhorn

fluid

fluidity

fluke

flume

flummox

flummoxed

flung
see **fling**

flunk

fluorescence

fluorescent

fluoridate

fluoridation

fluoride

fluoridize, -ise
fluoridized
fluoridizing

fluorocarbon

flurry
pl flurries
flurried
flurrying

flush

pl flushes

fluster
flustered
flustering

flute
fluted
fluting

flutter
fluttered
fluttering

fluvial

flux

fly
pl flies
flew
The bird flew away: He flew the plane
flown
The bird has flown away: He has flown the plane

fly-fishing

flying

flyleaf
pl flyleaves

flyover

flysheet

flyspray

flywheel

foal
foaled
foaling

foam
foamed
foaming

foamy

fob

fob off

fobbed off
fobbing off

focaccia

focal

fo'c'sle
see **forecastle**

focus
pl focuses, foci
focused, focussed
focusing, focussing

fodder

foe

foetal
see **fetal**

foetid
see **fetid**

foetus
pl foetuses
see **fetus**

fog

fogey

foggy

foghorn

foible

foil
foiled
foiling

foist

fold

folder

foliage

foliate

foliation

folio

folk

folklore

folksong

follicle

follow
 followed
 following

follower

follow-up

folly
 pl follies

foment
 to foment trouble

fomentation

fond

fondant

fondle
 fondled
 fondling

fondness

fondue

font
 the baptismal font

food

foodie

foodstuff

fool
 fooled
 fooling

foolhardy

foolish

foolishness

foolproof

foolscap

foot
 pl feet
 These shoes hurt my feet

foot-and-mouth

football

footbridge

foothill

foothold

footing

footlights

footloose

footman
 pl footmen

footnote

footpath

footprint

footsore

footstep

footstool

footwear

footwork

fop

foppish

for

forage
 foraged
 foraging

foray

forbade
 see forbid

forbear
 forbore
 forbearing

forbearance

forbearing

forbid
 forbade
 He forbade me to go
 forbidden
 He has forbidden me to go
 forbidding

forbore
 see forbear

force
 forced
 forcing

force-feed
 force-fed
 force-feeding

forceful

forcefully

forceps

forcible

forcibly

ford

fore
 well to the fore

forearm

foreboding

forecast
 forecast
 forecasting

forecastle, fo'c'sle

forecourt

forefather

forefinger

forefront

foregather

forego

foregone
 a foregone conclusion

foreground

forehand

forehead

foreign

foreigner

foreknowledge

foreleg

forelock

foreman
 pl foremen

foremost

forensic

foreplay

forerunner

foresee
 foresaw
 He foresaw the
 problem
 foreseen
 He has foreseen the
 problem
 foreseeing

foreseeable

foreshadow

foreshore

foresight

foreskin

forest

forestall
 forestalled
 forestalling

forestation

forested

forester

forestry

foretaste

foretell
 foretold
 foretelling

forethought

foretold
 see **foretell**

forever

forewarn

forewoman
 pl forewomen

foreword
 Who wrote the
 foreword to the book?

forfeit
 forfeited
 forfeiting

forfeiture

forgave
 see **forgive**

forge
 forged
 forging

forgery
 pl forgeries

forget
 forgot
 He forgot it
 forgotten
 He has forgotten it
 forgetting

forgetful

forgetfully

forgetfulness

forget-me-not

forgivable

forgive
 forgave
 He forgave her
 forgiven
 He has forgiven her
 forgiving

forgiveness

forgo
 forgoing
 forgone

 He has forgone
 privileges
 forwent
 He forwent privileges

forgot, forgotten
 see **forget**

fork

forked

forlorn

form

formal

formaldehyde

formality
 pl formalities

formalize
 formalized
 formalizing

formally

format
 formatted
 formatting

formation

formative

former

formerly

formidable

formidably

formless

formlessness

formula
 pl formulae, formulas

formulaic

formulate
 formulated
 formulating

formulation

fornicate

fornicated
fornicating
fornication
forsake
forsook
She forsook religion
forsaken
*She has forsaken
religion*
forsaking
forswear
forswore
He forswore alcohol
forsworn
*He has forsworn
alcohol*
forswearing
forsythia
fort
They besieged the fort
forte
Singing is his forte
forth
*issuing forth: giving
forth*
forthcoming
forthright
forthwith
forties
fortieth
fortification
fortify
fortified
fortifying
fortissimo
fortitude
fortnight
fortnightly

fortress
pl fortresses
fortuitous
fortunate
adv fortunately
fortune
fortune-teller
forty
He spent forty pounds
forum
pl forums
forward
forward not backward
forwards
forwent
see **forgo**
fossil
fossilization, -isation
fossilize, -ise
fossilized
fossilized
foster
fostered
fostering
fought
see **fight**
foul
*the foul smell of
tobacco: foul weather*
foul-mouthed
foul-up
found
see **find**
found
founded
*He founded the
business*
founding

foundation
founder
foundered
foundering
foundling
foundry
pl foundries
fount
*the fount of
knowledge*
fountain
four
*Four and four makes
eight*
four-poster
foursome
fourteen
fourteenth
fourth
*He was fourth in the
race*
fourthly
fowl
fish and fowl
fox
pl foxes
foxglove
foxhound
foxhunting
foxtrot
foxy
foyer
fracas
pl fracas
fractal
fraction
fractional

fractionally
fractious
fracture
  fractured
  fracturing
fragile
fragment
fragmentary
fragmentation
fragrance
fragrant
frail
frailty
  pl frailties
frame
  framed
  framing
framework
franc
  the French franc
francophone
franchise
frangipani
frank
  a frank statement:
  frank and honest
frank
  to frank a letter
frankfurter
frankincense
frantic
frantically
fraternal
fraternity
fraternization,
  -isation

fraternize, -ise
  fraternized
  fraternizing
fratricide
fraud
fraudulent
fraught
fray
  frayed
  fraying
frazzle
  frazzled
  frazzling
freak
freakish
freaky
freckle
free
freebie
freedom
free-for-all
freehand
freehold
freeholder
freelance
freelancer
freeload
freeloader
freely
free-range
freesia
freestyle
freeware
freeway
freewheel
freeze

to freeze vegetables
froze
She froze the meat
frozen
She has frozen the
peas
freezing
freight
freighter
French
frenetic
frenetically
frenzied
frenzy
frequency
  pl frequencies
frequent
fresco
  pl frescoes, frescos
fresh
freshen
  freshened
  freshening
fresher
freshman
  pl freshmen
freshness
freshwater
fret
  fretted
  fretting
fretful
fretfully
fretsaw
fretwork
friar
friary

pl friaries
fricative
friction
Friday
fridge
fried
  see fry
friend
friendless
friendliness
friendly
friendship
frieze
  a ceiling frieze
frigate
fright
frighten
  frightened
  frightening
frightful
frightfully
frigid
frigidity
frill
frilly
fringe
  fringed
  fringing
frippery
  pl fripperies
Frisbee®
frisk
friskily
frisky
frisson
fritillary

pl fritillaries
fritter
  frittered
  frittering
frivolity
  pl frivolities
frivolous
frizz
frizzy
fro
frock
frock-coat
frog
frogman
  pl frogmen
frog-march
frogspawn
frolic
  frolicked
  frolicking
frolicsome
from
fromage frais
frond
front
frontage
frontal
frontbench
frontbencher
frontier
frontispiece
front-runner
frost
frostbite
frostbitten
frosted

frostily
frosting
frosty
froth
frothy
frown
froze, frozen
  see freeze
fructification
fructose
frugal
frugality
frugally
fruit
fruitcake
fruiterer
fruitful
fruitfully
fruition
fruitless
fruitlessly
fruity
frump
frumpish
frustrate
  frustrated
  frustrating
frustration
fry
  fried
  frying
fryer
frying-pan
fuchsia
fuck
fucking

fuck-up
fuddle
  fuddled
  fuddling
fuddy-duddy
fudge
fuel
  fuelled
  fuelling
fug
fugitive
fugue
fulcrum
  pl fulcrums, fulcra
fulfil
  fulfilled
  fulfilling
fulfilment
full
full-blooded
full-blown
full-length
fullness
full-scale
full-time
fully
fulmar
fulminate
  fulminated
  fulminating
fulsome
fulsomely
fumble
  fumbled
  fumbling
fume
  fumed

fuming
fumes
fumigant
fumigate
  fumigated
  fumigating
fumigation
fun
function
  functioned
  functioning
functional
functionalism
functionality
functionally
functionary
  pl functionaries
fund
fundamental
fundamentalism
fundamentalist
fundamentally
funeral
  He attended her
  funeral
funereal
  solemn, funereal
  music
funfair
fungal
fungicidal
fungicide
fungus
  pl fungi, funguses
funicular railway
funnel
  funnelled

funnelling
funnily
funny
fur
  a fur coat: a cat's fur
furbish
furious
furl
furlong
furnace
furnish
furnishings
furniture
furore
furrier
furrow
furry
further
  furthered
  furthering
furtherance
furthermore
furthermost
furthest
furtive
furtively
furtiveness
fury
fuse
  fused
  fusing
fuselage
fusilier
fusillade
fusion
fuss

fussed
fussing
fussily
fusspot
fussy
fustiness

fusty
futile
futilely
futility
futon

future
futurist
futuristic
fuzz
fuzzy

g

If the word you're looking for sounds as if it begins with a straightforward **G** but you can't find it, try looking under **GH** for words like *ghastly* and *ghost*, and **GU** for words like *guard* and *guide*.

gab
 gabbed
 gabbing
gabardine
gabble
 the noisy gabble of the crowd: to gabble noisily
 gabbled
 gabbling
gaberdine
gable
 the gable of a house
gadfly
 pl gadflies
gadget
gadgetry
Gaelic
gaff
 a fishing gaff: blow the

gaff
gaffe
 a social gaffe
gag
 gagged
 gagging
gaga
gage
gaggle
gaiety
gaily
gain
 gained
 gaining
gainful
gait
 a shuffling gait
gaiter
gala

galactic
galaxy
 pl galaxies
gale
gall
gallant
gallantry
gallbladder
galleon
 a Spanish galleon
gallery
 pl galleries
galley
 pl galleys
galling
gallivant
gallon
 a gallon of petrol
gallop

galloped
galloping
gallows
gallstone
galore
galoshes
galumph
galvanize, -ise
galvanized
galvanizing
galvanometer
gambit
gamble
to gamble on a horse
gambled
gambling
gambler
gambol
The lambs gambol
gambolled
gambolling
game
gamekeeper
gamelan
gaming
gamma
gammon
gammy
gamut
gamy
gander
Gandhi
gang
gang-bang
ganger
gangland

ganglion
gangly
gangplank
gangrene
gangrenous
gangster
gang up
ganged up
ganging up
gangway
ganja
gannet
gantry
pl gantries
gaol
see jail
gaoler
see jailer
gap
gape
gaped
gaping
gappy
garage
garaged
garaging
garam masala
garb
garbage
garbed
garbled
garden
gardened
gardening
gardener
gardenia
gargantuan

gargle
gargled
gargling
gargoyle
garish
garishness
garland
garlic
garlicky
garment
garner
garnet
garnish
pl garnishes
garret
garrison
garrisoned
garrisoning
garrotte
garrotted
garrotting
garrulity
garrulous
garter
gas
pl gases
gassed
gassing
gasbag
gaseous
gash
pl gashes
gasket
gaslight
gasoline
gasometer
gasp

gassy
gastric
gastritis
gastroenteritis
gastronome
gastronomic
gastronomy
gastropod
gasworks
gate
  a garden gate
gâteau
  pl gâteaux
gatecrash
gatecrasher
gateleg
gateway
gather
  gathered
  gathering
gathering
gauche
gaucho
  pl gauchos
gaudily
gaudiness
gaudy
gauge
  gauged
  gauging
gaunt
gauntlet
gauntness
gauze
gave
  see give

gavel
gavotte
gawkily
gawkiness
gawky
gawp
gay
gaze
  gazed
  gazing
gazebo
gazelle
gazette
  gazetted
  gazetting
gazetteer
gazpacho
gazump
gazumper
gazumping
gazunder
gear
gearbox
gear to
  geared to
  gearing to
gecko
gee
geese
  see goose
geezer
geisha
gel
  gelled
  gelling
gelatine

gelatinous
geld
gelding
gelignite
gem
Gemini
gemstone
gen
  genned
  genning
gender
gender-bender
gene
genealogical
genealogist
genealogy
  pl genealogies
genera
  see genus
general
generality
generalization,
  -isation
generalize, -ise
  generalized
  generalizing
generally
generate
  generated
  generating
generation
generative
generator
generic
generosity
generous

genesis
genetic
genetically
geneticist
genetics
genial
genially
genie
a magic genie
genital
genitalia
genitals
genitive
genius
He is clever but not a genius
pl geniuses
genocide
genome
genre
gent
genteel
a genteel tea-party
genteelly
gentian
gentile
He is a gentile, not a Jew
gentility
gentle
She has a kind, gentle nature: a gentle breeze
gently
gentleman
pl gentlemen
gentlemanly

gentleness
gentrification
gentrify
gentrified
gentrifying
gentry
genuflect
genuflection
genuine
genuinely
genuineness
genus
To what genus does that plant belong?
pl genera
geode
geographer
geographical
geographically
geography
geological
geologically
geologist
geology
geometric
geometrically
geometry
geophysics
geothermal
geranium
gerbil
geriatric
germ
German
germane
germinate

germinated
germinating
germination
gerrymander
gerrymandering
gerund
gestalt
gestate
gestation
gesticulate
gesticulated
gesticulating
gesticulation
gesture
gestured
gesturing
get
got
getting
getaway
get-together
get-up-and-go
geyser
Ghanaian
ghastliness
ghastly
ghee
gherkin
ghetto
pl ghettos
ghetto-blaster
ghost
ghostliness
ghostly
ghoul
ghoulish

giant
giantess
gibber
  gibbered
  gibbering
gibberish
gibbet
gibbon
gibe
  see jibe
giblets
giddiness
giddy
gift
gifted
gift-wrap
gig
gigantic
giggle
  giggled
  giggling
giggly
gigolo
gigot
gild
  to gild a brooch: to gild
  the lilly
gilder
gill
gillie
gilt
  a brooch covered in
  gilt
gimcrack
gimlet
gimmick

gimmicky
gimp
gin
ginger
gingerbread
gingerly
gingham
gingivitis
ginkgo
ginormous
ginseng
gipsy
  see gypsy
giraffe
gird
girder
girdle
girl
girlfriend
girlhood
girlie
girlish
giro, Giro
  pl giros
girth
gist
git
gittern
give
  gave
  He gave her a present
  given
  He has given her a
  present
  giving
give-away

gizzard
glacé
glacial
glaciation
glacier
  The glacier is melting
glad
gladden
  gladdened
  gladdening
glade
gladiator
gladiolus
  pl gladioli,
  gadioluses
gladly
gladness
glamorize
  glamorized
  glamorizing
glamorous
glamour
glance
  glanced
  glancing
gland
glandular
glare
  glared
  glaring
glasnost
glass
  pl glasses
glasshouse
glassily
glasspaper
glassy

glaucoma
glaze
  glazed
  glazing
glazier
  The glazier mended the window
gleam
  gleamed
  gleaming
glean
  gleaned
  gleaning
glebe
glee
gleeful
gleefully
glen
glib
glibness
glide
  glided
  gliding
glider
glimmer
  glimmered
  glimmering
glimpse
  glimpsed
  glimpsing
glint
glisten
  glistened
  glistening
glitch
glitter
  glittered
  glittering

glitterati
glitz
glitzy
gloaming
gloat
global
globally
globe
globeflower
globetrotter
globular
globule
glockenspiel
gloom
gloomily
gloomy
glorification
glorify
  glorified
  glorifying
glorious
glory
  pl glories
gloss
  pl glosses
glossary
  pl glossaries
glossily
glossiness
glossy
glottal
glottis
  pl glottises, glottides
glove
glow
  glowed

glowing
glower
  glowered
  glowering
glow-worm
gloxinia
glucose
glue
  glued
  gluing
glue-sniffer
gluey
glum
glut
  glutted
  glutting
glutamate
gluten
glutinous
  a glutinous substance
glutton
gluttonous
  gluttonous diners
gluttony
glycerine
gnarled
gnash
gnashers
gnat
gnaw
gneiss
gnocchi
gnome
gnomish
gnostic
gnu

go
  went
  He went yesterday
  gone
  He has gone away
  going
goad
go-ahead
goal
  He scored a goal
goalie
goalkeeper
goalpost
goat
goatee
gob
gobbet
gobble
  gobbled
  gobbling
gobbledygook
go-between
goblet
goblin
gobsmacked
God
god
godchild
  pl godchildren
goddaughter
goddess
  pl goddesses
godfather
God-fearing
God-forsaken
godless
godlike

godliness
godly
godmother
godparent
godsend
godson
goer
gofer
go-getter
goggles
going
  see go
goitre
go-kart
gold
golden
goldfinch
goldfish
gold-plated
golem
golf
  golfed
  golfing
golfer
golliwog, gollywog
golly
gonad
gondola
gondolier
gone
  see go
goner
gong
gonorrhoea
goo
good

  compar better
  superl best
  adv well
goodbye
good-day
goodies
goodly
goodness
goodwill
goody-goody
gooey
goof
goofy
googly
goon
goose
  pl geese
gooseberry
  pl gooseberries
goose-pimples
goose-step
gopher
gore
  gored
  goring
gorge
  gorged
  gorging
gorgeous
gorgeousness
gorgon
gorgonzola
gorilla
  A gorilla is an ape
gormless
gorse

gory
gosh
gosling
gospel
gossamer
gossip
  gossiped
  gossiping
gossipy
got
  see get
gouache
gouge
  gouged
  gouging
goujon
goulash
  pl goulashes
gourd
gourmand
  He is a greedy gourmand
gourmandise
gourmet
  He likes good food and wine - he is a gourmet
gout
govern
  governed
  governing
governess
  pl governesses
government
governmental
governor
gown

grab
  grabbed
  grabbing
grace
  graced
  gracing
graceful
gracefully
gracefulness
graceless
gracious
graciousness
gradation
  gradation in order of difficulty
grade
  graded
  grading
gradient
gradual
gradually
gradualness
graduand
graduate
  graduated
  graduating
graduation
  graduation from University
graffiti
graft
grafter
Grail
grain
grainy
gram
  see gramme

grammar
grammarian
grammatical
grammatically
gramme, gram
gramophone
granary
  pl granaries
grand
grandad
grandchild
  pl grandchildren
grand-daughter
grandeur
grandfather
grandiloquence
grandiloquent
grandiose
grandma
grandmother
grandpa
grandparent
grandson
grandstand
grange
granite
granny
  pl grannies
grant
granular
granulate
granulated
granule
grape
grapefruit

grapevine
graph
graphic
graphically
graphics
graphite
graphologist
graphology
grappa
grapple
  grappled
  grappling
grasp
grass
  pl grasses
grasshopper
grassy
grate
  a fire in the grate
grateful
  adv gratefully
grater
gratification
gratify
  gratified
  gratifying
grating
gratis
gratitude
gratuitous
gratuity
  pl gratuities
gravadlax
  see gravlax
grave
gravely

gravel
gravelly
graven
gravestone
graveyard
gravid
gravitas
gravitate
  gravitated
  gravitating
gravitation
gravity
gravlax, gravadlax
gravy
gray
  see grey
graze
  grazed
  grazing
grease
  greased
  greasing
greasepaint
greasiness
greasy
great
  a great man: a great amount
great-aunt
greatcoat
greatness
great-uncle
grebe
greed
greedily
greediness

greedy
green
greenback
greenery
greenfinch
greenfly
greengage
greengrocer
greenhorn
greenhouse
greenish
greenness
Greenpeace
greenroom
greenstick
greet
  greeted
  greeting
greetings
gregarious
gremlin
grenade
grenadier
grenadine
grew
  see grow
grey, gray
greyhound
greyness
grid
griddle
gridiron
grief
  full of grief at his death
grievance

grieve
to grieve over his death
grieved
grieving
grievous
griffin, griffon
grill
a grill on a cooker: a mixed grill: to grill a steak
grille
a metal grille in a window
grim
grimace
grimaced
grimacing
grime
grimness
grimy
grin
grinned
grinning
grind
ground
He ground the coffee
grinding
grinder
grindstone
gringo
grip
gripped
He gripped her hand
gripping
gripe
griped
He griped about the

service
griping
gripped
see **grip**
grisly
a grisly, horrible sight
grist
gristle
gristly
gristly meat
grit
gritted
gritting
gritty
grizzled
grizzly
a grizzly bear
groan
groaned
groaning
groat
grocer
grocery
pl groceries
grog
groggily
grogginess
groggy
groin
grommet
groom
groomed
grooming
groove
groovy
grope
to grope one's way: to

grope for a handkerchief
groped
groping
gross
grossly
grossness
grotesque
grotesquely
grotesqueness
grottiness
grotto
pl grottos, grottoes
grotty
grouch
grouchy
ground
see **grind**
ground
grounded
They grounded the planes
grounding
grounding
groundless
groundnut
groundsel
groundsheet
groundswell
groundwork
group
a group of children: to group together
grouped
grouping
groupie
grouse

to shoot a grouse
pl grouse

grouse
a grouse about prices
pl grouses
groused
grousing

grout

grove

grovel
grovelled
grovelling

groveller

grow
grew
He grew tall
grown
He has grown tall
growing

growl

grown
see **grow**

grown-up

growth

groyne

grub
grubbed
grubbing

grubbily

grubbiness

grubby

grudge
grudged
grudging

gruel

gruelling

gruesome

gruff

grumble
grumbled
grumbling

grumbler

grummet

grump

grumpily

grumpiness

grumpy

grunge

grunt

G-string

guacamole

guano

guarantee
guaranteed
guaranteeing

guarantor

guard
guarded
guardedly

guardian

guardsman
pl guardsmen

guava

gubbins

gudgeon

Guernsey

guernsey

guerrilla
guerrilla warfare

guess
pl guesses
guessed
guessing

guesstimate

guesswork

guesthouse

guest

guff

guffaw

guidance

guide
guided
guiding

guidebook

guideline

guild
a guild of craftsmen

guilder

guile

guileful

guileless

guillemot

guillotine
guillotined
guillotining

guilt
the guilt of the prisoner

guiltily

guilty

guinea

guinea-fowl

guinea-pig

guise

guiser

guitar

guitarist

gulag

gulf
pl gulfs

gull

gullet
gullible
gullibly
gully
  pl gullies
gulp
gum
  gummed
  gumming
gumbo
gumboil
gumboot
gumdrop
gummy
gumption
gun
  gunned
  gunning
gunboat
gunfire
gunge
gung-ho
gungy
gunk
gunman
  pl gunmen
gunmetal
gunner
gunpoint

gunpowder
gunshot
gunwale, gunnel
guppy
gurgle
  gurgled
  gurgling
guru
  gurus
gush
gusset
gust
gustily
gusto
gusty
gut
  gutted
  gutting
guts
gutsy
gutta-percha
gutted
gutter
guttering
guttersnipe
guttural
gutturally
guv

guy
  pl guys
guzzle
  guzzled
  guzzling
guzzler
gym
gymkhana
gymnasium
  pl gymnasiums,
  gymnasia
gymnast
gymnastics
gynaecological
gynaecologist
gynaecology
gyp
gypsophila
gypsum
gypsy, gipsy
  pl gypsies, gipsies
gyrate
  gyrated
  gyrating
gyration
gyratory
gyroscope

h

If you can't find the word you're looking for under letter **H**, it could be that it starts with a different letter. Try looking under **WH** for words like *who*, *whole* and *whom*.

ha
haberdasher
haberdashery
habit
habitable
habitat
habitation
habitual
habitually
habituate
  habituated
  habituating
habituation
hacienda
hack
hacker
hackles
hackney
hackneyed
hacksaw
had
hadn't
haddock
Hades
haematology
haemoglobin
haemophilia
haemophiliac

haemorrhage
  haemorrhaged
  haemorrhaging
haemorrhoid
hag
haggard
haggis
  pl haggises
haggle
  haggled
  haggling
haggler
ha-ha
haiku
hail
  hail and wind: to hail a
  taxi
  hailed
  hailing
hail-fellow-
  well-met
hailstone
hailstorm
hair
  a hair of her head
hairbrush
haircut
hairdo
hairdresser
hairdryer

hair-grip
hairless
hairline
hair-piece
hairpin
hair-raising
hair's-breadth
hair-slide
hair-splitting
hairspray
hairstyle
hairy
hajj
hake
halal
halberd
halcyon
hale
  hale and hearty
half
  half an apple
  pl halves
halfback
half-baked
half-board
half-hearted
halfpenny
  pl halfpennies
half-term

half-timbered
half-time
halfway
halfwit
halibut
halitosis
hall
hallelujah
halliard
hallmark
hallo
 see **hello**
hallow
 to hallow a shrine
Hallowe'en
hallucinate
 hallucinated
 hallucinating
hallucination
hallucinatory
hallucinogen
hallucinogenic
hallway
halo
 a saint's halo
 pl halos, haloes
halogen
halt
halter
halterneck
halting
halva
halve
 to halve an apple
 halved
 halving

halves
 see **half**
halyard
ham
hamburger
hamfisted
hamlet
hammer
 hammered
 hammering
hammerhead
hammock
hamper
 hampered
 hampering
hamster
hamstring
 hamstrung
 hamstringing
hand
handbag
handball
handbill
handbook
handbrake
handcart
handcuffs
handful
 pl handfuls
hand-grenade
handgun
handicap
handicapped
handicraft
handily
handiness

handiwork
handkerchief
 pl handkerchiefs,
 handkerchieves
handle
 handled
 handling
handlebars
handler
handmade
hand-me-down
handout
handover
handshake
hands-off
handsome
handsomely
handsomeness
hands-on
handwriting
handwritten
handy
handyman
hang
 hung
 *A picture hung on the
 wall: He hung his coat
 up*
 hanged
 *They hanged the
 murderer*
 hanging
hangar
 *a hangar for two
 planes*
hanger
 a coat hanger

hanger-on
  pl hangers-on
hang-glider
hang-gliding
hangman
hangnail
hangover
hank
hanker
  hankered
  hankering
hankie, hanky
  pl hankies
hanky-panky
hansom-cab
Hanukkah
haphazard
hapless
happen
  happened
  happening
happily
happiness
happy
  compar happier
  superl happiest
happy-go-lucky
hara-kiri
harangue
  harangued
  haranguing
harass
  harassed
  harassing
harassment
harbinger
harbour

harboured
harbouring
hard
harden
  hardened
  hardening
hard-and-fast
hardback
hardcore
harden
  hardened
  hardening
hard-hearted
hard-hitting
hardily
hardiness
hardline
hardliner
hardly
hardness
hard-nosed
hard-on
hard-pressed
hard-pushed
hardship
hardware
hardy
hare
  a hare and a rabbit
harebell
hare-brained
hair-lip
harem
haricot
hark
hark back

harked back
harking back
harlequin
harlot
harlotry
harm
harmful
harmfully
harmless
harmonica
harmonics
harmonious
harmonium
harmonization
harmonize, -ise
  harmonized
  harmonizing
harmony
harness
  pl harnesses
harp
harpist
harpoon
harpsichord
harpy
  pl harpies
harridan
harrier
harrow
harrowing
harry
  harried
  harrying
harsh
harshness
hart

a hart and a hind
harum-scarum
harvest
harvester
has
has-been
hash
hashish
hasn't
 = has not
hassle
 hassled
 hassling
hassock
haste
hasten
 hastened
 hastening
hastily
hastiness
hasty
hat
hatch
 pl hatches
hatchback
hatchery
 pl hatcheries
hatchet
hatchway
hate
 hated
 hating
hateful
hatefully
hatpin
hatstand

hatred
hatter
haughtily
haughtiness
haughty
haul
 hauled
 hauling
haulage
haulier
haunch
 pl haunches
haunt
haunting
haute couture
haute cuisine
have
 had
 having
haven
haven't
 = have not
haversack
havoc
haw
Hawaii
hawk
hawker
hawk-eyed
hawkish
hawser
hawthorn
hay
hay-fever
haystack
haywire

hazard
hazardous
haze
hazel
hazelnut
hazily
haziness
hazy
H-bomb
he
head
 headed
 heading
headache
headband
headbanger
headboard
head-dress
header
headfirst
headgear
headhunter
headhunting
heading
headlamp
headland
headless
headlight
headline
headlong
headmaster
headmistress
 pl headmistresses
head-on
headphone

headquarters
headrest
headroom
headscarf
headset
headship
headshrinker
headstone
headstrong
headway
headwind
headword
heady
heal
  to heal a wound
  healed
  healing
healer
healing
health
healthily
healthy
heap
  heaped
  heaping
hear
  She cannot hear you
  heard
  hearing
hearsay
hearse
heart
  *heart disease: a loving
  heart*
heartache
heartbreaking
heartbroken

heartburn
hearten
  heartened
  heartening
heartfelt
hearth
hearthrug
heartily
heartland
heartless
heart-rending
heartstrings
heart-throb
hearty
heat
  heated
  heating
heater
heath
heathen
heather
heating
heatstroke
heatwave
heave
  heaved
  heaving
heaven
heavenly
heavens
heave to
  hove to
  heaving to
heavily
heaviness
heavy

  compar heavier
  superl heaviest
heavy-duty
heavy-handed
heavyweight
heckle
  heckled
  heckling
heckler
hectare
hectic
hectically
hector
  hectored
  hectoring
he'd
  = he had, he would
hedge
  hedged
  hedging
hedgehog
hedgerow
hedonism
hedonist
hedonistic
heebie-jeebies
heed
heedful
heedless
heel
  *the heel of a shoe: to
  heel a shoe*
  heeled
  heeling
hefty
hegemony
heifer

height
heighten
heightened
heightening
heinous
heinousness
heir
*heir to the throne: heir
to a fortune*
heiress
pl heiresses
heirloom
held
see hold
helicopter
heliotrope
helipad
heliport
helium
helix
pl helices, helixes
he'll
= he will
hell
hell-bent
hellebore
hellish
hello, hallo, hullo
*Hello there!: Hallo!
How are you?*
helm
helmet
helmsman
help
helper
helpful

helpfully
helpfulness
helping
helpless
helplessness
helter-skelter
hem
hemmed
hemming
hemisphere
hemispherical
hemline
hemlock
hemp
hemstitch
hen
hence
henceforth
henchman
henna
hennaed
hennaing
henpecked
hepatitis
heptagon
heptagonal
her
herald
heraldic
heraldry
herb
herbaceous
herbal
herbalism
herbalist
herbarium

pl herbaria
herbicide
herbivore
herbivorous
Herculean
herd
herdsman
here
*Here you are: I left it
here*
hereabouts
hereafter
hereby
hereditary
heredity
herein
hereinafter
heresy
pl heresies
heretic
heretical
heretically
hereto
heretofore
hereupon
herewith
heritage
hermaphrodite
hermeneutics
hermetically
hermit
hermitage
hernia
pl hernias, herniae
hero
pl heroes

heroic
heroically
heroin
  heroin addicts
heroine
  the hero and heroine
heroism
heron
  a heron eating fish
herpes
herring
  fried herring
herringbone
hers
herself
hertz
he's
  = he is, he has
hesitancy
hesitant
hesitate
  hesitated
  hesitating
hesitation
hessian
heterogeneous
heterosexual
het up
heuristic
hew
  to hew down a tree
  hewed
  He hewed down a tree
  hewed, hewn
  He has hewed down a tree: He has hewn it

down
hewing
hexagon
hexagonal
hey
heyday
hi
hiatus
  pl hiatuses
hibernate
  hibernated
  hibernating
hibernation
hibiscus
  pl hibiscuses
hiccup, hiccough
  hiccuped
  hiccuping
hickory
hide
  hid
  He hid the treasure
  hidden
  He has hidden the treasure
hide-and-seek
hidebound
hideous
hideout
hiding
hierarchical
hierarchy
hieroglyph
hieroglyphics
hi-fi
higgledy-piggledy

high
  compar higher
  at a higher level
  superl highest
highball
highbrow
high-chair
high fidelity
high-flier, high-flyer
high-handed
highland
Highlands
highlight
  highlighted
  highlighting
highlighter
highly
highly-strung
highness
high-pitched
high-rise
high-risk
hi-tech
highway
highwayman
hijack
  hijacked
  highjacking
hijacker
hike
  hiked
  hiking
hiker
hilarious
hilarity
hill

hillbilly
  pl hillbillies
hillock
hillside
hilly
hilt
him
  She killed him
Himalayas
himself
hind
hinder
  hindered
  hindering
hindmost
hindrance
hindsight
Hindu
Hinduism
hinge
  hinged
  hinging
hint
hinterland
hip
hip-hop
hippo
hippodrome
hippopotamus
  pl hippopotamuses,
  hippopotami
hippy
  pl hippies
hipsters
hiragana
hire

to hire a car
hired
hiring
hire purchase
hirsute
his
hiss
  pl hisses
histamine
histogram
historian
historic
historical
historically
history
  pl histories
histrionic
histrionically
histrionics
hit
  hit
  hitting
hit-and-miss
hit-and-run
hitch
  pl hitches
hitchhike
  hitchhiked
  hitchhiking
hitchhiker
hi-tech
hither
hitherto
HIV
hive
hoar
  hoar frost

hoard
  to hoard food
hoarding
hoarder
hoarse
  She is hoarse from
  shouting
hoarsely
hoary
hoax
  pl hoaxes
hob
hobble
  hobbled
  hobbling
hobby
  pl hobbies
hobby-horse
hobgoblin
hobnail
hobnob
  hobnobbed
  hobnobbing
hobo
  pl hobos, hoboes
hock
hockey
hocus-pocus
hod
hodgepodge
hoe
  hoed
  hoeing
hog
  hogged
  hogging
Hogmanay

hogshead
hogwash
hogweed
hoick
hoi polloi
hoist
hoity-toity
hold
  held
  holding
holdall
holder
holding
hold-up
hole
  a hole in the ground: a
  hole in her sock
holey
holiday
holidaymaker
holiness
holistic
holler
hollow
holly
hollyhock
holocaust
hologram
holster
holt
holy
homage
home
  homed
  homing
home-coming

homeland
homeless
homelessness
homeliness
homely
home-made
homeopath
homeopathic
homeopathy
homeostasis
homesick
homesickness
homespun
homestead
homewards
homework
homicidal
homicide
homily
  pl homilies
homing
homoeopath
  see **homeopath**
homoeopathic
  see **homeopathic**
homoeopathy
  see **homeopathy**
homoeostasis
  see **homeostasis**
homogeneity
homogeneous
homogenization,
  -isation
homogenize, -ise
  homogenized
  homogenizing

homogenous
homologous
homonym
homophobia
homophone
homophony
homosexual
homosexuality
homy
hone
  honed
  honing
honest
honestly
honesty
honey
honeycomb
honeyed
honeymoon
honeysuckle
honk
honky-tonk
honorarium
honorary
  He is honorary secre-
  tary of the club
honorific
honour
  honoured
  honouring
honourable
  He is an honest and
  honourable man
honourably
hooch
hood

hoodlum
hoodwink
hooey
hoof
  pl hooves, hoofs
hoo-ha
hook
hookah, hooka
hooked
hooker
hookey
hooligan
hooliganism
hoop
  a hoop round a barrel
hooray
hoot
  hooted
  hooting
hooter
Hoover®
hoover
  hoovered
  hoovering
hop
  hopped
  The bird hopped over
  hopping
hope
  hoped
  She hoped that he
  would come
  hoping
hopeful
hopefully
hopefulness
hopeless

hopelessness
hopped
  see hop
hopper
hopscotch
horde
  a horde of noisy
  children
horizon
horizontal
hormonal
hormone
horn
hornbill
hornet
hornpipe
horny
horological
horologist
horology
horoscope
horrendous
horrible
horribly
horrid
horrific
horrify
  horrified
  horrifying
horror
horror-stricken
horror-struck
hors d'œuvre
horse
  two dogs and a horse
horseback

horsefly
  pl horseflies
horseplay
horsepower
horse-racing
horseradish
horseshoe
horsy
horticultural
horticulture
horticulturist
hosanna
hose
hosepipe
hosier
hosiery
hospice
hospitable
hospitably
hospital
hospitality
hospitalization,
  -isation
hospitalize, -ise
host
hostage
hostel
hostelry
  pl hostelries
hostess
  pl hostesses
hostile
hostilely
hostility
  pl hostilities
hot

compar hotter
superl hottest
hotbed
hotchpotch
hot-dog
hotel
hotelier
hotfoot
hot-headed
hothouse
hotplate
hotpot
hot-wire
 hot-wired
 hot-wiring
hound
hour
hourglass
hourly
house
 housed
 housing
houseboat
housebound
housecoat
household
householder
housekeeper
housekeeping
houseman
house-proud
housetrain
house-warming
housewife
 pl housewives
housework

housing
hovel
hover
 hovered
 hovering
hovercraft
hove to
 see heave to
how
howdah
howdy
however
howl
howler
howzat
hub
hubble-bubble
hubbub
hubby
hubris
huckleberry
huddle
 huddled
 huddling
hue
 *the hue of the sky: a
 hue and cry*
huff
huffy
hug
 hugged
 hugging
huge
hugely
hugeness
huh

hula-hoop
hulk
hulking
hull
hullabaloo
hullo
 see hello
hum
 hummed
 humming
human
 a human being
humane
 cruel, not humane
humanely
humanism
humanist
humanitarian
humanity
humanization,
 -isation
humanize, -ise
 humanized
 humanizing
humankind
humble
humbly
humbug
humdinger
humdrum
humerus
humid
humidifier
humidify
 humidified
 humidifying
humidity

humiliate
  humiliated
  humiliating
humiliation
  full of shame and
  humiliation
humility
  meekness and
  humility
hummingbird
hummus
humongous,
  humungous
humorist
humorous
humour
humourless
hump
humpback
humpbacked
humph
humus
hunch
  pl hunches
hunchback
hundred
hundredth
hundredweight
hung
  see **hang**
hunger
  hungered
  hungering
hungrily
hungry
hunk
hunky

hunky-dory
hunt
hunter
huntress
  pl huntresses
huntsman
  pl huntsmen
hurdle
  hurdled
  hurdling
hurdler
hurdygurdy
hurl
hurling
hurlyburly
hurrah
hurray
hurricane
hurried
hurriedly
hurry
  hurried
  hurrying
hurt
hurtful
hurtfully
hurtfulness
hurtle
  hurtled
  hurtling
husband
husbandry
hush
hushed
hush-hush
husk

husky
  pl huskies
hussar
hussy
  pl hussies
hustings
hustle
  hustled
  hustling
hustler
hut
hutch
  pl hutches
hyacinth
hyaena
  see **hyena**
hybrid
hydra
hydrangea
hydrant
hydrate
  hydrated
  hydrating
hydraulic
hydro
hydrocarbon
hydrochloric
hydroelectric
hydrofoil
hydrogen
hydrogenate
  hydrogenated
  hydrogenating
hydrology
hydrolysis
hydrometer
hydropathic

hydrophobia
hydrotherapy
hydroxide
hyena, hyaena
hygiene
hygienic
hygienically
hymen
hymn
  The choir sang a hymn
hymnal
hymnary
  pl hymnaries
hype
  hyped
  hyping
hyper
hyperactive
hyperactivity
hyperbole
hyperglycaemia

hypermarket
hypersensitive
hypertension
hypertext
hyperventilation
hyphen
hyphenate
hyphenation
hypnosis
hypnotherapy
hypnotic
hypnotically
hypnotism
hypnotist
hypnotize, -ise
  hypnotized
  hypnotizing
hypochondria
hypochondriac
hypocrisy

hypocrite
hypocritical
hypocritically
hypodermic
hypoglycaemia
hyponym
hypotenuse
hypothermia
hypothesis
  pl hypotheses
hypothesize, -ise
hypothetical
hypothetically
hysterectomy
hysteria
hysterical
hysterically
hysterics

i

iambic
ibex
ibidem
ibis
ice
  iced
  icing

iceberg
icebreaker
icecap
icecream
ice-skate
ice-skater
ice-skating

icicle
icily
icing
icon, ikon
iconoclasm
iconoclast
iconoclastic

iconography
icy
id
I'd
 = I had, I should, I
 would
idea
ideal
idealism
idealist
idealistic
idealization, -isation
idealize, -ise
 idealized
 idealizing
ideally
idem
identical
identically
identifiable
identification
identify
 identified
 identifying
identikit (picture)
identity
 pl identities
ideological
ideologically
ideology
idiocy
 pl idiocies
idiolect
idiom
idiomatic
idiomatically

idiosyncrasy
 pl idiosyncrasies
idiosyncratic
idiosyncratically
idiot
idiotic
idiotically
idle
 a slow and idle worker;
 to idle away time
 idled
 idling
idleness
idler
idly
idol
 The pop-star is her
 idol: heathen idols
idolater
idolatry
idolization, -isation
idolize, -ise
 idolized
 idolizing
idyll
idyllic
idyllically
if
iffy
igloo
 pl igloos
igneous
ignite
 ignited
 igniting
ignition
ignoble

ignobly
ignominious
ignominy
ignoramus
 pl ignoramuses
ignorance
ignorant
ignore
 ignored
 ignoring
iguana
ikebana
ikon
 see icon
ilk
I'll
 = I shall, I will
ill
 compar worse
 superl worst
ill-advised
ill-bred
illegal
illegality
illegally
illegibility
illegible
 untidy and illegible
 handwriting
illegibly
illegitimacy
illegitimate
illegitimately
ill-fated
illicit
 an illicit love affair

illicitness
ill-informed
illiteracy
illiterate
He cannot read that letter — he is illiterate
ill-mannered
illness
pl illnesses
illogical
illogically
ill-tempered
ill-timed
ill-treat
ill-treatment
illuminate
illuminated
illuminating
illumination
illusion
an optical illusion: an illusion of grandeur
illusionist
illusory
illustrate
illustrated
illustrating
illustration
illustrative
illustrator
illustrious
ill-will
I'm
= I am
image
imagery

imaginable
imaginary
imagination
imaginative
imaginatively
imagine
imagined
imagining
imago
pl imagos or imagines
imam
imbalance
imbecile
imbecility
imbibe
imbibed
imbibing
imbroglio
imbue
imbued
imbuing
imitable
imitate
imitated
imitating
imitation
imitative
imitator
immaculate
immaculately
immanence
immanent
immaterial
immature
immaturity

immeasurable
immediacy
immediate
immediately
immemorial
immense
immensely
immensity
immerse
immersed
immersing
immersion
immigrant
immigrants to Britain
immigration
immigration into Britain
imminence
imminent
immobile
immobility
immobilize, -ise
immobilized
immobilizing
immoderacy
immoderate
immodest
immodesty
immoral
wicked and immoral
immorality
wickedness and immorality
immortal
People die — they are not immortal
immortality

the immortality of God

immortalize, -ise
immortalized
immortalizing

immovable

immovably

immune

immunity

immunization,
-isation

immunize, -ise
immunized
immunizing

immunologist

immunology

immure
immured
immuring

immutable

imp

impact

impacted

impair
impaired
impairing

impairment

impala
pl impalas, impala

impale
impaled
impaling

impalement

impalpable

impart

impartial

impartiality

impartially

impassable

impasse

impassioned

impassive

impassively

impassiveness

impassivity

impatience

impatient

impeach

impeachable

impeachment

impeccable

impeccably

impecunious

impede
impeded
impeding

impediment

impel
impelled
impelling

impending

impenetrable

impenitence

impenitent

imperative

imperatively

imperceptible

imperceptibly

imperfect

imperfection

imperial

imperialism

imperialist

imperialistic

imperil
imperilled
imperilling

imperious

imperiousness

imperishable

impermeable

impermanence

impermeable

impermissible

impersonal

impersonally

impersonate
impersonated
impersonating

impersonation

impersonator

impertinence

impertinent

imperturbable

impervious

imperviousness

impetigo

impetuosity

impetuous
rash and impetuous

impetus
*the impetus of the
blow*
pl impetuses

impi

impiety

impinge
impinged
impinging

impingement

impious

impish

implacable

implant

implantation

implausible

implement

implementation

implicate
 implicated
 implicating

implication

implicit

implode

implore

imply
 implied
 implying

impolite

impolitely

import

importance

important

importation

importer

importunate

importune
 importuned
 importuning

importunity

impose
 imposed
 imposing

imposition

impossibility

impossible

impossibly

impostor

impotence

impotent

impound

impoverish

impoverished

impracticability

impracticable
 an impracticable idea

impracticably

impractical
 an impractical person

impracticality

impractically

imprecise

imprecision

impregnable

impregnate

impregnation

impresario
 pl impresarios

impress

impression

impressionable

impressionism

impressive

impressively

imprint

imprison
 imprisoned
 imprisoning

imprisonment

improbability

improbable

improbably

impromptu

improper

impropriety
 pl improprieties

improve
 improved
 improving

improvidence

improvident

improvement

improvidence

improvident

improvisation

improvise
 improvised
 improvising

impudence

impudent

impugn

impugnment

impulse

impulsive

impulsively

impulsiveness

impunity

impure

impurity
 pl impurities

imputation

impute
 imputed
 imputing

in
 in the house: dressed in black: covered in dirt

inability
in absentia
inaccessible
inaccessibly
inaccuracy
  pl inaccuracies
inaccurate
inaccurately
inaction
inactive
inactivity
inadequacy
  pl inadequacies
inadequate
inadequately
inadmissible
inadvertent
inalienable
inane
inanely
inanimate
inanity
  pl inanities
inapplicable
inappropriate
inappropriately
inappropriateness
inapt
  an inapt remark
inaptness
inarticulate
inasmuch as
inattention
inattentive
inattentively

inaudible
inaudibly
inaugural
inaugurate
  inaugurated
  inaugurating
inauguration
inaugurator
inauspicious
inborn
inbred
inbreed
inbreeding
incalculable
incandesce
incandescence
incandescent
incantation
incapable
incapacitate
  incapacitated
  incapacitating
incapacitation
incapacity
incarcerate
  incarcerated
  incarcerating
incarceration
incarnate
incarnation
incendiary
in'cense
  incensed
  incensing
'incense
incentive

inception
incertitude
incessant
incest
incestuous
inch
  pl inches
incidence
incident
incidental
incidentally
incinerator
incipient
incise
incision
incisive
incisively
incisiveness
incisor
incite
  incited
  inciting
incitement
incivility
  pl incivilities
inclemency
inclement
inclination
incline
  inclined
  inclining
include
  included
  including
inclusion
inclusive

inclusively
incognito
incognizance
incognizant
incoherence
incoherent
incombustible
income
incomer
incoming
incommensurable
incommensurate
incommode
 incommoded
 incommoding
incommodious
incommunicado
incomparable
incomparably
incompatibility
incompatible
incompetence
incompetent
incomplete
incomprehensibility
incomprehensible
incomprehensibly
incomprehension
inconceivable
inconceivably
inconclusive
inconclusively
incongruity
incongruous
incongruously

inconsequent
inconsequential
inconsequentially
inconsiderable
inconsiderate
inconsiderately
inconsistency
 pl inconsistencies
inconsistent
inconsolable
inconspicuous
inconspicuousness
inconstancy
inconstant
incontestable
incontinence
incontinent
incontrovertible
incontrovertibly
inconvenience
inconvenient
incorporate
 incorporated
 incorporating
incorporation
incorporeal
incorrect
incorrigible
incorrigibly
incorruptible
increase
 increased
 increasing
increasingly
incredibility
incredible

an incredible story
incredibly
incredulity
incredulous
an incredulous person: an incredulous look
increment
incremental
incriminate
 incriminated
 incriminating
incrimination
incubate
 incubated
 incubating
incubation
incubator
incubus
 pl incubuses, incubi
inculcate
 inculcated
 inculcating
incumbency
 pl incumbencies
incumbent
incur
 incurred
 incurring
incurable
incurably
incursion
incus
 pl incudes
indebted
indebtedness
indecency

indecent
indecipherable
indecision
indecisive
indecisively
indecisiveness
indeed
indefatigable
indefatigably
indefensible
indefensibly
indefinable
indefinably
indefinite
indefinitely
indelible
indelibly
indelicacy
indelicate
indelicately
indemnify
  indemnified
  indemnifying
indemnity
indent
indentation
indenture
independence
independent
in-depth
indescribable
indescribably
indestructible
indeterminate
indeterminately

index
  pl indexes, indices
  indexes of books:
  indices of numbers
indexer
Indian
indicate
  indicated
  indicating
indication
indicative
indicator
indices
  see index
indict [*in'dīt*]
indictment
indie
indifference
indifferent
indigence
indigenous
  Tobacco is not
  indigenous to Britain
indigent
  the indigent widow
indigestible
indigestion
indignant
indignation
indignity
  pl indignities
indigo
indirect
indiscernible
indiscipline
indiscreet

indiscretion
indiscriminate
indiscriminately
indispensable
indispensably
indisposed
indisposition
indisputable
indisputably
indissoluble
indistinct
indistinguishable
indistinguishably
individual
individualism
individualist
individuality
individualize, -ise
  individualized
  individualizing
individually
indivisible
indoctrinate
  indoctrinated
  indoctrinating
indoctrination
indolence
indolent
indomitable
indomitably
indoor
indoors
indubitable
indubitably
induce
  induced

inducing
inducement
induct
induction
inductive
indulge
  indulged
  indulging
indulgence
indulgent
industrial
  an industrial process:
  an industrial worker
  (= in industry)
industrialism
industrialist
industrialization,
  -isation
industrialize, -ise
industrialized, -ised
industrializing,
  -ising
industrially
industrious
  an industrious child
  (= hardworking)
industriousness
industry
  pl industries
inebriated
inebriation
inedible
ineducable
ineffable
ineffably
ineffective

ineffectively
ineffectiveness
ineffectual
ineffectually
inefficacious
inefficacy
inefficiency
inefficient
inelegance
inelegant
ineligibility
ineligible
  ineligible for the post
  because of lack of
  qualifications
ineluctable
inept
  an inept attempt: an
  inept young man
ineptitude
ineptness
inequable
inequality
  pl inequalities
inequitable
inequity
inert
inertia
inertness
inescapable
inescapably
inestimable
inestimably
inevitability
inevitable
inevitably

inexact
inexcusable
inexcusably
inexhaustible
inexorable
inexorably
inexpedience
inexpediency
inexpedient
inexpensive
inexpensively
inexperience
inexperienced
inexpert
inexplicable
inexplicably
inexplicit
inexpressible
inexpressibly
inextinguishable
inextricable
inextricably
infallibility
infallible
infallibly
infamous
infamy
infancy
infant
infanticide
infantile
infantry
infatuate
infatuated
infatuation

infect
infection
infectious
infelicitous
infelicity
infer
  inferred
  inferring
inference
inferior
inferiority
infernal
infernally
inferno
  pl infernos
infertile
infertility
infest
infidel
infidelity
in-fighting
infiltrate
  infiltrated
  infiltrating
infiltration
infiltrator
infinite
infinitely
infinitesimal
infinitesimally
infinitive
infinity
infirm
infirmary
  pl infirmaries
infirmity

  pl infirmities
inflame
  inflamed
  inflaming
inflammable
*Petrol is highly inflam-
mable*
inflammation
inflammatory
inflatable
inflate
  inflated
  inflating
inflation
inflationary
inflect
inflection
  see inflexion
inflexible
inflexion, inflection
inflict
infliction
influence
  influenced
  influencing
influential
influentially
influenza
influx
info
inform
informal
informality
informally
informant
information

informative
informatively
informer
infotainment
infraction
infra-red
infrasound
infrastructure
infrequency
infrequent
infringe
  infringed
  infringing
infringement
infuriate
  infuriated
  infuriating
infuse
  infused
  infusing
infusion
ingenious
  an ingenious idea
ingenue
ingenuity
ingenuous
  young and ingenuous
ingenuousness
ingest
ingestion
inglenook
ingot
ingrained
ingratiate
  ingratiated
  ingratiating

ingratitude
ingredient
ingress
inhabit
  inhabited
  inhabiting
inhabitable
inhabitant
inhalant
inhalation
inhale
  inhaled
  inhaling
inhaler
inherent
inherit
  inherited
  inheriting
inheritance
inheritor
inhibit
  inhibited
  inhibiting
inhibition
inhibitor
inhospitable
inhospitably
inhuman
  The torturing of
  prisoners is inhuman:
  a strange inhuman
  laugh
inhumane
  inhumane treatment of
  animals
inhumanely
inimical

inimically
inimitable
inimitably
iniquitous
iniquity
  pl iniquities
initial
  initialled
  initialling
initially
initiate
  initiated
  initiating
initiation
initiative
initiator
inject
injection
injudicious
injunction
injure
  injured
  injuring
injurious
injury
  pl injuries
injustice
ink
inkblot
inkling
inkpad
inkwell
inky
inlaid
  see inlay
inland

in-law
inlay
  inlaid
  inlaying
inlet
inmate
inmost
inn
  to stay at an inn
innards
innate
inner
innermost
innings
innkeeper
innocence
innocent
innocuous
innovate
innovation
innovator
innuendo
  pl innuendoes
innumerable
innumeracy
innumerate
inoculate
  inoculated
  inoculating
inoculation
inoffensive
inoffensively
inoperable
inoperative
inopportune
inopportunely

inordinate
inordinately
inorganic
in-patient
input
inputting
inquest
inquietude
inquire, enquire
  inquired, enquired
  inquiring, enquiring
inquirer, enquirer
inquiry, enquiry
  pls inquiries,
  enquiries
inquisition
inquisitive
inquisitively
inquisitor
inroads
inrush
insalubrious
insane
insanely
insanitary
insanity
insatiability
insatiable
insatiably
inscribe
  inscribed
  inscribing
inscription
inscrutable
inscrutably
insect

insecticide
insectivore
insecure
insecurely
insecurity
inseminate
inseminated
inseminating
insemination
insensible
insensitive
insensitively
inseparable
inseparably
insert
insertion
in-service
inset
inshore
inside
insider
insidious
insidiousness
insight
insignia
insignificance
insignificant
insincere
insincerely
insincerity
insinuate
  insinuated
  insinuating
insinuation
insipid

insist
insistence
insistent
in situ
insole
insolence
insolent
insoluble
insolvency
insolvent
insomnia
insomniac
insomuch
insouciance
insouciant
inspect
inspection
inspector
inspectorate
inspiration
inspirational
inspire
  inspired
  inspiring
instability
instal, install
  installed
  installing
installation
instalment
instance
instant
instantaneous
instantly
instead

instep
instigate
  instigated
  instigating
instigation
instigator
instil
  instilled
  instilling
instinct
instinctive
instinctively
institute
  instituted
  instituting
institution
institutional
institutionalism
institutionalize, -ise
  institutionalized
  institutionalizing
instruct
instruction
instructive
instructively
instructor
instructress
instrument
instrumental
instrumentalist
instrumentation
insubordinate
insubordination
insubstantial
insufferable
insufferably

insufficiency
insufficient
insular
insularity
insulate
  insulated
  insulating
insulation
insulin
insult
insuperability
insuperable
insuperably
insupportable
insurable
insurance
insure
  to insure one's life: to
  insure one's house
  against theft
  insured
  insuring
insurer
insurgence
insurgent
insurmountable
insurmountably
insurrection
intact
intake
intangible
intangibly
integer
integral
integrate
  integrated

integrating
integration
integrity
intellect
intellectual
intellectualize, -ise
  intellectualized
  intellectualizing
intellectually
intelligence
intelligent
  bright and intelligent
intelligentsia
intelligibility
intelligible
  a scarcely intelligible
  account of the
  accident
intelligibly
intemperance
intemperate
intemperately
intend
intense
intensely
intensification
intensifier
intensify
  intensified
  intensifying
intensity
intensive
intensively
intent
intention
intentional

intentionally
intentness
inter
 interred
 interring
interact
interaction
interactive
inter alia
interbreed
 interbred
 interbreeding
intercede
 interceded
 interceding
intercept
interception
interceptor
intercession
interchange
 interchanged
 interchanging
interchangeable
intercom
interconnect
intercontinental
intercourse
interdependence
interdependent
interdict
interdiction
interdisciplinary
interest
interested
interesting
interface

interfere
 interfered
 interfering
interference
interferon
intergalactic
interim
interior
interject
interjection
interlace
interlink
interlock
interlocutor
interloper
interlude
intermarriage
intermarry
 intermarried
 intermarrying
intermediary
 pl intermediaries
intermediate
interment
 the interment of the corpse
interminable
interminably
intermingle
intermission
intermittent
intern
internal
internally
internalize, -ise
 internalized

internalizing
international
internationalism
internationalist
internationally
internee
Internet, internet
internment
 the internment of the prisoner
internship
interpellate
 interpellated
 interpellating
interpellation
interpersonal
interplay
Interpol
interpolate
interpolation
interpret
 interpreted
 interpreting
interpretation
interpreter
interracial
interregnum
 pl interregnums, interregna
interrelate
interrelated
interrogate
 interrogated
 interrogating
interrogation
interrogative

interrogator
interrupt
interruption
intersect
intersection
intersperse
  interspersed
  interspersing
interstice
intertwine
interval
intervene
  intervened
  intervening
intervention
interventionism
interventionist
interview
interviewee
interviewer
interweave
  interwove
  interweaving
  interwoven
intestate
intestinal
intestines
intifada
intimacy
intimate
intimately
  intimated
  intimating
intimation
intimidate
  intimidated
  intimidating

intimidation
into
intolerable
intolerably
intolerance
intolerant
intonation
intone
  intoned
  intoning
intoxicant
intoxicate
  intoxicated
  intoxicating
intoxication
intractable
intramural
intransigence
intransigent
intransitive
intrauterine
intravenous
intrusive
intrusively
intrepid
intrepidity
intricacy
  pl intricacies
intricate
intricately
intrigue
  intrigued
  intriguing
intrinsic
intrinsically
introduce

introduced
introducing
introduction
introductory
introspection
introspective
introspectively
introversion
introvert
intrude
  intruded
  intruding
intruder
intrusion
intrusive
intuit
intuition
intuitive
intuitively
inundate
  inundated
  inundating
inundation
inure
  inured
  inuring
invade
  invaded
  invading
invader
invalid
invalidate
  invalidated
  invalidating
invalidation
invalidity

invaluable
invaluably
invariable
invariably
invariant
invasive
invasion
invective
inveigh
inveigle
  inveigled
  inveigling
invent
invention
inventive
inventiveness
inventor
inventory
  pl inventories
inverse
inversely
inversion
invert
invertebrate
  A worm is an inverte-
  brate creature
invest
investigate
  investigated
  investigating
investigation
investigative
investigator
investiture
investment
investor

inveterate
  an inveterate liar
invidious
invigilate
  invigilated
  invigilating
invigilator
invigorate
  invigorated
  invigorating
invincible
inviolable
inviolate
invisibility
invisible
invisibly
invitation
invite
  invited
  inviting
in vitro
invocation
invoice
invoke
  invoked
  invoking
involuntary
involuntarily
involve
  involved
  involving
involvement
inward
inwardly
inwards
iodine

ion
ionic
ionization, -isation
ionize, -ise
  ionized
  ionizing
ionizer, -iser
ionosphere
iota
IOU
Iowa
ipecacuanha
Iraqi
irascibility
irascible
irascibly
irate
irately
ire
iridescence
iridescent
iris
  pl irises
Irish
irk
irksome
iron
  ironed
  ironing
ironic, ironical
ironically
ironing
ironmonger
irony
  pl ironies
irradiate

irrational
irrationally
irreconcilable
irrecoverable
irredeemable
irrefutable
irregular
irregularity
  pl irregularities
irrelevance
irrelevancy
irrelevant
irremediable
irreparable
irreparably
irreplaceable
irrepressible
irrepressibly
irreproachable
irreproachably
irresistible
irresistibly
irresolute
irresolutely
irrespective
irrespectively
irresponsible
irresponsibly
irretrievable
irreverence
irreverent
irreversible
irrevocable
irrevocably
irrigate

irrigated
irrigating
irrigation
irritable
irritably
irritant
irritate
  irritated
  irritating
irritation
irrupt
irruption
is
  see be
isinglass
Islam
Islamic
island
islander
isle
  Isle of Man
islet
isn't
  = is not
isobar
isolate
  isolated
  isolating
isolation
isometric
isomorph
isomorphic
isosceles
isotherm
Israeli
issue
  issued

issuing
isthmus
  pl isthmuses
it
Italian
italicize, -ise
  italicized
  italicizing
italics
itch
  pl itches
itchiness
itchy
it'd
  = it would
item
itemize
iterate
iterated
iterating
iterative
itinerant
itinerary
  pl itineraries
it'll
  = it shall, it will
it's
  = it is
  It's fine
its
  its leg
itself
itsy-bitsy
I've
  = I have
ivory
ivy

j

If you can't find the word you're looking for under letter **J**, it could be that it starts with a different letter. Try looking under **G** for words like *gem*, *gin* and *gymnast*.

jab
  jabbed
  jabbing
jabber
  jabbered
  jabbering
jack
jackal
jackass
  pl jackasses
jackboot
jackdaw
jacket
jack-in-the-box
jack-knife
jack-of-all-trades
jackpot
Jacuzzi®
jade
jaded
jag
  jagged
  jagging
jaguar
jail, gaol
  He was sent to jail/ gaol
jailer, gaoler

jalopy
jam
  strawberry jam: in a jam: Did the machine jam?: to jam full
  jammed
  jamming
jamb
  the door jamb
jamboree
jammy
jangle
  jangled
  jangling
janitor
January
jape
japonica
jar
  jarred
  jarring
jargon
jasmine
jaundice
jaunt
jauntily
jaunty
javelin
jaw

jawbone
jay
jaywalk
jaywalker
jaywalking
jazz
jazzily
jazzy
jealous
jealousy
jeans
jeep
jeer
  jeered
  jeering
Jekyll and Hyde
jellied
jelly
  pl jellies
jellyfish
jeopardize, -ise
  jeopardized
  jeopardizing
jeopardy
jerboa
jerk
jerkily
jerkin

jerky

jeroboam

jersey
  pl jerseys

jest

jester

jet
  jetted
  jetting

jet-black

jetfoil

jet-lagged

jetsam

jet-setter

jettison
  jettisoned
  jettisoning

jetty
  pl jetties

Jew

jewel

jeweller, jeweler

jewellery, jewelry

Jewish

jib
  to jib at paying a lot
  jibbed
  jibbing

jibe, gibe
  to sneer and jibe
  jibed, gibed
  jibing, gibing

jiffy

jig
  jigged
  jigging

jiggery-pokery

jiggle

jigsaw

jihad

jilt

jingle
  jingled
  jingling

jingoism

jingoistic

jinx

jitterbug

jittery

jive

job

jobber

jobbing

job centre,
  Jobcentre

jobless

joblessness

job-sharing

jockey
  pl jockeys
  jockeyed
  jockeying

jockstrap

jocular

jocularity

jodhpurs

jog
  jogged
  jogging

jogger

joggle
  joggled
  joggling

Johannesburg

join
  joined
  joining

joiner

joinery

joint

joist

jojoba

joke
  joked
  joking

joker

jokey

jokiness

jokingly

jollification

jollity

jolly
  compar jollier
  superl jolliest

jollily

jolt

josh

joss-stick

jostle
  jostled
  jostling

jot
  jotted
  jotting

jotter

joule

journal

journalese

journalism

journalist

journey
  pl journeys
  journeyed
  journeying
joust
jovial
jovially
jowl
joy
joyful
joyfully
joyfulness
joyless
joyous
joyride
  joyrode
  joyriding
joyrider
joystick
jubilant
jubilation
jubilee
judge
  judged
  judging
judgement,
  judgment
judicial
  a judicial inquiry
judiciary
judicious
  *a judicious choice of
  books*

judo
jug
jugged
juggernaut
juggle
  juggled
  juggling
juggler
jugular (vein)
juice
juiciness
juicy
ju-jitsu
jukebox
July
jumble
  jumbled
  jumbling
jumble sale
jumbo
jump
jumper
jump-start
jumpsuit
jumpy
junction
  a road junction
juncture
  at this juncture
June
jungle
junior

juniper
junk
junket
junketing
junkie
Junoesque
jurisdiction
jurisprudence
jurist
juror
jury
  pl juries
just
justice
justiciary
justifiable
justifiably
justification
justify
  justified
  justifying
justly
jut
  jutted
  jutting
jute
juvenile
juxtapose
  juxtaposed
  juxtaposing
juxtaposition

k

If you can't find the word you're looking for under letter **K**, it could be that it starts with a different letter. Try looking under **C** for words like *can*, **CH** for words like *character*, and **Q** for words like *quite*. Also don't forget **KH** for words like *khaki*.

kabaddi
Kafkaesque
kaftan, caftan
kaiser
kale
kaleidoscope
kaleidoscopic
kaleidoscopically
kana
kangaroo
  pl kangaroos
kaolin
kapok
karaoke
karbovanets
karate
karma
kart
  a go-kart
kasbah
kayak
kazoo
kebab
kedgeree
keel
  keeled
  keeling
keelhaul

keen
keenness
keep
  kept
  keeping
keeper
keepsake
keg
kelp
kelvin
kennel
kepi
kept
  see **keep**
kerb
  She stood on the kerb
kerb-crawler
kerb-crawling
kerbstone
kernel
kerosene
kestrel
ketch
  pl ketches
ketchup
kettle
kettledrum
key

  the key to the door
keyboard
keyboarder
keyed-up
keyhole
keynote
key-ring
keystroke
keyword
khaki
Khyber
kibbutz
  pl kibbutzim
kibosh
kick
kicker
kick-off
kick-start
kid
kidnap
  kidnapped
  kidnapping
kidnapper
kidney
  pl kidneys
kill
killer
killjoy

kiln
kilo
kilobyte
kilocalorie
kilogramme
kilohertz
kilometre
kilowatt
kilt
kimono
  pl kimonos
kin
kind
kindergarten
kind-hearted
kindle
  kindled
  kindling
kindliness
kindly
kindness
kindred
kinesis
kinetic
kinetically
kinetics
king
kingdom
kingfisher
kingly
kingpin
kink
kinky
kinsfolk
kinship

kinswoman
kinsman
kiosk
kipper
kiss
  pl kisses
kissable
kisser
kissogram
kit
kitbag
kitchen
kitchenette
kite
kitsch
kitten
kittenish
kittiwake
kitty
kiwi
  pl kiwis
klaxon
kleptomania
kleptomaniac
knack
knacker
knackered
knapsack
knapweed
knave
  the knave of hearts
knavery
knavish
knead
  knead the bread

knee
  kneed
  He kneed him in the stomach
  kneeing
kneecap
kneecapped
kneecapping
knee-deep
knee-jerk
kneel
  knelt
  kneeling
knees-up
knell
knelt
  see kneel
knew
  see know
knickerbockers
knickers
knick-knack
knife
  pl knives
  knifed
  knifing
knight
  a knight in shining armour
knighted
knighthood
knightly
  Bravery is a knightly quality
knit
  to knit a cardigan
  knitted
  knitting

knitwear
knob
knock
knockdown
knocker
knock-kneed
knock-on
knockout
knoll
knot
a knot in the string
knotted
knotting
knotty
a knotty problem

know
I know her well
knew
I knew it
known
I should have known
knowing
know-all
know-how
knowingly
knowledge
knowledgeable
knowledgeably
known
see **know**

knuckles
knuckle under
knuckled under
knuckling under
koala bear
kookaburra
Koran
kosher
kowtow
kowtowed
kowtowing
kudos
kung-fu

l

la
lab
label
labelled
labelling
labial
labium
pl labia
laboratory
pl laboratories
laborious
labour
laboured
labouring

labourer
laburnum
labyrinth
lace
laced
lacing
lacerate
lacerated
lacerating
laceration
lace-up
lachrymose
lack

lackadaisical
lackadaisically
lackey
pl lackeys
lacklustre
laconic
laconically
lacquer
lacquered
lacquering
lacrosse
lactate
lactated

lactating

lactation

lactic

lactose

lacuna
 pl lacunae, lacunas

lad

ladder
 laddered
 laddering

laden

ladies
 see lady

lading

ladle
 ladled
 ladling

lady
 pl ladies

ladybird

ladylike

ladyship

lag
 lagged
 lagging

lager

laggard

lagoon

laid
 see lay

lain
 see lie

lair
 a wolf's lair

laird

laissez-faire

laity

lake

lama
 Tibetans respect the lama

lamb

lambada

lambaste, lambast
 lambasted
 lambasting

lambswool

lame

lamé

lameness

lament

lamentable

lamentation

lamina

laminate
 pl laminae

lamination

lamp

lampoon
 lampooned
 lampooning

lampoonist

lamppost

lampshade

lance
 lanced
 lancing

lance-corporal

lancet

land

landau

landlady
 pl landladies

landlocked

landlord

landlubber

landmark

landmass

landowner

landscape

landslide

landslip

lane
 a country lane

language

languid

languish

languor

languorous

languorously

laniard
 see lanyard

lank

lanky

lanolin

lantern

lanyard, laniard

lap
 lapped
 lapping

lapdog

lapel

lapidary
 pl lapidaries

lapse
 lapsed
 lapsing

laptop

lapwing

larcenist

larceny
larch
  pl larches
lard
larder
large
largely
largeness
largesse
largo
lariat
lark
larkspur
larva
  pl larvae
laryngitis
larynx
lasagne
lascivious
laser
lash
  pl lashes
lass
  pl lasses
lassi
lassie
lassitude
lasso
  pl lassos, lassoes
last
lastly
Las Vegas
latch
  pl latches
latchkey
late

lately
latency
lateness
latent
lateral
lateralization
laterally
  A crab moves laterally
latex
lath
  a lath of wood
lathe
  A mechanic uses a lathe
lather
  lathered
  lathering
lathery
Latin
latitude
latitudinal
latrine
latter
latterly
  Latterly he has grown senile
lattice
laud
  lauded
  lauding
laudable
laudably
laudanum
laudatory
laugh
laughable
laughably

laughing-stock
laughter
launch
  pl launches
launder
  laundered
  laundering
launderette
laundry
  pl laundries
laureate
laurel
lav
lava
lavatorial
lavatory
  pl lavatories
lavender
lavish
law
law-abiding
lawful
lawfully
lawless
lawlessness
lawn
lawnmower
lawsuit
lawyer
lax
laxative
laxity
lay
  see lie
lay
  to lay it on the table

laid
She laid it on the bed
laying

layabout

layby
pl laybys

layer
two layers of cloth

layette

layman
pl laymen

layout

layperson
pl laypeople

laywoman
pl laywomen

laze
lazed
lazing

lazily

laziness

lazy
compar lazier
superl laziest

lazy-bones

lea
the green lea

leach
to leach harmful substances into the water

lead [*lēd*]
to lead into battle
led
He led me to the king
leading

lead [*led*]
lead pipes

leaden

leader

leadership

leading

leaf
pl leaves

leafless

leaflet

leafy

league

leak
a gas leak: Does this kettle leak?

leakage

lean
leant, leaned
leaning

leanness

leant
see lean

leap
leapt, leaped
leaping

leapfrog

leapt
see leap

learn
learned, learnt
learning

learner

lease
leased
leasing

leasehold

leash
pl leashes

least

see little

leather
leathered
leathering

leathery

leave
left
leaving

leaves
see leaf

leaven

leavings

lecher

lecherous

lechery

lecithin

lectern

lecture
lectured
lecturing

lecturer

lectureship

led
see lead

ledge

ledger

lee
in the lee of the boat

leech
clinging to her like a leech
pl leeches

leek
leek soup

leer
leered
leering

lees
leeward
leeway
left
see **leave**
left-hand
left-handed
left-handedness
left-hander
leftism
leftist
left-over
leftovers
left-wing
left-winger
leg
legacy
pl legacies
legal
legality
pl legalities
legalize, -ise
legalized
legalizing
legally
legate
legatee
legation
legend
legendary
legerdemain
leggings
leggy
legibility
legible
clear, legible writing

legibly
legion
legionary
legionnaire
legislate
legislated
legislating
legislation
legislative
legislator
legislature
legitimacy
legitimate
legitimately
legitimize, -ise
legless
legume
leguminous
leisure
leisured
leisurely
lemming
like lemmings to the sea
lemon
an orange and a lemon
lemonade
lemony
lemur
lend
lent
lending
length

lengthen
lengthened
lengthening
lengthily
lengthiness
lengthways
lengthy
lenience
leniency
lenient
lens
pl lenses
Lent
lent
see **lend**
lentil
Leo
leonine
leopard
a tiger and a leopard
leotard
leper
a leper dressed in rags
leprechaun
leprosy
lesbian
lesbianism
lesion
less
see **little**
lessee
lessen
to lessen the pain
lessened
lessening

lesser
lesson
  a French lesson
lessor
lest
let
  let
  letting
lethal
lethargic
lethargically
lethargy
letter
lettered
letterhead
lettering
lettuce
leucine
leucocyte
leukaemia
levee
level
  levelled
  levelling
level-headed
lever
leverage
leveret
leviathan
levied
  see **levy**
levitate
  levitated
  levitating
levitation
levity

levy
  pl levies
  levied
  levying
lewd
lewdness
lexeme
lexical
lexicographer
lexicography
lexicology
lexicon
lexis
liability
  pl liabilities
liable
  You are liable to slip on ice: liable for her debts
liaise
  liaised
  liaising
liaison
liana
liar
  Don't believe a liar
libation
libel
  guilty of libel: Did the newspaper libel him?
  libelled
  libelling
libellous
liberal
liberally
liberalism
liberalization
liberalize, -ise

liberalized
liberalizing
liberality
liberate
  liberated
  liberating
liberation
liberator
libertine
liberty
  pl liberties
libidinal
libidinous
libido
Libra
librarian
librarianship
library
  pl libraries
librettist
libretto
  pl libretti, librettos
lice
  see **louse**
licence
  a TV licence: poetic licence
license
  to license a TV
  licensed
  licensing
licensee
licentiate
licentious
licentiousness
lichen
lichgate

licit
lick
lid
lido
lie
 lied
 He lied about his age
 lying
lie
 lay
 He lay down
 lain
 He has lain down: He'd
 lain there for three
 days
 lying
liege
lie-in
lieu
lieutenant
life
 pl lives
lifebelt
lifeboat
life cycle
lifeguard
life-jacket
lifeless
life-like
lifeline
lifelong
lifer
life-saver
lifestyle
lifetime
lift
lift-off

ligament
ligature
light
 lit, lighted
 lighting
lighten
 lightened
 lightening
 lightening the load
lighter
light-hearted
lighthouse
lighting
lightness
lightning
 thunder and lightning
lightweight
like
 liked
 liking
likeable, likable
likelihood
likely
like-minded
liken
 likened
 likening
likeness
likewise
lilac
Lilliputian
lilt
lily
 pl lilies
lily-of-the-valley
limb
limber

limbered
 limbering
limbless
limbo
lime
limelight
limerick
limestone
limit
 limited
 limiting
limitation
limitless
limousine
limp
limpet
limpid
limpness
linchpin
linctus
line
 lined
 lining
lineage
lineal
lineally
lineament
 the lineaments of her
 face
linear
linen
liner
linesman
lineswoman
 pl lineswomen
line-up

ling
linger
  lingered
  lingering
lingerer
lingerie
lingua franca
  pl lingua francas
linguist
linguistic
linguistically
linguistics
liniment
  to rub some liniment
  on his leg
lining
link
links
link-up
linnet
lino
linocut
linoleum
linseed
lint
lintel
lion
lioness
  pl lionesses
lionize, -ise
  lionized
  lionizing
lip
lipid
lipogram
liposuction

lip-read
  lip-read
  lip-reading
lip-reader
lip-service
lipstick
liquefy
  liquefied
  liquefying
liqueur
  Cointreau is an
  orange liqueur
liquid
liquidate
  liquidated
  liquidating
liquidation
liquidator
liquidize, -ise
  liquidized
  liquidizing
liquidizer, -iser
liquor
  whisky and other
  strong liquors
liquorice
lira
lisp
lissom, lissome
list
listen
  listened
  listening
listener
listeria
listless
lit

  see light
litany
  pl litanies
literacy
literal
  a literal translation
literally
literary
  He has literary tastes
literate
  He is scarcely literate
literati
literature
lithe
litheness
lithium
lithograph
lithographer
lithographer
lithosphere
litigant
litigate
  litigated
  litigating
litigation
litigious
litmus
litotes
litre
litter
  littered
  littering
little
  compar less
  superl least
littoral

liturgical

liturgy
pl liturgies

live [*liv*]
lived
living

liveable

live [*līv*]

livelihood

liveliness

livelong

lively
compar livelier
superl liveliest

liven up
livened up
livening up

liver

liveried

livery
pl liveries

livestock

livid

living

living-room

lizard

llama
The llama is of the camel family

lo!

loach

load
a load of coal: to load the lorry with coal

loaded

loaf
pl loaves

loaf
loafed
loafing

loam

loamy

loan
a book on loan

loanword

loath, loth
I am loath to go

loathe
I loathe cruelty
loathed
loathing

loathsome

lob
lobbed
lobbing

lobby
pl lobbies

lobbyist

lobe

lobelia

lobotomy
pl lobotomies

lobster

local
local people: drinking in his local

locale
the locale of the film

locality

localize, -ise
localized
localizing

locate
located
locating

location

loch

loci

lock

lockable

locker

locket

lockjaw

locomotion

locomotive

lockout

locksmith

lockup

locomotion

locomotive

locum
pl locums

locus
pl loci

locust

locution

lode
A lode is a vein in rock containing metal

lodestar

lodestone

lodge
lodged
lodging

lodger

loess

loft

loftily

loftiness

lofty

log

logged
logging
loganberry
pl loganberries
logarithm
logbook
loggerheads
logic
logical
logically
logistic
logistical
logistics
logo
loin
loincloth
loiter
loitered
loitering
loiterer
loll
lolled
lolling
lollipop
lollop
lolloped
lolloping
lolly
pl lollies
lone
a lone cottage: a lone star
loneliness
lonely
lonesome
long
longboat

longbow
longhand
longevity
longing
longitude
longship
long-suffering
long-term
long-winded
loo
loofah
look
lookalike
lookout
loom
loomed
looming
loony
loop
looped
The pilot looped the loop
looping
loophole
loose
a loose-fitting coat: This screw is loose: a loose end
loosely
loosen
loosened
loosening
loot
the burglar's loot
looter
lop
lopped

He lopped a branch from the tree
lopping
lope
loped
The large dog loped along
loping
lopped
see lop
lop-sided
loquacious
loquacity
lord
lordly
lordship
lore
lorgnette
lorry
pl lorries
Los Angeles
lose
to lose a glove: to lose weight: to lose time
lost
losing
loser
loss
pl losses
loss-leader
lost
see lose
lot
loth
see loath
lotion
lottery

pl lotteries
lotto
lotus
louche
loud
loudhailer
loudness
loudspeaker
lounge
 lounged
 lounging
lour
 see lower
louse
 pl lice
lousy
lout
louvre
louvred
lovable
lovage
love
 loved
 loving
lovebird
loveless
loveliness
lovelorn
lovely
 compar lovelier
 superl loveliest
love-making
lover
lovesick
loving
low

lower ['lōər]
 lowered
 lowering
lower, lour ['lowər]
lower-case
lowland
lowlander
lowliness
lowly
lowness
loyal
loyalist
loyally
loyalty
lozenge
lubricant
lubricate
 lubricated
 lubricating
lubrication
lubricator
lucid
lucidity
luck
luckily
lucky
 compar luckier
 superl luckiest
lucrative
lucre
ludicrous
ludo
luff
lug
 lugged
 lugging

luge
luggage
lugubrious
lugworm
lukewarm
lull
 lulled
 lulling
lullaby
 pl lullabies
lumbago
lumbar
 lumbar pain
lumber
 rubbish and lumber:
 Elephants lumber
 through the forests: to
 lumber him with the
 work
 lumbered
 lumbering
lumberjack
luminary
luminescence
luminescent
luminosity
luminous
lump
lumpectomy
lumpfish
lumpy
lunacy
lunar
lunatic
lunch
 pl lunches
luncheon

lunchtime
lung
lunge
  lunged
  lunging
lupin
lupine
lurch
lurcher
lure
  lured
  luring
lurid
lurk
luscious
lush
lust
lustful

lustfully
lustily
lustre
lustrous
lusty
lute
  to play a lute
luxuriance
luxuriant
luxuriate
  luxuriated
  luxuriating
luxurious
luxury
  pl luxuries
lycanthropy
lychee

lying
  see lie
lymphatic
lymph gland
lynch
lynx
  pl lynxes
lyre
  A lyre is like a harp
lyrebird
lyric
lyrical
lyrically
lyricism
lyricist

m

ma'am
macabre
macadamize, -ise
  macadamized
  macadamizing
macaroni
  macaroni cheese
macaroon
  biscuits and macaroons

macaw
mace
macerate
  macerated
  macerating
maceration
machete
Machiavellian
machinate
  machinated

machinating
machination
machine
machine-gun
machinery
machinist
machismo
macho
Mach number
mackerel

mackintosh
 pl mackintoshes
macro
macrobiotic
macrocosm
macroeconomics
mad
 compar madder
 superl maddest
madam
madcap
madden
 maddened
 maddening
made
 see make
Madeira
madhouse
madman
 pl madmen
madness
Madonna
madrigal
madwoman
maelstrom
maestro
 pl maestros
magazine
magenta
maggot
maggoty
magic
magical
magically
magician
magisterial

magistrate
magma
magnanimity
magnanimous
magnate
 He is a shipping magnate
magnesia
magnesium
magnet
 A magnet attracts iron
magnetic
magnetically
magnetism
magnetization, -isation
magnetize, -ise
 magnetized
 magnetizing
magnificat
magnification
magnificence
magnificent
magnify
 magnified
 magnifying
magnitude
magnolia
magnum
magpie
magus
 pl magi
Maharajah
mah-jong
mahogany
maid

 a chamber-maid
maiden
maidservant
mail
 first-class mail; mail the letter
mailed
mailing
mailbag
mail-order
mailshot
maim
 maimed
 maiming
main
 the main points of his speech
mainbrace
mainframe
mainland
mainline
mainly
mainsail
mainstay
mainstream
maintain
 maintaining
 maintained
maintenance
maisonette
maize
 fields of maize
majestic
majestically
majesty
 pl majesties
major

majorette
majority
  pl majorities
make
  made
  She made a cake
  making
maker
makeshift
make-up
malachite
maladjusted
maladroit
malady
  pl maladies
malaise
malapropism
malaria
malarkey
male
  male and female
malediction
maledictory
maleness
malevolence
malevolent
malformation
malformed
malfunction
  malfunctioned
  malfunctioning
malice
malicious
malign
  maligned
  maligning

malignant
malinger
  malingered
  malingering
malingerer
mall
mallard
malleable
mallet
malleus
  pl mallei
mallow
malnutrition
malodorous
malpractice
malt
maltreat
maltreatment
mamba
mambo
mamma, mama
mammal
mammalian
mammary
mammography
mammoth
man
  pl men
  manned
  manning
manacle
manage
  managed
  managing
manageable
management

manager
manageress
managerial
mandarin
mandate
mandatory
mandible
mandoline,
  mandolin
mane
  a horse's mane
manful
manfully
manga
manganese
mange
manger
mangetout
mangle
  mangled
  mangling
mango
  pl mangoes
mangrove
mangy
manhandle
  manhandled
  manhandling
manhole
manhood
manhunt
mania
maniac
  *The murderer was a
  maniac*
maniacal

manic
a manic depressive
manicure
manicurist
manifest
manifestation
manifesto
pl manifestos,
manifestoes
manifold
manikin
manipulate
manipulated
manipulating
manipulation
mankind
manky
manliness
manly
manna
manned
see man
mannequin
manner
a manner of speaking:
a pleasant manner
mannerism
mannerly
mannish
manoeuvrable
manoeuvre
manor
the lord of the manor
manorial
manpower
mansard

manse
manservant
pl manservants
mansion
manslaughter
mantel
mantelpiece
mantilla
mantis
mantle
mantra
manual
manually
manufacture
manufactured
manufacturing
manufacturer
manure
manuscript
Manx cat
many
map
mapped
mapping
maple
maquette
mar
marred
marring
marabou
maraschino
marathon
maraud
marauder
marauding
marble

marcasite
March
march
pl marches
marchioness
pl marchionesses
mare
a mare and her foal
margarine
margin
marginal
marginally
marguerite
marigold
marijuana
marimba
marina
yachts in the marina
marinade
marinaded
marinading
marinate
marinated
marinating
marine
mariner
marionette
marital
maritime
marjoram
mark
marked
marker
market
marketed
marketing

marketable
marksman
  pl marksmen
marksmanship
marl
marmalade
marmoset
marmot
maroon
  marooned
  marooning
marquee
marquess, marquis
  pls marquesses,
  marquises
marquetry
marriage
marriageable
marrow
marrowbone
marrowfat
marry
  married
  marrying
marsh
  pl marshes
marshal
  an air marshal: a US
  marshal: to marshal
  the troops
  marshalled
  marshalling
marshmallow
marshy
marsupial
mart
martello tower

marten
  the fur of a marten
martial
  martial music: martial
  law
martin
  a martin's nest
martinet
martyr
  martyred
  martyring
martyrdom
marvel
  marvelled
  marvelling
marvellous
Marxism
Marxist
marzipan
mascara
mascarpone
mascot
masculine
masculinity
mash
mask
  The surgeon wore a
  mask: The burglar
  wore a mask
masochism
masochist
masochistic
masochistically
mason
masonic
masonry

masque
  The minstrels took part
  in the masque
masquerade
  masqueraded
  masquerading
masquerader
mass
  pl masses
Massachusetts
massacre
  massacred
  massacring
massage
  massaged
  massaging
masseur
masseuse
massive
mass-produce
  mass-produced
  mass-producing
mass-production
mast
mastectomy
master
masterful
masterfully
masterliness
masterly
mastermind
masterpiece
mastery
masthead
masticate
  masticated
  masticating

mastication
mastiff
mastitis
masturbate
 masturbated
 masturbating
masturbation
mat
 see matt
mat
 *a mat by the front
 door: This material
 tends to mat*
 matted
 matting
matador
match
 pl matches
matchbox
 pl matchboxes
matchless
matchmaker
matchstick
mate
 mated
 mating
mater
material
materially
materialism
materialistic
materialistically
materialization,
 -isation
materialize, -ise
 materialized
 materializing

maternal
maternally
maternity
mathematical
mathematically
mathematician
mathematics
maths
matinée, matinee
matins
matriarch
matriarchal
matricide
matriculate
 matriculated
 matriculating
matriculation
matrimonial
matrimony
matrix
 pl matrices, matrixes
matron
matronly
matt, matte, mat
 matt paint
matter
 mattered
 mattering
matter-of-fact
matting
mattress
 pl mattresses
mature
 matured
 maturing
maturity

maudlin
maul
 mauled
 mauling
mausoleum
mauve
maverick
mawkish
maxim
maximal
maximization,
 -isation
maximize, -ise
 maximized
 maximizing
maximum
 pl maxima
May
may
 might
maybe
mayday
mayfly
 pl mayflies
mayhem
mayonnaise
mayor
 *the Lord Mayor of
 London*
mayoress
maypole
maze
 lost in a maze
me
mea culpa
mead
meadow

meagre
meagrely
meal
mealie
mealy-mouthed
mean
  a mean old miser:
  What does the word
  mean?
  meant
  meaning
meander
  meandered
  meandering
meaning
meaningful
meaningfully
meaningless
meanness
meant
  see **mean**
meantime
meanwhile
measles
measly
measurable
measure
  measured
  measuring
measurement
meat
  Vegetarians don't eat
  meat
meatball
meaty
mecca
mechanic

mechanical
mechanically
mechanics
mechanism
mechanization,
  -isation
mechanize, -ise
  mechanized
  mechanizing
medal
  a gold medal
medallion
medallist
meddle
  to meddle in people's
  affairs
  meddled
  meddling
meddler
media
  see **medium**
**mediaeval,
  medieval**
median
mediate
  to mediate in a dispute
  mediated
  mediating
mediation
mediator
medic
medical
medically
medicated
medication
medicinal
medicine

medieval
  see **mediaeval**
mediocre
mediocrity
meditate
  to pray and meditate
  meditated
  meditating
meditation
meditative
Mediterranean
medium
  pl media
  the mass media
  pl mediums
  Mediums are psychic
medley
  pl medleys
medusa
  pl medusae
meek
meerschaum
meet
  They meet in the
  church hall
  met
  meeting
mega
megabyte
megalith
megalomania
megalomaniac
megaphone
megaton
Meissen
melamine
melancholia

melancholic
melancholy
melanin
melanoma
mellifluous
mellow
melodic
melodious
melodrama
melodramatic
melodramatically
melody
　pl melodies
melon
melt
meltdown
melting-pot
member
membership
membrane
membranous
memento
　pl mementos
memo
memoir
memorabilia
memorable
memorably
memorandum
　pl memoranda
memorial
memorize, -ise
　memorized
　memorizing
memory
　pl memories

men
　see **man**
menace
　menaced
　menacing
ménage
menagerie
mend
mendacious
mendacity
mendicant
menfolk
menhir
menial
meningitis
meniscus
　pl meniscuses,
　menisci
menopausal
menopause
menses
menstrual
menstruate
　menstruated
　menstruating
menstruation
mental
mentally
mentality
　pl mentalities
menthol
mentholated
mention
　mentioned
　mentioning
mentor
menu

　pl menus
mercantile
mercantilism
mercenary
　pl mercenaries
merchandise
merchant
merciful
mercifully
merciless
mercurial
mercury
mercy
mere
merely
merge
　merged
　merging
merger
meridian
meridional
meringue
merino
　merino wool
merit
　merited
　meriting
meritocracy
　pl meritocracies
meritorious
mermaid
merman
merrily
merriment
merry
　compar merrier

superl merriest

merry-go-round

merrymaking

mescal

mescalin

mesh
pl meshes

mesmerism

mesmerize, -ise
mesmerized
mesmerizing

mess
pl messes

message

messenger

messy

met
see **meet**

metabolic

metabolism

metabolize, -ise
metabolized
metabolizing

metacarpal

metal
a metal box

metallic

metallurgical

metallurgy

metamorphose
metamorphosed
metamorphosing

metamorphosis
pl metamorphoses

metaphor

metaphorical

metaphorically

metaphysical

metaphysics

metastasis
pl metastases

metatarsal

meteor

meteoric

meteorite

meteorological

meteorologically

meteorologist

meteorology

mete out
*to mete out
punishment*
meted out
meting out

meter
a gas meter

methadone

methane

methanol

method

methodical

methodically

methodological

methodology

meths

methylated spirits

meticulous

metonymy

metre
a metre of cloth

metric

metrical

metricate

metricated
metricating

metrication

metronome

metropolis
pl metropolises

metropolitan

mettle
*That horse has plenty
of mettle*

mew

mews
a mews flat

mezzanine

mezzo-soprano

miaow

miasma
pl miasmata,
miasmas

mica

mice
see **mouse**

Michaelmas daisy

mickey

micro

microbe

microbiologist

microbiology

microchip

microclimate

microcomputer

microcosm

microdot

microfiche

microfilm

microlight

micrometer
micro-organism
microphone
microprocessor
microscope
microscopic
microsurgery
microwave
microwaveable
mid-air
midday
middle
middle-aged
middle-class
middleman
middleweight
middling
midge
midget
midnight
midpoint
midriff
midst
midstream
midsummer
midway
midweek
midwife
  pl midwives
midwifery
midwinter
mien
  a solemn mien
miffed
might

see may
might
  the might of the army
mightily
mightiness
mightn't
  = might not
mighty
  compar mightier
  superl mightiest
migraine
migrant
migrate
  migrated
  migrating
migratory
mike
mild
mildew
mile
mileage
mileometer
milestone
milieu
militancy
militant
militarism
militaristic
military
militate
  militated
  militating
militia
militiaman
  pl militiamen
milk

milkmaid
milkman
  pl milkmen
milkshake
milky
mill
millennium
  pl millennia
miller
millet
millibar
milligramme
millilitre
millimetre
milliner
millinery
million
millionaire
millionairess
millipede
millpond
millstone
milord
mime
  mimed
  miming
mimesis
mimic
  mimicked
  mimicking
mimicry
mimosa
minaret
mince
  minced
  mincing

mincemeat
mincer
mind
mind-blowing
mindful
mindless
mine
minefield
miner
  a coal miner
mineral
mineralogical
mineralogically
mineralogist
mineralogy
minestrone
mingle
  mingled
  mingling
mini
  pl minis
miniature
miniaturize
  miniaturized
  miniaturizing
minibus
  pl minibuses
minicab
minim
minimal
minimalism
minimalist
minimize, -ise
  minimized
  minimizing
minimum

  pl minima
mining
minion
miniskirt
minister
  *a minister of the
  church: to minister to
  her needs*
  ministered
  ministering
ministerial
ministerially
ministration
ministry
  pl ministries
mink
minneola
minnow
minor
  *of minor importance:
  legally, a minor*
minority
  pl minorities
minster
  York Minster
minstrel
mint
minty
minuet
minus
minuscule
minute
minutiae
minx
  pl minxes
miracle
miraculous

mirage
mire
mirin
mirror
  mirrored
  mirroring
mirth
mirthful
misadventure
misanthropic
misanthropist
misanthropy
misappropriate
  misappropriated
  misappropriating
misappropriation
misbehave
  misbehaved
  misbehaving
misbehaviour
miscalculate
  miscalculated
  miscalculating
miscalculation
miscarriage
miscarry
  miscarried
  miscarrying
miscellaneous
miscellany
  pl miscellanies
mischance
mischief
mischievous
misconception
misconduct
misconstrue

misconstrued
misconstruing
miscreant
misdeed
misdemeanour
miser
miserable
miserably
misericord
miserly
misery
　pl miseries
misfire
　misfired
　misfiring
misfit
misfortune
misgiving
misguided
mishandle
　mishandled
　mishandling
mishap
mishear
mishmash
misinform
misinformation
misjudge
　misjudged
　misjudging
mislay
　mislaid
　mislaying
mislead
　misled
　misleading
mismanage

mismanaged
mismanaging
mismatch
misnomer
misogynist
misogynous
misplace
misprint
mispronounce
misquote
misread
misrepresent
miss
　pl misses
　missed
　missing
missal
　The choirboy carried a
　missal
misshapen
missile
　a nuclear missile
mission
missionary
　pl missionaries
Mississippi
missive
misspell
　misspelled, misspelt
　misspelling
misspent
mist
mistake
　mistaken
　We were mistaken
　mistook
　I mistook her for you

mistaking
mister
mistletoe
mistook
　see mistake
mistral
mistreat
mistress
　pl mistresses
mistrust
misty
misunderstand
　misunderstood
　misunderstanding
misuse
mite
　a poor little mite
mitigate
　mitigated
　mitigating
mitigation
mitre
mitt
mitten
mix
　pl mixes
mixer
mixture
mnemonic
moan
　moaned
　moaning
moat
　a moat round the
　castle
mob
　mobbed

mobbing
mobile
mobility
mobilization,
 -isation
mobilize, -ise
 mobilized
 mobilizing
moccasin
mocha
mock
mockery
mocking
mockingbird
mock-up
modal
 a modal verb
modality
mode
model
 a model aeroplane
 modelled
 modelling
modem
moderate
moderately
moderation
moderato
moderator
modern
modernity
modernization,
 -isation
modernize, -ise
 modernized
 modernizing
modernizer, -iser

modest
modesty
modicum
modification
modify
 modified
 modifying
modish
modular
modulate
 modulated
 modulating
modulation
module
 a space module
mogul
mohair
Mohammedan
mohican
moist
moisten
 moistened
 moistening
moistness
moisture
moisturize, -ise
 moisturized
 moisturizing
molar
molasses
mole
molecular
molecule
molehill
moleskin
molest

mollification
mollify
 mollified
 mollifying
mollusc
mollycoddle
 mollycoddled
 mollycoddling
molten
moment
momentary
 a momentary pause
momentarily
momentous
 *a momentous
 discovery*
momentum
 to gather momentum
monandrous
monandry
monarch
monarchy
 pl monarchies
monastery
 pl monasteries
monastic
monasticism
Monday
monetarism
monetarist
monetary
money
moneyed, monied
mongol
mongolism
mongoloid
mongoose

pl mongooses

mongrel

monistic

monitor
  monitored
  monitoring

monitory

monk

monkey
  pl monkeys
  monkeyed
  monkeying

monkfish

monochrome

monocle

monogamous

monogamy

monogram

monolingual

monolith

monolithic

monologue

monopolize, -ise
  monopolized
  monopolizing

monopoly
  pl monopolies

monosodium

monosyllabic

monosyllable

monotone

monotonous

monotony

monotype

monoxide

monsoon

monster

monstrosity
  pl monstrosities

monstrous

montage

month

monthly
  pl monthlies

monument

monumental

moo

mooch

mood

moodiness

moody

moon

moonbeam

moonlight

moonlighting

moonlit

moonshine

moonstone

moor
  moored
  mooring

moorhen

moorings

moorland

moose
  the antlers of a moose
  pl moose

moot point

mop
  mopped
  She mopped the floor
  mopping

mope
  moped
  She moped and sulked
  moping

moped ['mōped]
  She arrive on a moped

mopped
  see **mop**

moquette

moraine

moral
  the moral of the story

morally

morale
  Morale was low in the army

moralist

morality
  goodness and morality

moralize, -ise
  moralized
  moralizing

moralizer

morass
  pl morasses

moratorium
  pl moratoria

moray

morbid

morbidity

mordant

more

morello

moreover

morgue

moribund

morn

mornay

morning

moron

moronic

morose

morosely

moroseness

morpheme

morphia

morphine

morphological

morphology

morris dance

morrow

morse

morsel

mortal

mortality
the mortality rate in car crashes

mortally

mortar

mortarboard

mortgage
mortgaged
mortgaging

mortice
see **mortise**

mortician

mortification

mortify
mortified
mortifying

mortise, mortice

mortuary
pl mortuaries

mosaic

Moslem

mosque

mosquito
pl mosquitos, mosquitoes

moss
pl mosses

mossy

most

mostly

mote
a mote in the eye

motel

moth

mothball

moth-eaten

mother
mothered
mothering

motherboard

motherhood

mother-in-law
pl mothers-in-law

motherland

motherliness

motherly

mother-of-pearl

motif
a motif of flowers

motion

motionless

motivate
motivated
motivating

motive
a motive for murder

motley

motocross

motor

motor-bike

motorcade

motorcycle

motorcyclist

motorist

motorize, -ise
motorized
motorizing

motorway

mottled

motto
pl mottoes

mould

moulder

mouldering

mouldy

moult

mound

mount

mountain

mountaineer

mountainous

mountebank

mourn

mourner

mournful

mournfully

mourning

mouse
The cat ate the mouse: computer mouse

pl mice
mousetrap
moussaka
mousse
  lemon mousse
moustache
mousy
mouth
  mouthed
  mouthing
mouthful
  pl mouthfuls
mouthpiece
mouthwash
movable, moveable
move
  moved
  moving
movement
mover
movie
  pl movies
moving
mow
  mowed
  mowing
mower
mozzarella
Mr
Mrs
Ms
much
muck
mucous
  a mucous substance
mucus
  mucus from the nose

mud
muddle
  muddled
  muddling
muddy
mudguard
mudpack
muesli
muezzin
muff
muffin
muffle
  muffled
  muffling
muffler
mufti
mug
  mugged
  mugging
mugger
muggins
muggy
mugshot
mulatto
  pl mulattos
mulberry
  pl mulberries
mulch
mule
mulish
mull
mulled
mullet
mulligatawny
multi-coloured
multicultural

multifarious
multilingual
multimedia
multimillionaire
multinational
multiple
  multiple injuries: 8 is a
  multiple of 4
multiplex
multiplication
multiplicity
multiply
  is the sign for multiply
  multiplied
  multiplying
multipurpose
multiracial
multistorey
multitasking
multitude
multitudinous
mum
mumble
  mumbled
  mumbling
mumbo-jumbo
mummification
mummify
  mummified
  mummifying
mummy
  pl mummies
mumps
munch
munchies
mundane

municipal
municipality
  pl municipalities
munificence
munificent
munitions
mural
muralist
murder
  murdered
  murdering
murderer
murderess
murderous
murky
murmur
  murmured
  murmuring
murrain
muscat
muscatel
muscle
  well-developed
  muscles
muscular
muse
  to muse on the beauty
  of nature
  mused
  musing
museum
  pl museums
mush
mushroom
  mushroomed
  mushrooming
mushy

music
musical
musically
musician
musicologist
musicology
musings
musk
musket
musketeer
muskrat
musky
Muslim
muslin
musquash
mussel
  I love fresh mussels
must
mustachio
mustachioed
mustang
mustard
muster
  mustered
  mustering
mustiness
mustn't
  = must not
musty
mutability
mutable
mutant
mutate
  mutated
  mutating
mutation

mute
muted
mutilate
  mutilated
  mutilating
mutilation
mutineer
mutinous
mutiny
  pl mutinies
  mutinied
  mutinying
mutter
  muttered
  muttering
mutton
mutual
mutuality
mutually
muzzle
  muzzled
  muzzling
muzzy
my
myalgia
mycology
myna
myopia
myopic
myopically
myriad
myrrh
myrtle
myself
mysterious
mystery

pl mysteries

mystic
mystic philosophy

mystical

mystically

mysticism

mystification

mystify
mystified
mystifying

mystique
the mystique of the stage

myth

mythical

mythically

mythological

mythology

myxomatosis

n

If you can't find the word you're looking for under letter **N**, it could be that it starts with a different letter. Try looking under **KN** for words like *knot* and *know*, **GN** for words like *gnat*, **PN** for words like *pneumonia*, and **MN** for words like *mnemonic*.

nab
nabbed
nabbing

nacre

nadir

naff

nag
nagged
nagging

naiad

nail
nailed
nailing

Nairobi

naïve, naive

naïvety, naivety

naked

nakedness

namby-pamby

name
named
naming

name-drop
name-dropped
name-dropping

name-dropper

nameless

namely

namesake

nana

nanny
pl nannies

nap
napped
napping

napalm

nape

naphtha

naphthalene

napkin

nappy
pl nappies

narcissism

narcissistic

narcissus
pl narcissi

narcolepsy

narcotic

nark

narky

narrate
narrated
narrating

narration
narrative
narrator
narrow
narrowly
narrow-minded
narrow-mindedness
narrowness
nasal
nasalize, -ise
 nasalized
 nasalizing
nascent
nastily
nastiness
nasturtium
nasty
natal
nation
national
nationalism
nationalistic
nationality
 pl nationalities
nationalization,
 -isation
nationalize, **-ise**
 nationalized
 nationalizing
nationally
nationwide
native
nativity
natter
natterjack
nattily

natty
natural
naturalist
naturalization,
 -isation
naturalize, -ise
 naturalized
 naturalizing
naturally
naturalness
nature
naturism
naturopathy
naught
 *He cared naught for
 her*
naughtily
naughtiness
naughty
 a naughty child
nausea
nauseate
 nauseated
 nauseating
nauseous
nautical
naval
 a naval battle
nave
 the nave of a church
navel
 *The baby's navel has
 healed*
navigability
navigable
navigate
 navigated

navigating
navigation
navigational
navigator
navvy
 *a navvy on a building
 site*
 pl navvies
navy
 to join the navy
 pl navies
nay
 Nay, he will not come
neaptide
near
nearby
nearly
nearness
nearside
near-sighted
neat
neaten
neatness
nebulous
necessarily
necessary
necessitate
 necessitated
 necessitating
necessity
 pl necessities
neck
neckerchief
necklace
neckline
necromancer

necromancy
necrophilia
necrophiliac
necropolis
  pl necropolises
nectar
nectarine
née
  Ann Smith née Jones
need
  Animals need water
needful
needle
needlecord
needlepoint
needless
needlewoman
needlework
needn't
  = need not
needy
ne'er
ne'er-do-well
nefarious
negate
  negated
  negating
negation
negative
neglect
neglectful
negligée
negligence
negligent
  *a careless, negligent
  mother*

negligible
  a negligible amount
negligibly
negotiable
negotiate
  negotiated
  negotiating
  negotiation
negotiator
negro
  pl negroes
negroid
neigh
  to neigh like a horse
  neighed
  neighing
neighbour
neighbourhood
neighbouring
neighbourliness
neighbourly
neither
nemesis
neoclassical
neolithic
neologism
neonatal
neon lighting
neophyte
nephew
nephritis
nephrology
nepotism
nerd
nerve
nerve-racking

nervous
nervousness
nervy
nest
nestle
  nestled
  nestling
net, nett
  nett profit
net
  *a ball in the net: to net
  a fish*
  netted
  netting
netball
nether
nethermost
nett
  see net
netting
nettle
network
neuralgia
neurone
neurosis
neurotic
neuter
  neutered
  neutering
neutral
neutrality
neutralization,
  -isation
neutralize, -ise
  neutralized
  neutralizing
neutrally

neutron
never
nevertheless
new
  a new dress
newborn
newcomer
newfangled
newly
newness
news
newsagent
newscaster
newsflash
newsletter
newspaper
newsreader
newsy
newt
newton
next
niacin
nib
nibble
  nibbled
  nibbling
niblick
nice
nicely
nicety
  pl niceties
niche
nick
nickel
nick-nack
nickname

nicotine
niece
niff
niffy
nifty
niggard
niggardly
niggle
  niggled
  niggling
nigh
night
  a cold, dark night
nightcap
nightclub
nightdress
nightfall
nightie
nightingale
nightjar
nightlife
nightly
  a new show nightly
nightmare
nightmarish
nightshade
nightshirt
night-time
nightwatchman
  pl nightwatchmen
nihilism
nihilist
nihilistic
nil
nimble
nimbly

nimbus
nincompoop
nine
ninepins
nineteen
nineteenth
ninetieth
ninety
  pl nineties
ninny
ninth
nip
  nipped
  nipping
nipple
nippy
nirvana
nisi
nit
  a stupid nit: nits in her hair
nit-picking
nitrate
nitric
nitrogen
nitty-gritty
nitwit
no
  We have no money: She answered 'No'
  pl noes
no-ball
nobble
nobility
noble
nobly

nobleman
pl noblemen
noblewoman
pl noblewomen
nobody
nocturnal
nocturnally
nod
nodded
nodding
node
nodule
Noël, Nowell
nog
noggin
noise
noiseless
noisily
noisy
nomad
nomadic
nom de plume
pl noms de plume
nomenclature
nominal
nominally
nominate
nominated
nominating
nomination
nominative
nominee
= a person who has
been nominated
nonagenarian
nonagon

nonce
nonchalance
nonchalant
non-committal
nonconformism
nonconformist
nondescript
none
nonentity
pl nonentities
nonetheless
non-event
non-flammable
no-no
no-nonsense
nonplussed
nonsense
nonsensical
nonsensically
non sequitur
non-starter
non-stick
non-stop
noodle
nook
noon
no-one
noose
nor
norm
normal
normalcy
normality
normalization,
-isation

normalize, -ise
normalized
normalizing
normally
normative
north
northbound
north-east
north-easterly
north-eastern
northerly
in a northerly direction
northern
northern lands
northerner
northernmost
northward
north-west
north-westerly
north-western
Norwegian
nose
nosebag
nosedive
nosey, nosy
nosh
nostalgia
nostalgic
nostalgically
nostril
nostrum
not
He is not here
notability
pl notabilities
notable

notably
notary public
  pl notaries public
notation
notch
  pl notches
note
  noted
  noting
notebook
notelet
notepad
notepaper
noteworthy
nothing
nothingness
notice
  noticed
  noticing
noticeable
noticeably
notice-board
notifiable
notification
notify
  notified
  notifying
notion
notional
notoriety
notorious
notwithstanding
nougat ['nōōgä]
  This nougat is sticky
nought
  The telephone number
  contains two noughts

noun
nourish
nourishing
nourishment
nous
nouvelle cuisine
novel
novelist
novella
novelty
  pl novelties
November
novice
now
nowadays
Nowell
  see Noël
nowhere
noxious
nozzle
nuance
nub
nubile
nuclear
nucleus
  pl nuclei
nude
nudge
  nudged
  nudging
nudism
nudist
nudity
nudge
  nudged
  nudging

nugget
  a gold nugget
nuisance
null
nullification
nullify
  nullified
  nullifying
nullity
numb
number
  numbered
  numbering
numbness
numeracy
numeral
numerate
numerator
numerical
numerically
numerology
numerous
numinous
numismatics
numismatist
numskull
nun
nuncio
nunnery
  pl nunneries
nuptial
nurse
  nursed
  nursing
nursery
  pl nurseries

nurture
  nurtured
  nurturing
nut
nutcase
nutcracker
nuthatch
nutmeg
nutrient

nutriment
nutrition
nutritional
nutritious
nutshell
nutter
nutty
nuzzle

nuzzled
nuzzling
nylon
nymph
nymphet
nymphomania
nymphomaniac

O

o
  see oh
oaf
  pl oafs
oafish
oafishness
oak
oak-apple
oar
  an oar for a boat
oarsman
  pl oarsmen
oarsmanship
oarswoman
  pl oarswomen
oasis
  pl oases
oast-house
oatcake

oath
  pl oaths
oatmeal
oats
obduracy
obdurate
obdurately
obedience
obedient
obeisance
obelisk
obese
obesity
obey
  obeyed
  obeying
obfuscate
  obfuscated
  obfuscating

obfuscation
obituary
  pl obituaries
object
objection
objectionable
objectionably
objective
objectively
objectivism
objectivity
objector
oblate
oblation
obligate
  obligated
  obligating
obligation
obligatory

obligatorily
oblige
obliged
obliging
oblique
obliqueness
obliterate
obliterated
obliterating
obliteration
oblivion
oblivious
oblong
obloquy
pl obloquies
obnoxious
oboe
pl oboes
oboist
obscene
obscenely
obscenity
pl obscenities
obscure
obscurely
obscurity
obsequious
obsequiousness
observable
observance
observant
observation
observational
observatory
pl observatories
observe

observed
observing
observer
obsess
obsession
obsessional
obsessive
obsessively
obsessiveness
obsolescence
obsolescent
obsolete
obstacle
obstetric
obstetrical
obstetrician
obstetrics
obstinacy
obstinate
obstinately
obstreperous
obstruct
obstruction
obstructive
obtain
obtained
obtaining
obtainable
obtrude
obtrusion
obtrusive
obtrusively
obtuse
obtusely
obverse

obviate
obviated
obviating
obvious
obviously
ocarina
occasion
occasional
occasionally
occidental
occiput
occlude
occlusion
occult
occultism
occultist
occupancy
occupant
occupation
occupier
occupy
occupied
occupying
occur
occurred
occurring
occurrence
ocean
oceanic
oceanographer
oceanography
ocelot
ochre
octagon
octagonal

octagonally
octahedron
octane
octant
octave
octet
October
octogenarian
octopus
  pl octopuses
ocular
oculist
odd
oddball
oddity
  pl oddities
oddment
oddness
odds
ode
odious
odium
odorous
odour
odourless
odyssey
oesophagus
  pl oesophagi
oestrogen
of
  a cup of tea: made of
  silver: to die of hunger
off
  to switch off a light: to
  run off: to finish off a
  job: badly off: The

meat is off
offal
offbeat
off-chance
offcut
offence
offend
offender
offensive
offensively
offer
  offered
  offering
offertory
offhand
office
officer
official
  official action: official
  duties
officialdom
officialese
officially
officiate
  officiated
  officiating
officious
  rude and officious
offing
off-licence
off-line
offload
off-peak
off-putting
offset
  offset

offsetting
offshoot
offshore
offside
offspring
oft
often
ogle
  ogled
  ogling
ogre
oh, o
ohm
oil
  oiled
  oiling
oilfield
oiliness
oil-paint
oil-painting
oilrig
oilskin
oily
oink
ointment
OK
okay
  okayed
  okaying
okey-dokey
okra
old
olden
old-fashioned
oldie
olfactory

oligarch
oligarchy
olive
ombudsman
omega
omelette, omelet
omen
ominous
omission
He apologized for the omission of her name from the list
omit
omitted
omitting
omnibus
pl omnibuses
omnipotence
omnipotent
omnipresent
omniscience
omniscient
omnivore
omnivorous
on
once
oncologist
oncology
oncoming
one
one-liner
onerous
oneself
one-upmanship
one-way
ongoing

onion
on-line
onlooker
only
onomatopoeia
onomatopoeic
onrush
onset
onshore
onslaught
onto
ontology
onus
pl onuses
onwards
onyx
oodles
oomph
oops
ooze
oozed
oozing
opacity
opal
opalescent
opaque
opaqueness
open
opened
opening
opencast
opener
openly
open-minded
open-mindedness
openness

opera
operable
operate
operated
operating
operatic
operation
operational
operative
operator
operetta
ophthalmic
ophthalmologist
opiate
opine
opined
opining
opinion
opinionated
opium
opossum
opponent
opportune
opportunism
opportunist
opportunistic
opportunity
pl opportunities
oppose
opposed
opposing
opposer
opposite
opposition
oppress
oppression

oppressive
oppressor
opprobrious
opprobrium
opt
optic
optical
optically
optician
optics
optimal
optimism
optimist
optimistic
optimistically
optimize, -ise
  optimized
  optimizing
optimum
option
optional
optionally
optometrist
opulence
opulent
opus
  pl opera
or
oracle
oral
  The dentist spoke about oral hygiene
orally
orange
orang-utan
oration

orator
oratorio
  pl oratorios
oratory
  pl oratories
orb
orbit
  orbited
  orbiting
orbital
orchard
orchestra
orchestral
orchestrate
  orchestrated
  orchestrating
orchestration
orchid
ordain
ordainment
ordeal
order
  ordered
  ordering
orderly
  pl orderlies
ordinal
ordinance
ordinarily
ordinary
ordination
Ordnance Survey
ore
  iron ore
oregano
organ

organdie
organic
organically
organism
  This poison kills all known organisms
organist
organization, -isation
organize, -ise
  organized
  organizing
organza
orgasm
  sexual orgasm
orgasmic
orgiastic
orgy
  pl orgies
orient
oriental
orientate
  orientated
  orientating
oriented
orienteering
orifice
origami
origin
original
originality
originally
originate
  originated
  originating
originator
ornament

ornamental
ornamentally
ornamentation
ornate
ornithological
ornithologist
ornithology
orphan
orphanage
orthodontic
orthodontist
orthodox
orthodoxy
orthographic
orthography
orthopaedic
oscillate
  oscillated
  oscillating
oscillation
osmosis
osprey
  pl ospreys
ostensible
ostensibly
ostentation
ostentatious
osteopath
osteopathic
osteopathy
osteoporosis
ostracism
ostracize, -ise
  ostracized
  ostracizing

ostrich
  pl ostriches
other
otherwise
otiose
otitis
otter
ottoman
ouch
ought
ounce
our
ours
ourselves
oust
out
outback
outboard
outbreak
outburst
outcast
outcome
outcrop
outcry
outdated
outdo
  outdid
  She outdid her
  neighbours
  outdone
  She has outdone them
  outdoing
outdoor
outdoors
outer
outermost

outfit
outfitter
outgoing
outgrow
  outgrew
  outgrowing
  outgrown
outhouse
outing
outlandish
outlaw
outlay
outlet
outline
outlive
  outlived
  outliving
outlook
outlying
outmoded
outnumber
  outnumbered
  outnumbering
out-patient
outpost
outpouring
output
outrage
outrageous
outright
outset
outshine
  outshine
  outshining
outside
outsider

outsize
outskirts
outspoken
outstanding
outstay
outstretched
outstrip
 outstripped
 outstripping
outtake
outward
outweigh
outwit
 outwitted
 outwitting
outworker
oval
ovarian
ovary
 pl ovaries
ovation
oven
ovenproof
over
overact
overall
overarm
overawe
 overawed
 overawing
overbalance
overbearing
overboard
overcame
 see overcome
overcast

overcharge
overcoat
overcome
 overcame
 He overcame his
 enemies
 overcome
 He has overcome
 them
 overcoming
overcrowded
overcrowding
overdo
 overdid
 She overdid the meat
 overdone
 She has overdone it
 overdoing
overdose
overdraft
overdrawn
overdrive
overdue
overestimate
overestimation
overexpose
overexposure
overflow
overgrown
overhang
overhaul
overheads
overhear
 overheard
 overhearing
overheat
overjoyed

overkill
overlap
 overlapped
 overlapping
overlay
overleaf
overload
overlook
overly
overnight
overpass
overpowering
overran
 see overrun
overrate
 overrated
 overrating
overreach
overreact
override
overrule
overrun
 overran
 The enemy overran the
 country
 overrun
 They have overrun the
 country
 overrunning
overseas
oversee
overseer
overshadow
oversight
oversimplify
 oversimplified
 oversimplifying

oversleep
overslept
oversleeping

overstatement

overstep
overstepped
overstepping

overt

overtake
overtook
He overtook the car
overtaken
He has overtaken the car
overtaking

overthrow
overthrew
He overthrew the king
overthrown
He has overthrown the king
overthrowing

overtime

overtook
see **overtake**

overtone

overture

overturn

overview

overweight

overwhelm

overwhelming

overworked

overwrite

overwrought

ovulate

ovulation

ovum
pl ova

owe
owed
owing

owl

owlish

own
owned
owning

owner

ownership

ox
pl oxen

oxidant

oxide

oxidize, -ise

oxtail

oxygen

oxygenate

oyster

oystercatcher

ozone

p

pace
  paced
  pacing
pacemaker
pacesetter
Pacific
pacifier
pacifism
pacifist
pacify
  pacified
  pacifying
pack
  packed
  We packed the cases:
  a packed hall
  packing
package
packaging
packed
  see pack
packet
pact
  a pact between
  nations
pad
  padded
  padding
paddle
  paddled
  paddling
paddock
padlock

paediatrician
paediatrics
paedophile
paedophilia
paella
pagan
paganism
page
  paged
  paging
pageant
pageantry
pageboy
pager
paginate
pagination
pagoda
paid
  see pay
pail
  a pail of water
pain
  a pain in his chest
pained
painful
painfully
painkiller
painless
painstaking
paint
paintbrush
painter

painting
pair
  a pair of shoes
  paired
  pairing
pakora
pal
palace
palaeontologist
palaeontology
palatable
palate
  the soft palate of the
  mouth
palatial
palaver
pale
  thin and pale: of a pale
  colour
paleness
palette
  an artist's palette
palindrome
palindromic
paling
palisade
pall
  palled
  palling
palladium
pallet
  a straw pallet
palliative

pallid
pallor
palm
palmist
palmistry
palomino
palpable
palpably
palpitate
  palpitated
  palpitating
palpitation
palsy
paltry
pampas
pamper
  pampered
  pampering
pamphlet
pan
  panned
  panning
panacea
panache
panama
pancake
pancreas
panda
pandemic
pandemonium
pander
  pandered
  pandering
pane
  a pane of glass
panegyric

panel
panelling
panellist
pang
panic
  panicked
  panicking
panicky
panic-stricken
pannier
panoply
panorama
panoramic
panpipes
pansy
  pl pansies
pant
pantechnicon
pantheism
pantheist
pantheon
panther
panties
pantomime
pantry
  pl pantries
pants
panty hose,
  pantihose
papa
papacy
papal
paparazzo
  pl paparazzi
papaya
paper

papered
papering
paperback
paperweight
paperwork
papier mâché
papoose
paprika
papyrus
par
  *not up to par: on a par
  with his brother*
parable
parabola
parabolic
paracetamol
parachute
parachutist
parade
  paraded
  parading
paradigm
paradigmatic
paradise
paradox
  pl paradoxes
paradoxical
paradoxically
paraffin
paraglider
paragliding
paragon
paragraph
parakeet
parallel
parallelogram

paralyse
 paralysed
 paralysing
paralysis
paralytic
paramedic
parameter
paramilitary
paramount
paramour
paranoia
paranoid
paranormal
parapet
paraphernalia
paraphrase
paraplegia
paraplegic
parapsychology
parasite
parasitic
parasol
paratrooper
paratroops
parboil
 parboiled
 parboiling
parcel
 parcelled
 parcelling
parch
parchment
pardon
 pardoned
 pardoning
pardonable

pare
 to pare an apple: to
 pare one's toenails
 pared
 paring
parent
parentage
parental
parenthesis
 pl parentheses
parenthetic
parenthetical
parenthood
pariah
parish
 pl parishes
parishioner
parity
park
parka
parkin
Parkinsonism
parlance
parley
 pl parleys
 parleyed
 parleying
parliament
parliamentary
parlour
parlourmaid
Parmesan
parochial
parody
 pl parodies
 parodied
 parodying

parole
paroxysm
parquet
parr
 A parr is a young
 salmon
parricide
parrot
parry
 parried
 parrying
parse
 parsed
 parsing
parsimonious
parsimony
parsley
parsnip
parson
parsonage
part
partake
 partook
 partaken
 partaking
parterre
partial
partiality
partially
participant
participate
 participated
 participating
participation
participial
participle

particle
particular
particularly
parting
partisan
partition
partitive
partly
partner
  partnered
  partnering
partook
  see partake
partridge
part-time
part-timer
party
  pl parties
parvenu
pascal
pass
  passed
  He passed out of
  sight: The bus passed
  the house: The feeling
  soon passed
  passing
passable
passage
passageway
passed
  see pass
passata
passé
passenger
passer-by
  pl passers-by

passim
passion
passionate
passionately
passive
passively
passiveness
passivity
passport
password
past
  The old think about the
  past: We walked past
  the church
pasta
paste
pastel
  pastel colours
pasteurization,
  -isation
pasteurize, -ise
  pasteurized
  pasteurizing
pastiche
pastille
  a throat pastille
pastime
pastiness
pastor
pastoral
pastrami
pastry
  pl pastries
pasturage
pasture
pasty ['pāsti]

pasty ['pasti]
  pl pasties
pat
  patted
  patting
patch
  pl patches
patchouli
patchwork
patchy
pate
  a bald pate
pâté
  pâté on toast
patella
  pl patellae, patellas
patent
patently
pater
paternal
paternalism
paternalistic
paternally
paternity
paternoster
path
pathetic
pathetically
pathogen
pathological
pathologist
pathology
pathos
patience
patient
patina

patio
 pl patios
patisserie
patois
patriarch
patriarchal
patriarchy
patrician
patricide
patriot
patriotic
patriotically
patriotism
patrol
 patrolled
 patrolling
patron
patronage
patronize, -ise
 patronized
 patronizing
patronymic
patter
 pattered
 pattering
pattern
patterned
patty
 a mince patty
 pl patties
paucity
paunch
 pl paunches
pauper
pause
 paused
 pausing

pave
 paved
 paving
pavement
pavilion
pavlova
paw
pawn
pawnbroker
pawnshop
pawpaw
pay
 paid
 paying
payable
payee
 = the person to
 whom money is paid
payment
payphone
payroll
pea
peace
 peace and quiet
peaceable
peaceably
peaceful
peacefully
peacemaker
peacetime
peach
 pl peaches
peacock
peahen
peak
 a mountain peak

peakiness
peaky
peal
 a peal of bells: Bells peal
 pealed
 pealing
peanut
pear
 an apple and a pear
pearl
 a pearl necklace
peasant
 a simple peasant
pea-shooter
peat
peaty
pebble
pebbledash
pebbly
pecan
peccadillo
 pl peccadillos,
 peccadilloes
peck
pecker
peckish
pectin
peculiar
peculiarity
 pl peculiarities
pecuniary
pedagogic
pedagogical
pedagogue
pedagogy

pedal
to pedal a bicycle
pedalled
pedalling

pedalo

pedant

pedantic

pedantically

pedantry

peddle
to peddle one's wares
peddled
peddling

peddler
a dope peddler

pederast

pederasty

pedestal

pedestrian

pedestrianize, -ise
pedestrianized
pedestrianizing

pedicure

pedigree

pedlar
a pedlar came to the door

pedometer

pee
peed
peeing

peek
a peek through the window

peel
to peel an apple
peeled
peeling

peeler

peelings

peep
peeped
peeping

peephole

peepshow

peer
to peer through the window: a peer of the realm
peered
peering

peerage

peerless

peeved

peevish

peevishness

peewit

peg
pegged
pegging

pejorative

Pekinese, Pekingese

pelican

pellet

pell-mell

pelmet

pelota

pelt

pelvis

pen
penned
penning

penal

penalize, -ise
penalized

penalizing

penalty

penance

pence
see **penny**

penchant

pencil
pencilled
pencilling

pendant
a silver pendant

pendent
a pendent light

pending

pendulous

pendulum

penetrable

penetrate
penetrated
penetrating

penetration

penfriend

penpal

penguin

penicillin

penile

peninsula

peninsular

penis
pl penises

penitence

penitent

penitential

penitentiary

penknife
pl penknives

pen-name
pennant
pennies
 see **penny**
penniless
penny
 pl pence
 This costs ten pence
 pl pennies
 This machine takes
 pennies
penny-pincher
penny-pinching
pennyworth
pen-pusher
pension
pensionable
pensioner
pensive
pensively
pentagon
pentathlon
pentatonic
penthouse
pent-up
penultimate
penumbra
penurious
penury
peony
 pl peonies
people
 peopled
 peopling
pep
 pepped
 pepping

pepper
 peppered
 peppering
peppercorn
peppermill
peppermint
peppery
pep-talk
per
perambulation
perambulator
per capita
perceivable
perceive
 perceived
 perceiving
per cent
percentage
percentile
perceptible
perceptibly
perception
perceptive
perch
 pl perches
percolate
 percolated
 percolating
percolator
percussion
perdition
peregrine
peremptorily
peremptory
perennial
perennially

perestroika
perfect
perfectible
perfection
perfectionism
perfectionist
perfidious
perfidy
perforate
 perforated
 perforating
perforation
perforce
perform
performance
performer
perfume
perfumery
perfunctorily
perfunctory
perhaps
peril
perilous
perimeter
period
periodic
periodically
periodical
peripatetic
peripheral
periphery
 pl peripheries
periphrasis
 pl periphrases
periphrastic

periscope
perish
perishable
peristalsis
periwinkle
perjure
 perjured
 perjuring
perjurer
perjury
perk
perky
perm
permafrost
permanence
permanency
permanent
permanganate
permeable
permeate
 permeated
 permeating
permissible
permission
permissive
permissiveness
permit
 permitted
 permitting
permutation
pernicious
pernickety
peroxide
perpendicular

perpetrate
 perpetrated
 perpetrating
perpetrator
perpetual
perpetually
perpetuate
 perpetuated
 perpetuating
perpetuation
perpetuity
perplex
perplexity
 pl perplexities
perquisite
 A company car is one
 of the perquisites of
 the job
persecute
 persecuted
 persecuting
persecution
persecutor
perseverance
persevere
 persevered
 persevering
persist
persistence
persistent
person
personable
personage
personal
 She is his personal
 assistant: a personal
 letter

personality
 pl personalities
personalize, -ise
 personalized
 personalizing
personally
personification
personify
 personified
 personifying
personnel
 the company's per-
 sonnel officer
perspective
Perspex®
perspicacious
perspicacity
perspicuity
perspicuous
perspiration
perspire
 perspired
 perspiring
persuade
 persuaded
 persuading
persuasion
persuasive
persuasively
pert
pertain
 pertained
 pertaining
pertinacious
pertinacity
pertinence
pertinent

pertness
perturb
perturbation
pertussis
perusal
peruse
 perused
 perusing
pervade
 pervaded
 pervading
pervasive
perverse
perversely
perversion
perversity
pervert
peseta
pesky
peso
pessary
 pl pessaries
pessimism
pessimist
pessimistic
pessimistically
pest
pester
 pestered
 pestering
pesticide
pestilence
pestilent
pestle
pesto
pet

petted
petting
petal
petard
peter out
 petered out
 petering out
petite
petition
 petitioned
 petitioning
petitioner
petit mal
petrel
 a gull and a petrel
petrify
 petrified
 petrifying
petrochemical
petrol
 two gallons of petrol
petroleum
petticoat
pettily
pettiness
petty
petulance
petulant
petunia
pew
pewter
peyote
pfennig
phalanges
phalanx
 pl phalanxes,

phalanges
phallic
phallus
 pl phalluses, phalli
phantasmagoria
phantasmagoric
phantom
Pharaoh
 pl Pharaohs
pharmaceutical
pharmacist
pharmacological
pharmacologist
pharmacology
pharmacy
 pl pharmacies
pharyngeal
pharyngitis
pharynx
phase
 phased
 phasing
phatic
pheasant
 pheasant feathers
phenomenal
phenomenon
 pl phenomena
pheromone
phew
phial
philander
 philandered
 philandering
philanderer
philanthropic

philanthropically
philanthropist
philanthropy
philatelist
philately
philharmonic
Philippines
philistine
philological
philologist
philology
philosopher
philosophical
philosophically
philosophize
  philosophized
  philosophizing
philosophy
phlegm
phlegmatic
phlox
  phlox growing in the garden
phobia
  pl phobias
phobic
phoenix
phone
phonecard
phoneme
phonemic
phonetic
phonetically
phonetics
phoney, phony
phonic

phonological
phonologically
phonology
phosphate
phosphorescent
phosphorous
photo
photocopiable
photocopier
photocopy
  photocopied
  photocopying
Photofit®
photogenic
photogenically
photograph
photographer
photographic
photographically
photography
photon
photosynthesis
photosynthesize, -ise
  photosynthesized
  photosynthesizing
phrasal
phrase
  phrased
  phrasing
phraseology
phrenology
physical
physically
physician
physicist

physics
physiognomy
physiological
physiologically
physiologist
physiology
physiotherapist
physiotherapy
physique
pi
pianissimo
pianist
piano
  pl pianos
pianoforte
piazza
  a church in the piazza
pibroch
picador
picaresque
Picasso
piccalilli
piccolo
  pl piccolos
pick
pickaxe
picker
picket
  picketed
  picketing
pickle
  pickled
  pickling
pick-me-up
pickpocket
picnic

picnicked
picnicking
picnicker
pictogram
pictorial
pictorially
picture
picturesque
picturesquely
piddling
pidgin
pie
piebald
piece
  a piece of paper
pièce de résistance
piecemeal
piecework
pied
pied-à-terre
  pl pieds-à-terre
pie-eyed
pier
  the pier at the seaside
pierce
  pierced
  piercing
Pierrot
piety
piffle
pig
pigeon
pigeon-hole
piggery
piggish
piggy

piggyback
pigheaded
piglet
pigment
pigmentation
pigmy
  see **pygmy**
pigskin
pigsty
pigswill
pigtail
pike
pikestaff
pilaff
pilchard
pile
  piled
  piling
pile-up
pilfer
  pilfered
  pilfering
pilferer
pilgrim
pilgrimage
pill
pillage
pillar
pillbox
pillion
pillory
  pl pillories
  pilloried
  pillorying
pillow
pillowcase

pillowslip
pilot
  piloted
  piloting
pimento
  = allspice
pimiento, pimento
  = red pepper
pimp
pimpernel
pimple
pimply
pin
  pinned
  flowers pinned to her dress
  pinning
pinafore
pinball
pince-nez
pincers
pinch
  pl pinches
pinched
pincushion
pine
  pined
  The dog pined and died
  pining
pineapple
ping
ping-pong
pinhead
pinion
  pinioned
  pinioning

pink
pinkie
pinnacle
pinned
  see pin
pinpoint
pinprick
pint
Pinyin
pioneer
  pioneered
  pioneering
pious
pip
  pipped
  He was pipped at the post
  pipping
pipe
  piped
  a cake piped with white icing: The members of the band piped away all night
  piping
pipe-cleaner
pipeline
piper
pipette
piping
pipped
  see pip
pipistrelle
pipsqueak
piquancy
piquant
pique

to resign out of pique: to pique one's curiosity
piqued
piquing
piracy
piranha
pirate
pirouette
  pirouetted
  pirouetting
Pisces
piss
pissed
pistachio
  pl pistachios
piste
pistil
  the pistil of a flower
pistol
  shot by a pistol
piston
pit
  pitted
  pitting
pitch
  pl pitches
pitcher
pitchfork
piteous
pitfall
pith
pithy
pitiable
pitiful
pitifully
pitiless

piton
pitstop
pitta
pittance
pituitary
pity
  pitied
  pitying
pivot
  pivoted
  pivoting
pivotal
pixel
pixie, pixy
  pl pixies
pizza
  a tomato and cheese pizza
pizzazz
pizzeria
pizzicato
placard
placate
  placated
  placating
placatory
place
  a place in the sun: to place the book on the table
  placed
  placing
placebo
placement
placenta
placid
plagiarism

plagiarize, -ise
  plagiarized
  plagiarizing
plague
plaice
  plaice and chips
plaid
plain
  Wheat grows on the plain: a plain dress
plainness
plainsong
plaintiff
  The plaintiff lost the case
plaintive
  a plaintive cry
plait
  to plait hair
  plaited
  plaiting
plan
  planned
  planning
plane
  The plane landed: The joiner uses a plane: a plane-tree: a plane surface
planet
planetarium
  pl planetaria, planetariums
planetary
plangent
plank
plankton
planner

plant
plantain
plantation
planter
plaque
plasma
plaster
  plastered
  plastering
plasterboard
plastered
plasterer
plastic
Plasticine®
plasticity
plate
  a plate of food: to plate with silver
  plated
  plating
plateau
  pl plateaux, plateaus
plateful
platelet
platform
plating
platinum
platitude
platitudinous
platonic
platoon
platter
platypus
  pl platypuses
plaudit
plausibility

plausible
plausibly
play
  played
  playing
playback
playboy
player
playful
playfully
playground
playgroup
playing-card
playmate
playpen
playschool
playwright
plaza
plea
plead
pleasant
pleasantness
pleasantry
  pl pleasantries
please
  pleased
  pleasing
pleasurable
pleasurably
pleasure
pleat
  pleated
  pleating
pleb
plebeian
plebiscite

plectrum
pledge
  pledged
  pledging
plenary
plenitude
plenteous
plentiful
plentifully
plenty
plethora
pleurisy
plexus
  pl plexus, plexuses
pliability
pliable
pliant
pliers
plight
plimsoll
plinth
plod
  plodded
  plodding
plodder
plonk
plop
  plopped
  plopping
plosive
plot
  plotted
  plotting
plough
  ploughed
  ploughing

ploughshare
plover
ploy
pluck
plucky
pluckily
plug
  plugged
  plugging
plughole
plum
  a red plum
plumage
plumb
  to plumb the depths
  plumbed
  plumbing
plumbago
plumber
plumbline
plume
plummet
  plummeted
  plummeting
plummy
plump
plunder
  plundered
  plundering
plunderer
plunge
  plunged
  plunging
plunger
pluperfect
plural
pluralism

pluralist
plurality
plus
plush
plutocracy
plutocrat
plutocratic
plutonic
plutonium
ply
  plied
  plying
plywood
pneumatic
pneumatically
pneumonia
poach
poacher
pock
pocket
  pocketed
  pocketing
pocketbook
pockmark
pockmarked
pod
podgy
podiatrist
podiatry
podium
  pl podiums, podia
poem
poet
poetic
poetical
poetically

poetry
pogo
pogrom
poignance
poignancy
poignant
poinsettia
point
pointed
pointedly
pointedness
pointer
pointless
poise
poised
poison
poisoner
poisonous
poke
 poked
 poking
poker
poker-faced
poky
polar
polarity
polarization, -isation
polarize, -ise
 polarized
 polarizing
pole
polecat
polemic
polemicist
polemics
polenta

police
 policed
 policing
policeman
 pl policemen
policewoman
 pl policewomen
policy
 pl policies
polio
poliomyelitis
polish
 pl polishes
polisher
polite
politely
politeness
politic
 It is politic to do as the
 king says
political
 a political figure
politically
politician
politicize, -ise
 politicized
 politicizing
politics
polka
poll
 polled
 polling
pollard
pollen
pollinate
 pollinated
 pollinating

pollination
pollster
pollutant
pollute
 polluted
 polluting
pollution
polo
poltergeist
polyester
polyamide
polyandrous
polyandry
polyanthus
polyester
polygamist
polygamous
polygamy
polyglot
polygon
polymath
polymer
polyp
polyphonic
polyphony
polystyrene
polysyllabic
polytechnic
polythene
polyunsaturated
polyurethane
pomade
pomander
pomegranate
pomelo

pommel
pomp
pompom
pomposity
pompous
ponce
  ponced
  poncing
poncho
  pl ponchos
pond
ponder
  pondered
  pondering
ponderous
pong
pongy
pontiff
pontificate
  pontificated
  pontificating
pontoon
pony
  pl ponies
pony-trekking
poodle
poof
pooh-pooh
pool
  a swimming pool:
  football pools: to pool
  their resources
  pooled
  pooling
poop
poor
poorly

pop
  popped
  popping
popcorn
pope
popery
poplar
  a poplar and a yew
  tree
poplin
poppadum
popper
poppet
poppy
  pl poppies
populace
popular
  a popular entertainer
popularity
popularize, -ise
  popularized
  popularizing
populate
  populated
  populating
population
populist
populous
porcelain
porch
  pl porches
porcine
porcupine
pore
  a blocked pore
  pored
  He pored over his

  books
  poring
pork
porky
porn
porno
pornographic
pornography
porosity
porous
porpoise
porridge
porringer
port
portable
portal
portcullis
  pl portcullises
portend
portent
portentous
porter
portfolio
  pl portfolios
port-hole
portico
  pl porticos,
  porticoes
portion
portly
portmanteau
  pl portmanteaux,
  portmanteaus
portrait
portraiture
portray

portrayed
portraying
portrayal
pose
  posed
  posing
poser
  a poser before the camera: That question is quite a poser
poseur
  He is a poseur and a sham
posh
posit
  posited
  positing
position
  positioned
  positioning
positive
positively
positivism
positivist
posse
possess
  possessed
  possessing
possession
possessive
possessively
possessiveness
possessor
possibilities
possibility
possible
possibly

possum
post
postage
postal
postbag
postbox
postcard
postcode
postdate
  postdated
  postdating
poster
poste restante
posterior
posterity
postern
postgraduate
posthumous
postman
postmark
postmeridian
postmortem
postnatal
postpone
  postponed
  postponing
postponement
postprandial
postscript
postulate
  postulated
  postulating
posture
postviral
postwar
postwoman

posy
  pl posies
pot
  potted
  potting
potash
potassium
potato
  pl potatoes
pot-belly
potboiler
poteen
potency
potent
potentate
potential
potentially
potentiometer
pothole
potholing
potholer
potion
pot-pourri
potter
  pottered
  pottering
pottery
  pl potteries
potty
pouch
  pl pouches
pouffe
poulterer
poultice
poultry
pounce

pounced
pouncing

pound

pour
Did the rain pour down?
poured
She poured milk from the jug
pouring

pout
pouted
pouting

poverty

poverty-stricken

powder
powdered
powdering

powdery

power

powerboat

powered

powerful

powerfully

powerhouse

powerless

pow-wow

pox

practicable
It is not practicable to try to make the journey in one day

practical
a practical knowledge of carpentry: He is a dreamer but his wife is very practical

practicality

practically

practice
She is at dancing practice: a doctor's practice

practise
You must practise your dance steps
practised
practising

practitioner

pragmatic

pragmatism

pragmatist

prairie

praise
praised
praising

praiseworthy

praline

pram

prance
pranced
prancing

prang

prank

prankster

prat

prate
prated
prating

prattle
prattled
prattling

prawn

pray
I heard the minister pray

prayed
praying

prayer

preach

preacher

preamble

prearrange
prearranged
prearranging

precancerous

precarious

precaution

precautionary

precede
She always precedes him into the room
preceded
preceding

precedence

precedent

precept

precinct

precious

precipice

precipitate
precipitated
precipitating

precipitation

precipitous

précis
pl précis

precise

precisely

preciseness

precision

preclude

precluded
precluding
preclusion
precocious
precocity
preconceive
  preconceived
  preconceiving
preconception
precondition
precursor
pre-date
predator
predatory
predecessor
predestined
predetermined
predicament
predication
predicative
predict
predictable
predictably
prediction
predilection
predispose
  predisposed
  predisposing
predisposition
predominant
pre-eminent
pre-empt
pre-emptive
preen
  preened
  preening

prefab
prefabricated
preface
prefect
prefer
  preferred
  preferring
preferable
preference
preferential
preferment
prefix
  pl prefixes
pregnancy
  pl pregnancies
pregnant
prehistoric
prehistorically
prejudge
  prejudged
  prejudging
prejudice
  prejudiced
  prejudicing
prejudicial
prelate
preliminary
  pl preliminaries
prelims
prelude
premarital
premature
prematurely
premeditated
premenstrual
premier

*Who is the Italian
premier?*
première
  *the première of the
  play*
premise
  pl premises
  false premises
premises
  *They moved to new
  premises*
premium
  pl premiums
premolar
premonition
preoccupation
preoccupy
  preoccupied
  preoccupying
preordain
prepacked
prepaid
  see **prepay**
preparation
preparatory
prepare
  prepared
  preparing
prepay
  prepaid
  prepaying
prepayment
preponderance
preposition
prepositional
prepossessing
preposterous

prerequisite
  Patience is a prerequisite for teaching
prerogative
presage
  presaged
  presaging
Presbyterian
presbytery
pre-school
prescient
prescribe
  prescribed
  prescribing
prescription
prescriptive
prescriptivism
presence
present
presentable
presentably
presentation
presenter
presentiment
presently
preservation
preservative
preserve
  preserved
  preserving
preset
preside
  presided
  presiding
presidency
president

presidential
press
pressgang
press-up
pressure
pressurize, -ise
  pressurized
  pressurizing
prestige
prestigious
presto
presumably
presume
  presumed
  presuming
presumption
presumptive
presumptuous
presuppose
presupposition
pretence
pretend
pretender
pretension
pretentious
preterite
preternatural
preternaturally
pretext
prettily
prettiness
pretty
pretzel
prevail
  prevailed
  prevailing

prevalence
prevalent
prevaricate
  prevaricated
  prevaricating
prevarication
prevaricator
prevent
preventable
preventative
prevention
preventive
preview
previous
previously
pre-war
prey
  Mice are prey for owls:
  Owls prey on mice
  preyed
  preying
price
  What is the price of
  that house?: I would
  price that hat at £15
  priced
  pricing
priceless
pricey
prick
prickle
  prickled
  prickling
prickly
pride
  prided
  priding

priest
priestess
priesthood
priestly
prig
priggish
prim
primacy
prima donna
prima facie
primal
primarily
primary
primate
prime
  primed
  priming
primer
primeval
primitive
primitively
primness
primordial
primrose
primula
  pl primulae, primulas
prince
princedom
princely
princess
  pl princesses
principal
  *the principal of the
  college*
principality
  pl principalities

principally
principle
  *the principle of the
  steam engine: a man
  of principle*
principled
print
printable
printer
printing
printout
prior
prioress
  pl prioresses
prioritize, -ise
  prioritized
  prioritizing
priority
  pl priorities
priory
  pl priories
prise
  to prise open a lid
  prised
  prising
prism
prison
prisoner
prissy
pristine
privacy
private
  *private information: a
  private secretary*
privately
privateer
privation

privatization,
  -isation
privatize, -ise
privet
  a privet hedge
privilege
privileged
privy council
prize
  *to win a prize: to prize
  a possession dearly*
  prized
  prizing
pro
proactive
probability
  pl probabilities
probable
probably
probate
probation
probationary
probationer
probe
  probed
  probing
probity
problem
problematic
problematical
proboscis
  pl proboscises
procedural
procedure

proceed
Proceed along the corridor!
proceeded
proceeding
proceeds
process
pl processes
processed
processing
procession
processor
proclaim
proclamation
proclivity
pl proclivities
procrastinate
procrastinated
procrastinating
procrastination
procreate
procreated
procreating
procreation
proctor
procurator fiscal
procure
procured
procuring
procurement
procurer
prod
prodded
prodding
prodigal
prodigious
prodigy

pl prodigies
produce
produced
producing
producer
product
production
productive
productively
productivity
profane
profanely
profanity
profess
profession
professional
professionally
professor
professorial
professorship
proffer
proffered
proffering
proficiency
proficient
profile
profit
profit and loss
profitability
profited
profiting
profitable
profitably
profiteer
profiteered
profiteering

profiterole
profligacy
profligate
pro forma
profound
profundity
profuse
profusely
profusion
progenitor
progeny
progesterone
prognosis
pl prognoses
prognosticate
prognosticated
prognosticating
prognostication
program
a computer program:
to program a
computer
programmed
programming
programmable
programme
a theatre programme
programmer
progress
progression
progressive
progressively
prohibit
prohibited
prohibiting
prohibition
prohibitionist

prohibitive
prohibitively
prohibitory
project
projectile
projection
projectionist
projector
prolapse
prole
proletarian
proletariat
pro-life
proliferate
  proliferated
  proliferating
prolific
prolix
prolixity
prologue
prolong
promenade
promenader
prominence
prominent
promiscuity
promiscuous
promise
  pl promises
  promised
  promising
promissory
promontory
  pl promontories
promote
  promoted

promoting
promoter
promotion
prompt
prompter
promptly
promptness
promulgate
  promulgated
  promulgating
prone
prong
pronominal
pronoun
pronounce
  pronounced
  pronouncing
pronounceable
pronouncement
pronunciation
proof
  Do they have proof of
  his guilt?: 70% proof
  spirit
proof-read
  proof-read
  proof-reading
proof-reader
prop
  propped
  propping
propaganda
propagandist
propagate
  propagated
  propagating
propagation

propagator
propel
  propelled
  propelling
propellant
  = something that
  propels
propellent
  = driving, propelling
propeller
propensity
  pl propensities
proper
properly
property
  the lost property office
  pl properties
prophecy
  to make a prophecy
  pl prophecies
prophesy
  to prophesy about the
  future
  prophesied
  prophesying
prophet
  an Old Testament
  prophet
prophetic
prophylactic
propinquity
propitiate
  propitiated
  propitiating
propitiator
propitious
proponent
proportion

proportional
proportionally
proportionate
proportionately
proposal
propose
  proposed
  proposing
proposer
proposition
propound
proprietary
proprietor
proprietorial
proprietress,
  proprietrix
propriety
  She behaved with
  dignity and propriety
  pl proprieties
propulsion
pro rata
prosaic
prosaically
prosciutto
proscribe
  proscribed
  proscribing
proscription
proscriptive
prose
prosecute
  prosecuted
  prosecuting
prosecution
prosecutor

proselytize
prosodic
prosody
prospect
prospective
prospector
prospectus
  pl prospectuses
prosper
  prospered
  prospering
prosperity
prosperous
prostate
  the prostate gland
prosthesis
  pl prostheses
prostitute
prostitution
prostrate
  to prostrate with grief:
  He lay prostrate on the
  floor
  prostrated
  prostrating
prostration
protagonist
protect
protection
protectionism
protectionist
protective
protectively
protector
protectorate
protégé

protein
protest
Protestant
protestation
protester
protocol
proton
prototype
Protozoa
protozoan
protract
protracted
protractor
protrude
  protruded
  protruding
protrusion
protuberance
protuberant
proud
prove
  Can you prove that he
  murdered her?
  proved
  proving
provenance
provender
proverb
proverbial
proverbially
provide
  provided
  providing
providence
provident
providential

providentially
provider
province
provincial
provincially
provision
provisional
provisionally
proviso
  pl provisos
provisory
provocation
provocative
provocatively
provoke
  provoked
  provoking
provost
prow
prowess
prowl
prowler
proximity
proxy
  pl proxies
prude
prudence
prudent
prudery
prudish
prudishness
prune
  pruned
  pruning
prurient
pry

pried
prying
psalm
psalmist
psalter
pseud
pseudo
pseudonym
psoriasis
psych
psyche
psychedelic
psychiatric
psychiatrist
psychiatry
psychic
psycho
psychoanalyse
  psychoanalysed
  psychoanalysing
psychoanalysis
psychoanalyst
psychological
psychologically
psychologist
psychology
psychopath
psychosis
  pl psychoses
psychosomatic
psychotherapist
psychotherapy
psychotic
ptarmigan
pterodactyl

pub
puberty
pubescence
pubescent
pubic
pubis
public
publicly
publican
publication
publicity
publicize, -ise
  publicized
  publicizing
publish
publisher
publishing
puce
puck
pucker
  puckered
  puckering
pudding
puddle
pudenda
puerile
puff
puffin
puffy
pug
pugilist
pugnacious
pugnacity
pug-nosed
puke
pukka

pull
to pull a cart
pullet
pulley
pl pulleys
pullover
pulmonary
pulp
pulpit
pulsar
pulsate
pulsated
pulsating
pulse
pulsed
pulsing
pulverize, -ise
pulverized
pulverizing
puma
pumice stone
pummel
pummelled
pummelling
pump
pumpernickel
pumpkin
pun
punned
punning
punch
pl punches
punchline
punchy
punctilious
punctual
punctuality

punctually
punctuate
punctuated
punctuating
punctuation
puncture
punctured
puncturing
pundit
pungent
punish
punishable
punishing
punishment
punitive
punk
punnet
punt
puny
pup
pupa
pl pupae
pupil
puppet
puppeteer
puppetry
puppy
pl puppies
purchase
purchased
purchasing
purchaser
pure
purée
purely
purgative

purgatory
purge
purged
purging
purification
purifier
purify
purified
purifying
purism
purist
puritan
puritanical
puritanically
purity
purl
knit one, purl one
purled
purling
purloin
purple
purport
purpose
purposeful
purposefully
purposely
purr
purred
purring
purse
purser
pursue
pursued
pursuing
pursuer
pursuit

purulence
purulent
purveyor
pus
push
push-chair
pusher
pushover
pushy
pusillanimous
pussy
pussyfoot
pussyfooting
pustule
put
to put a cup on the

table
put
putting
putative
putrefaction
putrefy
putrefied
putrefying
putrid
putt
to putt a ball
putted
putting
putter
putty
puzzle
puzzled

puzzling
puzzlement
pygmy, pigmy
pl pygmies, pigmies
pyjamas
pylon
pyramid
pyre
Pyrex®
pyrite
pyromania
pyromaniac
pyrotechnics
Pyrrhic
python

q

qi
qi gong
quack
quackery
quad
quadrangle
quadrangular
quadrant
quadraphonic
quadrilateral
quadrille

quadruped
quadruple
quadrupled
quadrupling
quadruplet
quaff
quagmire
quail
quailed
quailing
quaint
quake

quaked
quaking
qualification
qualifier
qualify
qualified
qualifying
qualitative
quality
pl qualities
qualm
quandary

pl quandaries

quango

quantify
quantified
quantifying

quantitative

quantity
pl quantities

quantum

quarantine

quark

quarrel
quarrelled
quarrelling

quarrelsome

quarry
pl quarries
quarried
quarrying

quart

quarter

quarterly

quartermaster

quartet

quarto

quartz

quasar

quash
to quash a rebellion

quasi-

quassia

quaver
quavered
quavering

quay
the boat tied to the quay

queasily

queasiness

queasy

queen

queenly

queer

quell

quench

quenelle

querulous

query
pl queries
queried
querying

quest

question
questioned
questioning

questionable

questionably

questioner

questionnaire

queue
a cinema queue: to queue for the cinema
queued
queuing, queueing

quibble
quibbled
quibbling

quiche

quick

quicken
quickened
quickening

quicklime

quickness

quicksand

quicksilver

quickstep

quid

quiddity

quiescence

quiescent

quiet
a shy, quiet child

quieten
quietened
quietening

quietness

quietude

quiff

quill

quilt

quilted

quin

quince

quinine

quinquennial

quintessence

quintessential

quintet

quintuplet

quip
quipped
quipping

quire
a quire of paper

quirk

quirky

quit
quitted, quit
quitting

quite
  quite pretty
quits
quiver
  quivered
  quivering
quixotic
quixotically
quiz
  pl quizzes

quizzed
quizzing
quizmaster
quizzical
quizzically
quoin
quoits
quorate
quorum

quota
  pl quotas
quotable
quotation
quote
  quoted
  quoting
quotient
qwerty

r

If you can't find the word you're looking for under letter **R**, it could be that it starts with a different letter. Try looking under **WR** for words like *wrap*, *wrist* and *wrong*. Also, don't forget **RH** for words like *rhetoric*, *rhyme* and *rhinoceros*.

rabbet
  = a groove cut in a
  piece of wood, to cut
  such a groove
  rabbeted
  rabbeting
rabbi
  pl rabbis
rabbit
  rabbited
  rabbiting
rabble
rabble-rouser
rabid
rabies

raccoon, racoon
race
racecourse
racehorse
racer
racial
racially
racialism
racialist
racism
racist
rack
racket, racquet
  a tennis racket

racket
  *a noisy racket: an
  illegal racket*
racketeer
raconteur
racoon
  see raccoon
racquet
  see racket
racy
radar
  a radar beam
radial
radian
radiance

radiant
radiate
 radiated
 radiating
radiation
radiator
radical
radically
radio
 pl radios
 radioed
 radioing
radioactive
radioactivity
radiologist
radiographer
radiography
radiologist
radiology
radiotherapist
radiotherapy
radish
 pl radishes
radium
radius
 pl radii
raffia
raffish
raffle
 raffled
 raffling
raft
rafter
rag
 ragged
 They ragged the new boy

ragging
raga
ragamuffin
rag-bag
rage
 raged
 He raged and swore
 raging
ragga
ragged [*ragd*]
 see **rag**
ragged ['*ragid*]
 ragged clothes
raglan
ragout
ragtime
ragwort
raid
raider
 The police caught the raider
rail
railcard
railing
raillery
railroad
railway
raiment
rain
 wind and rain: to rain heavily
 rained
 raining
rainbow
raincoat
rainfall
rainforest

rainy
raise
 to raise a family: to raise one's arm
 raised
 raising
raisin
raita
rajah
rake
 raked
 raking
rakish
rakishness
rally
 pl rallies
 rallied
 rallying
ram
 rammed
 ramming
Ramadan
ramble
 rambled
 rambling
rambler
rambutan
ramekin
ramification
ramp
rampage
 rampaged
 rampaging
rampant
 the lion rampant: Violence is rampant
rampart
 the rampart round the

castle
ram-raid
ramrod
ramshackle
ran
  see **run**
ranch
  pl ranches
rancher
rancid
rancorous
rancour
rand
randy
random
rang
  see **ring**
range
  ranged
  ranging
ranger
rank
rankle
  rankled
  rankling
rankness
ransack
ransom
  ransomed
  ransoming
rant
rap
  rapped
  He rapped on the door
  rapping
rapacious
rape

raped
  He raped and
  murdered her
  raping
rapid
rapidity
rapier
rapist
rapped
  see **rap**
rapper
rapport
rapprochement
rapscallion
rapt
  gazing with rapt
  attention
rapture
rapturous
rare
rarefied
rarely
raring
rarity
  pl rarities
rascal
rascally
rash
rasher
rashness
rasp
raspberry
  pl raspberries
rasping
Rasta
Rastafarian

rat
ratted
  The dog ratted: His
  friends ratted on him
  ratting
ratafia
ratatouille
ratbag
ratchet
rate
  rated
  They rated him the
  best pilot
  rating
rateable
ratepayer
rather
ratification
ratify
  ratified
  ratifying
rating
ratio
  pl ratios
ration
  rationed
  rationing
rational
rationale
rationalism
rationalist
rationality
rationalization,
  -isation
rationalize, -ise
  rationalized
  rationalizing

rationally

ratted
see rat

rattan

rattle
rattled
rattling

rattlesnake

ratty

raucous

raunchy

ravage
ravaged
ravaging

rave
raved
raving

raven

ravenous

raver

ravine

ravioli

ravishing

raw

rawness

ray
pl rays

rayon

raze
to raze a city to the ground
razed
razing

razor

razzle

razzmatazz

reach

react

reaction

reactionary

reactivate
reactivate
reactivating

reactivation

reactive

reactor

read [*rēd*]
to read a book
read [*red*]
*He read that book:
She has read that book*
reading

readable

reader

readership

readily

readiness

ready

real
a real diamond: a real friend

realign

realignment

realism

realist

realistic

realistically

reality
pl realities

realizable, -isable

realization, -isation

realize, -ise
realized
realizing

really

realm

realtor

ream

reap
reaped
reaping

reaper

reapply
reapplied
reapplying

rear
reared
rearing

rearguard

rearm

rearmament

reason
reasoned
reasoning

reasonable

reasonably

reassurance

reassure
reassured
reassuring

rebate

rebel
rebelled
rebelling

rebellion

rebellious

rebirth

reboot

reborn
rebound
rebuff
rebuild
 rebuilt
 rebuilding
rebuke
 rebuked
 rebuking
rebut
 rebutted
 rebutting
rebuttal
recalcitrance
recalcitrant
recall
 recalled
 recalling
recant
recap
 recapped
 recapping
recapitulate
 recapitulated
 recapitulating
recapitulation
recapture
 recaptured
 recapturing
recede
 receded
 receding
receipt
receive
 received
 receiving
receiver
receivership

recent
recently
receptacle
reception
receptionist
receptive
recess
 pl recesses
recession
recessive
recidivism
recidivist
recipe
recipient
reciprocal
reciprocally
reciprocate
 reciprocated
 reciprocating
reciprocation
reciprocity
recital
recitalist
recitation
recitative
recite
 recited
 reciting
reckless
reckon
 reckoned
 reckoning
reclaim
reclamation
recline
 reclined

reclining
recliner
recluse
recognition
recognizable, -isable
recognizably, -isably
recognize, -ise
 recognized
 recognizing
recoil
 recoiled
 recoiling
recollect
recollection
recommend
recommendation
recompense
reconcile
 reconciled
 reconciling
reconciliation
recondite
recondition
 reconditioned
 reconditioning
reconnaissance
reconnoitre
 reconnoitred
 reconnoitring
reconsider
reconstitute
 reconstituted
 reconstituting
reconstitution
reconstruct
reconstruction

record
recorder
recording
recount
re-count
recoup
  recouped
  recouping
recourse
recover
  recovered
  recovering
re-cover
recoverable
recovery
recreate
  recreated
  recreating
re-creation
  a skilful re-creation of
  the Victorian
  atmosphere in the film
recreation
  She swims for
  recreation
recreational
recrimination
recriminatory
recruit
  recruited
  recruiting
recruitment
rectal
rectangle
rectangular
rectifiable
rectify

rectified
rectifying
rectitude
recto
rector
rectory
  pl rectories
rectum
recumbent
recuperate
  recuperated
  recuperating
recuperation
recuperative
recur
  recurred
  recurring
recurrence
recurrent
recyclable
recycle
  recycled
  recycling
red
  a red dress
redbreast
redcurrant
redden
  reddened
  reddening
redeem
Redeemer
redeeming
redemption
redemptive
redeploy
  redeployed

redeploying
redeployment
redevelop
  redeveloped
  redeveloping
redevelopment
red-handed
redhead
redness
redo
  redid
  redoing
  redone
redolence
redolent
redouble
  redoubled
  redoubling
redoubtable
redress
redstart
reduce
  reduced
  reducing
reduction
redundancy
  pl redundancies
redundant
redwood
reed
  a broken reed: a reed
  by the pond: a reed of
  a musical instrument
reedy
reef
reefer
reek

reel
a Scottish reel: to reel drunkenly
reeled
reeling
re-entry
refectory
pl refectories
refer
referred
referring
referee
reference
referendum
pl referenda, referendums
referential
referral
refill
refillable
refine
refined
refining
refinement
refinery
pl refineries
refit
refitted
refitting
reflect
reflection
reflective
reflectively
reflector
reflex
reflexive
reflexologist

reflexology
reform
reformation
reformatory
reformer
reformism
refract
refraction
refractory
refrain
refrained
refraining
refresh
refresher course
refreshment
refrigerate
refrigerated
refrigerating
refrigeration
refrigerator
refuel
refuelled
refuelling
refuge
to find refuge from danger
refugee
He is a war refugee
refulgent
refund
refundable
refurbish
refurbishment
refusal
refuse [rə'fūz]
Did you refuse to go?
refused

refusing
refuse ['refūs]
kitchen refuse
refusenik
refutable
refute
refuted
refuting
regain
regained
regaining
regal
a stately and regal carriage
regally
regale
to regale him with humorous stories
regaled
regaling
regalia
regard
regarding
regardless
regatta
pl regattas
regency
regenerate
regenerated
regenerating
regeneration
regenerative
regent
reggae
regicide
régime
regimen

regiment
regimental
regimentation
region
regional
regionally
register
  registered
  registering
registrar
registration
registry
  pl registries
regress
regression
regressive
regret
  regretted
  regretting
regretful
regretfully
regrettable
regrettably
regular
regularity
regularization,
  -isation
regularize, -ise
  regularized
  regularizing
regulate
  regulated
  regulating
regulation
regulator
regulo

regurgitate
  regurgitated
  regurgitating
rehabilitate
  rehabilitated
  rehabilitating
rehabilitation
rehash
rehearsal
rehearse
  rehearsed
  rehearsing
reheat
rehouse
reign
  *How long did Victoria
  reign?*
  reigned
  reigning
reiki
reimburse
  reimbursed
  reimbursing
rein
  *the reins of a horse: to
  rein in the horse*
  reined
  reining
reincarnate
  reincarnated
  reincarnating
reincarnation
reindeer
  pl reindeer
reinforce
  reinforced
  reinforcing
reinforcements

reinstate
  reinstated
  reinstating
reinstatement
reiterate
  reiterated
  reiterating
reiteration
reiterative
reject
rejection
rejoice
  rejoiced
  rejoicing
rejoinder
rejuvenate
  rejuvenated
  rejuvenating
relapse
  relapsed
  relapsing
relate
  related
  relating
relation
relationship
relative
relatively
relativism
relativity
relax
relaxant
relaxation
relaxed
relaxing
relay
  relayed

relaying

release
released
releasing

relegate
relegated
relegating

relegation

relent

relentless

relevance

relevant

reliability

reliable

reliably

reliance

reliant

relic

relief
a sigh of relief

relieve
to relieve her pain
relieved
relieving

religion

religious

relinquish

relish
pl relishes

relive
relived
reliving

reload

relocate
relocated
relocating

relocation

reluctance

reluctant

rely
relied
relying

remain
remained
remaining

remainder

remains

remake

remand

remark

remarkable

remarkably

remarry
remarried
remarrying

remedial

remedy
pl remedies
remedied
remedying

remember
remembered
remembering

remembrance

remind

reminder

reminisce
reminisced
reminiscing

reminiscence

reminiscent

remiss

remission

remit
remitted
remitting

remittance

remix

remnant

remonstrance

remonstrate
remonstrated
remonstrating

remonstration

remorse

remorseful

remorsefully

remorseless

remote

remote-controlled

remotely

remoteness

remould

removable

removal

remove
removed
removing

remover

remunerate
remunerated
remunerating

remuneration

remunerative

renaissance

renal

rename

renascent

rend

render
  rendered
  rendering
rendezvous
  pl rendezvous
rendition
renegade
renege
  reneged
  reneging
renew
renewable
renewal
rennet
renounce
  renounced
  renouncing
renouncement
renovate
  renovated
  renovating
renovation
renovator
renown
renowned
rent
rental
renunciation
reorganization,
  -isation
reorganize, -ise
  reorganized
  reorganizing
rep
repaid
  see repay
repair

repaired
repairing
repairable
reparable
reparation
repartee
repast
repatriate
  repatriated
  repatriating
repatriation
repay
  repaid
  repaying
repayment
repeal
  repealed
  repealing
repeat
  repeated
  repeating
repeatable
repeatedly
repel
  repelled
  repelling
repellent, repellant
repent
repentance
repentant
repercussion
repertoire
repertory
repetition
repetitious
repetitive
repetitively

replace
  replaced
  replacing
replaceable
replacement
replay
replenish
replenishment
replete
replica
  pl replicas
replicate
  replicated
  replicating
reply
  pl replies
  replied
  replying
report
reporter
repose
repository
  pl repositories
repossess
  repossessed
  repossessing
repossession
reprehensible
reprehensibly
represent
representation
representative
repress
repression
repressive

reprieve
reprieved
reprieving
reprimand
reprint
reprisal
reproach
  pl reproaches
reproachful
reproachfully
reprobate
reproduce
  reproduced
  reproducing
reproduction
reproductive
reproof
  a look of reproof
reprove
  to reprove the naughty child
  reproved
  reproving
reptile
reptilian
republic
republican
republicanism
repudiate
  repudiated
  repudiating
repudiation
repugnance
repugnant
repulsion
repulsive

repulsively
reputable
reputation
repute
reputed
reputedly
request
requiem
require
  required
  requiring
requirement
requisite
requisition
reroute
  rerouted
  rerouteing
rerun
  reran
  rerunning
  rerun
rescind
rescue
  rescued
  rescuing
rescuer
research
  pl researches
researcher
resemblance
resemble
  resembled
  resembling
resent
resentful
resentfully
resentment

reservation
reserve
  reserved
  reserving
reserved
reservist
reservoir
reshuffle
reside
  resided
  residing
residence
resident
residential
residual
residue
resign
  resigned
  resigning
resignation
resilience
resilient
resin
resinous
resist
resistance
resistible
resistor
resolute
resolutely
resolution
resolve
  resolved
  resolving
resonance
resonant

resonate
  resonated
  resonating
resort
resounding
resource
resourceful
respect
respectability
respectable
respectably
respectful
  a respectful salute
respectfully
respective
  They went to their respective homes
respectively
respiration
respirator
respiratory
respite
resplendent
respond
respondent
response
responsibility
  pl responsibilities
responsible
responsibly
responsive
rest
  take a rest: rest in peace
restaurant
restaurateur

restful
restfully
restitution
restive
restively
restless
restlessness
restorable
restoration
restorative
restore
  restored
  restoring
restorer
restrain
  restrained
  restraining
restraint
restrict
restriction
restrictive
result
resultant
resume
  resumed
  resuming
résumé
resumption
resurgence
resurgence
resurgent
resurrect
resurrection
resuscitate
  resuscitated
  resuscitating

resuscitation
retail
  retailed
  retailing
retailer
retain
  retained
  retaining
retainer
retake
  retook
  retaking
  retaken
retaliate
  retaliated
  retaliating
retaliation
retard
retarded
retardant
retch
  The sight of blood makes him retch
retention
retentive
rethink
  rethought
  rethinking
reticence
reticent
reticule
retina
  pl retinas, retinae
retinue
retiral
retire
  retired

retiring
retirement
retort
retrace
retraced
retracing
retract
retractable
retraction
retrain
retreat
retreated
retreating
retrench
retrenchment
retribution
retrievable
retrieval
retrieve
retrieved
retrieving
retriever
retrograde
retrospect
retrospective
retrospectively
retroussé
return
returnable
reunion
reunite
reunited
reuniting
rev
revved
revving

revamp
reveal
revealed
revealing
reveille
revel
revelled
revelling
revelation
revelatory
reveller
revelry
revenge
revenged
revenging
revengeful
revenue
reverberate
reverberated
reverberating
reverberation
revere
revered
revering
reverence
Reverend
reverent
reverential
reverentially
reverie
reversal
reverse
reversed
reversing
reversible
reversion
revert

review
*the review of his new
play*: *to review a novel*
reviewer
revile
reviled
reviling
revilement
revise
revised
revising
revision
revisionism
revisionist
revitalize, -ise
revitalized
revitalizing
revival
revivalist
revive
revived
reviving
revoke
revoked
revoking
revolt
revolting
revolution
revolutionary
pl revolutionaries
revolutionize, -ise
revolutionized
revolutionizing
revolve
revolved
revolving
revolver

revue
  a musical revue

revulsion

reward

rewind
  rewound
  rewinding

rewire
  rewired
  rewiring

reword

rewrite

rhapsodic

rhapsodize, -ise
  rhapsodized
  rhapsodizing

rhapsody
  pl rhapsodies

rhesus

rhetoric

rhetorical

rhetorically

rheumatic

rheumatism

rheumatoid

rhinitis

rhinoceros
  pl rhinoceroses

rhizome

rhododendron

rhombus

rhubarb

rhyme
  Cat is a rhyme for rat:
  Do these words
  rhyme?
  rhymed
  rhyming

rhythm

rhythmic,
  rhythmical

rhythmically

rib

ribald

ribaldry

ribbed

ribbon

riboflavin

rice

rich

riches

richness

rickets

rickety

rickshaw

ricochet
  ricocheted
  ricocheting

rid
  rid
  ridding

riddance

ridden
  see **ride**

riddle
  riddled
  riddling

ride
  rode

He rode on a horse
ridden
He has ridden on a
horse
riding

rider

ridge

ridicule
  ridiculed
  ridiculing

ridiculous

ridiculousness

rife

riff-raff

rifle
  rifled
  rifling

rift

rig
  rigged
  rigging

right
  the road on the right:
  the right answer: the
  right to vote

righteous

righteousness

rightful

rightfully

right-hand

right-handed

right-wing

right-winger

rigid

rigidity

rigmarole

rigor mortis

rigorous

rigour

rile
 riled
 riling

rim

rimmed

rime
 the rime on the grass

rind

ring
 an engagement ring:
 to ring a racing pigeon
 ringed
 He ringed the pigeons
 ringing

ring
 to ring the bells
 rang
 The bell rang
 rung
 I have rung the bell
 ringing

ringed
 see ring

ringer

ringleader

ringlet

ring-pull

ringworm

rink

rinse
 rinsed
 rinsing

riot
 rioted
 rioting

rioter

riotous

rip
 ripped
 ripping

ripcord

ripe

ripen
 ripened
 ripening

ripeness

rip-off

riposte

ripple
 rippled
 rippling

rip-roaring

rise
 rose
 The sun rose
 risen
 The sun has risen
 rising

risible

risk

risky

risotto

rissole

rite
 to perform a religious
 rite

ritual

ritualist

ritualistic

ritually

rival
 rivalled
 rivalling

rivalry
 pl rivalries

river

rivet
 riveted
 riveting

rivulet

roach

road
 a main road

roadie

roadside

roadster

roadworthy

roam
 roamed
 roaming

roar
 roared
 roaring

roast

rob
 robbed
 robbing

robber

robbery
 pl robberies

robe

robin

robot

robotic

robotics

robust

rock

rockabilly

rocker

rockery

pl rockeries
rocket
  rocketed
  rocketing
rock 'n' roll
rocky
rococo
rod
rode
  see ride
rodent
rodeo
roe
  a roe deer: cod roe
rogue
roguish
role
  the role of Hamlet
roll
  a roll of carpet: to roll a
  ball
roller
rollercoaster
roller-skate
  roller-skated
  roller-skating
rollicking
rolling-pin
rollmop
roll-on
roly-poly
Roman
romance
romantic
romantically
romanticize, -ise
  romanticized

romanticizing
romp
rondo
rood
roof
  pl roofs
roofing
rooftop
rook
rookery
  pl rookeries
room
roommate
roomy
roost
rooster
root
  rooted
  rooting
rope
  roped
  roping
ropy
rosary
  pl rosaries
rose
  see rise
rose
rosehip
rosemary
rosette
rosewood
roster
rostral
rostrum
  pl rostrums, rostra

rosy
rot
  rotted
  rotting
rota
  pl rotas
rotary
rotate
  rotated
  rotating
rotation
rote
  He learnt the answers
  by rote
rotisserie
rotor
rotten
rotter
rotund
rotundity
rouble
rouge
rough
  a rough surface: a
  rough sea
roughage
roughen
  roughened
  roughening
roughshod
roulette
round
roundabout
roundel
rounders
roundworm
rouse

rouseed
rousing

rout
the rout of Napoleon's army

route
the quickest route to Edinburgh

routine

routinely

roux

rove
roved
roving

rover

row [*rō*]
a row of cabbages: to row a boat
rowed
He rowed the boat
rowing

row [*row*]
a noisy row

rowan

rowdy

rowdyism

rowdiness

rowed
see **row**

rower

rowing boat

rowlock

royal

royalist

royally

royalty
pl royalties

rub
rubbed
rubbing

rubber

rubbery

rubbish

rubble

rubella

rubicund

rubric

ruby
pl rubies

ruche

ruched

rucksack

ruction

rudder

ruddy

rude

rudely

rudeness

rudimentary

rudiments

rue
rued
ruing

rueful

ruefully

ruff
a ruff round the neck

ruffian

ruffle
ruffled
ruffling

rug

Rugby

rugged

ruin
ruined
ruining

ruination

ruinous

ruinously

rule
ruled
ruling

ruler

rum

rumba

rumble
rumbled
rumbling

ruminant

ruminate
ruminated
ruminating

rumination

rummage
rummaged
rummaging

rumour

rump

rumple
rumpled
rumpling

rumpus

run
ran
He ran away
run
He has run away
running

runaway

run-down
rune
rung
  see ring
rung
  the rung of the ladder
runic
run-in
runner
runner-up
  pl runners-up
runny
runt
run-up

runway
rupee
rupture
  ruptured
  rupturing
rural
ruse
rush
  pl rushes
rusk
russet
rust
rustic
rustiness

rustle
  rustled
  rustling
rustler
rustproof
rusty
rut
  rutted
  rutting
ruthless
ruthlessness
rye
  rye bread

S

If you can't find the word you're looking for under letter **S**, it could be that it starts with a different letter. Try looking under **C** for words like *century*, *city* and *cycle*, and **PS** for words like *psychology*. Also, don't forget **SC** for words like *scent*, **SCH** for words like *schism*, and **SW** for words like *sword*. If the word you're looking for sounds as if it begins **SH** but you can't find it there, remember that **CH** is sometimes pronounced *sh* (as in *chivalry*), as is **SCH** (*schnapps*).

Sabbath
sabbatical
sable
sabotage
saboteur
sabre
sac
saccharine
sachet
sack
sackcloth
sacking
sacral
sacrament
sacred
sacrifice
  sacrificed
  sacrificing
sacrificial
sacrilege
sacrilegious
sacrosanct
sad
  compar sadder
  superl saddest

sadly
sadden
  saddened
  saddening
saddle
  saddled
  saddling
saddler
sadism
sadist
sadistic
sadistically
sadness
sado-masochism
sado-masochist
safari
safe
safely
safeguard
safekeeping
safety
safflower
saffron
sag
  sagged

sagging
saga
  pl sagas
sagacious
sagacity
sage
sagely
saggy
Sagittarius
sago
said
  see say
sail
  a sail round the bay: to
  sail a boat
  sailed
  sailing
sailboard
sailboarding
sailor
saint
sainthood
saintliness
saintly
sake

salaam
salacious
salad
salamander
salami
salary
  pl salaries
sale
  a furniture sale
saleable
salesman
salesperson
saleswoman
salient
saline
saliva
salivary
salivate
  salivated
  salivating
sallow
sally
  pl sallies
  sallied
  sallying
salmon
salmonella
salon
  a hairdressing salon
saloon
  a saloon car: a saloon bar
salopettes
salsa
salsify
salt

salted
saltiness
saltpetre
salty
salubrious
salutary
salutation
salute
  saluted
  saluting
salvage
  salvaged
  salvaging
salvation
salve
  salved
  salving
salver
salvo
  pl salvos, salvoes
samba
same
sameness
samey
samosa
samovar
sampan
sample
  sampled
  sampling
sampler
samurai
sanatorium
  pl sanatoriums, sanatoria
sanctify
  sanctified

sanctifying
sanctimonious
sanction
  sanctioned
  sanctioning
sanctity
sanctuary
  pl sanctuaries
sanctum
  pl sanctums, sancta
sand
sandal
sandalwood
sandbag
sandblast
sander
sandpaper
sandpit
sandstone
sandwich
  pl sandwiches
sandy
sane
sanely
saneness
sang
  see sing
sangfroid
sangria
sanguine
sanguinely
sanitary
sanitation
sanitization, -isation
sanitize, -ise
  sanitized

sanitizing
sanity
sank
 see sink
sanserif
sap
 sapped
 sapping
sapling
sapphire
saraband
sarcasm
sarcastic
sarcastically
sarcophagus
 pl sarcophagi,
 sarcophaguses
sardine
sardonic
sardonically
sari
sarong
sartorial
sash
 pl sashes
sat
 see sit
Satan
satanic
satchel
sated
satellite
satiable
satiate
 satiated
 satiating

satiety
satin
satinwood
satire
satirical
satirically
satirist
satirize, -ise
 satirized
 satirizing
satisfaction
satisfactorily
satisfactory
satisfy
 satisfied
 satisfying
satsuma
saturate
 saturated
 saturating
saturation
Saturday
saturnine
satyr
sauce
saucepan
saucer
saucily
sauciness
saucy
sauerkraut
sauna
saunter
 sauntered
 sauntering
sausage

sauté
savage
savagely
savagery
savannah
save
 saved
 saving
saveloy
savings
saviour
 Christ the Saviour
savoir-faire
savour
 to savour the delicious
 wine
savoury
 pl savouries
savoy
savvy
saw
 see see
saw
 sawed
 He sawed the tree
 down
 sawn
 He has sawn off the
 branch
 sawing
sawdust
sawfish
saxophone
saxophonist
say
 said
 saying
scab

scabbard

scabby

scabies

scabious

scabrous

scaffold

scaffolding

scalar

scald

scale

scalene

scallion

scallop

scalloped

scallywag

scalp

scalpel

scaly

scam

scamp

scamper
  scampered
  scampering

scampi

scan
  scanned
  scanning

scandal

scandalize, -ise
  scandalized
  scandalizing

scandalmonger

scandalous

scanner

scansion

scant

scantily

scanty

scapegoat

scapula
  pl scapulae,
  scapulas

scar
  scarred
  His cheek is scarred
  scarring

scarab

scarce

scarcely

scarcity
  pl scarcities

scare
  scared
  *She was scared of the
  dark*
  scaring

scarecrow

scaremonger

scaremongering

scarf
  pl scarves, scarfs

scarlet

scarper

scarred
  see scar

scary

scat

scathing

scatological

scatology

scatter
  scattered
  scattering

scatterbrain

scatty

scavenger

scenario

scene
  *the first scene of the
  play: the scene of the
  crime*

scenery

scenic

scent
  *the scent of spring
  flowers*

sceptic
  *A sceptic doesn't
  believe anyone*

sceptical

sceptically

scepticism

sceptre

schedule

schema
  pl schemata

schematic

schematize, -ise
  schematized
  schematizing

scheme
  schemed
  scheming

schemer

schism

schizoid

schizophrenia

schizophrenic

schlep

schmaltz

schmaltzy
schnapps
scholar
scholarly
scholarship
scholastic
scholastically
school
 schooled
 schooling
schoolfellow
schoolmarm
schoolmarmish
schoolmaster
schoolmistress
schoolteacher
schooner
schwa
sciatica
science
scientific
scientifically
scientist
sci-fi
scimitar
scintillate
 scintillated
 scintillating
scissors
sclerosis
scoff
scold
scolding
sconce
scone

scoop
 scooped
 scooping
scooter
scope
scorch
scorcher
scorching
score
 scored
 scoring
scoreboard
scorer
scorn
scornful
scornfully
Scorpio
scorpion
scotch
scot-free
scoundrel
scour
 scoured
 scouring
scourer
scourge
 scourged
 scourging
scout
scowl
scrabble
 scrabbled
 scrabbling
scrag
scragginess
scraggy

scram
scramble
 scrambled
 scrambling
scrap
 scrapped
 *They have scrapped
 the plans*
 scrapping
scrapbook
scrape
 scraped
 *She scraped her arm
 on the stone wall*
 scraping
scraper
scrapie
scrapped
 see scrap
scrappy
scratch
 pl scratches
scratchy
scrawl
scrawny
scream
 screamed
 screaming
scree
screech
 pl screeches
screed
screen
 screened
 screening
screenplay
screen-saver
screw

screwed
screwing

screwball

screwdriver

scribble
scribbled
scribbling

scribbler

scribe

scrimp

script

scripture

scriptwriter

scroll

scrotal

scrotum
pl scrota, scrotums

scrounge
scrounged
scrounging

scrounger

scrub
scrubbed
scrubbing

scrubby

scrubland

scruff

scruffily

scruffy

scrum

scrummage

scrummy

scrumptious

scrumpy

scrunch

scrunch-dry

scrunch-dried
scrunch-drying

scrunchie

scruple

scrupulous

scrupulously

scrutineer

scrutinize, -ise
scrutinized
scrutinizing

scrutiny

scuba

scud

scuff

scuffle

scullery
pl sculleries

sculpt

sculptor
He is an artist and a sculptor

sculpture
a beautiful piece of sculpture

scum

scumbag

scummy

scupper
scuppered
scuppering

scurf

scurrilous

scurry
scurried
scurrying

scurvy

scuttle

scuttled
scuttling

scythe

sea
ships on the sea

seafarer

seafaring

seafood

seagoing

seagull

seal
sealed
sealing
the sealing of the envelope: sealing wax

sealant

sealskin

seam
to sew a seam: a coal seam

seaman
pl seamen

seamless

seamstress

seamy

séance

sear
to sear meat
seared
searing

search
pl searches

seashell

seashore

seasick

seasickness

seaside

season
  seasoned
  seasoning
seasonable
seasonal
seasonally
seat
  seated
  seating
seaweed
sebaceous
sebum
secateurs
secede
  seceded
  seceding
secession
secluded
seclusion
second
secondary
seconder
second-hand
secondment
secrecy
secret
  They kept their marriage a secret: a secret plan
secretaire
secretarial
secretariat
secretary
  pl secretaries
secrete
  to secrete a dagger under a cloak

secreted
secreting
secretion
secretive
secretively
sect
sectarian
sectarianism
section
  sectioned
  sectioning
sectional
sector
secular
secularism
secularize, -ise
  secularized
  secularizing
secure
  secured
  securing
securely
security
  pl securities
sedan
sedate
sedately
sedation
sedative
sedentary
sedge
sediment
sedimentary
sedition
seditious
seduce

seduced
seducing
seduction
seductive
seductively
see
  Did you see him?: to see clearly
  saw
  I saw you
  seen
  I have seen him
  seeing
seed
seedless
seedling
seedy
seek
  sought
  seeking
seem
  They seem friendly
  seemed
  seeming
seemingly
seemly
seen
  see **see**
seep
  seeped
  seeping
seepage
seer
  The seer foretold her death
seersucker
seesaw
seethe

seethed
seething
segment
segregate
segregated
segregating
segregation
seine
seismic
seismograph
seismography
seismological
seismologist
seismology
seize
seized
seizing
seizure
seldom
select
selection
selective
selector
selenium
self
pl selves
self-addressed
self-appointed
self-assurance
self-assured
self-catering
self-centred
self-confessed
self-confidence
self-confident
self-conscious

self-control
self-defence
self-effacing
self-employed
self-esteem
self-evident
self-explanatory
self-help
self-importance
self-indulgence
self-indulgent
self-interest
selfish
selfishness
selfless
selflessness
self-made
self-pity
self-raising
self-righteous
selfsame
self-satisfied
self-service
self-sufficient
sell
to sell flowers from a
stall
sold
selling
Sellotape®
sell-out
selvage
semantic
semantically
semantics
semaphore

semblance
semen
semester
semibreve
semicircle
semicolon
semi-detached
semi-final
seminal
seminar
semiology
semiotic
semiotics
semiquaver
Semitic
semitone
semolina
senate
senator
send
sent
I sent a letter
sending
sender
senile
senility
senior
seniority
senna
sensation
sensational
sensationalist
sensationally
sense
sensed
sensing

senseless
sensibility
  pl sensibilities
sensible
sensibly
sensitive
sensitively
sensitivity
sensitize, -ise
  sensitized
  sensitizing
sensor
sensory
sensual
  a sensual face
sensuality
sensually
sensuous
  the sensuous quality of the sculpture
sent
  see send
sentence
  sentenced
  sentencing
sententious
sentient
sentiment
sentimental
sentimentality
sentimentally
sentinel
sentry
Seoul
sepal
separable

separate
separately
  separated
  separating
separatism
separatist
separation
sepia
September
septet
septic
  a septic wound: a septic tank
septicaemia
septuagenarian
sepulchral
sepulchre
sequel
sequence
sequential
sequestered
sequestrate
sequestration
sequin
seraph
  pl seraphs, seraphim
seraphic
sere
  withered and sere
serenade
serendipitous
serendipity
serene
serenely
serenity
serf

serfdom
serge
sergeant
serial
  a television serial: a magazine serial
serialization, -isation
serialize, -ise
  serialized
  serializing
series
  a series of plays
  pl series
serif
serious
  in a serious mood
seriousness
sermon
seropositive
serotonin
serpent
serrated
serried
serum
servant
serve
  served
  serving
server
service
serviceable
serviceman
serviette
servile
servilely
servility

serving
servitude
sesame
session
set
  set
  setting
setback
settee
setter
settle
  settled
  settling
settlement
settler
seven
seventeen
seventeenth
seventh
seventieth
seventy
sever
  severed
  severing
several
severance
severe
severely
severity
sew
  to sew a seam
  sewed
  She sewed the seam
  sewn
  She has sewn it
  sewing
sewage

sewed
  see **sew**
sewer ['sūər]
sewer ['sōər]
  a sewer and a knitter
sewerage
sewn
  see **sew**
sex
sexagenarian
sexily
sexiness
sexism
sexist
sextant
  a ship's sextant
sextet
sexton
  The sexton tolled the bell
sextuplet
sexual
sexuality
sexually
sexy
shabbily
shabby
shack
shackles
shade
  shaded
  shading
shadow
shady
shaft
shag

shaggy
shah
shake
  shook
  She shook the child
  shaken
  She has shaken the child
  shaking
shaker
shakily
shaky
shale
shall
  should
shallot
shallow
shalom
sham
  shammed
  shamming
shaman
shamanism
shambles
shambolic
shame
  shamed
  shaming
shameful
shamefully
shameless
shammy
  see **chamois**
shampoo
  shampooed
  shampooing
shamrock

shandy
shanty
shape
  shaped
  shaping
shapeless
shapely
shard
share
  shared
  sharing
shareholder
shareware
shark
sharp
sharpen
  sharpened
  sharpening
sharpener
shatter
  shattered
  shattering
shave
  shaved
  shaving
shaven
shaver
shawl
sheaf
  pl sheaves
shear
  to shear sheep
  sheared
  He sheared the sheep
  shorn
  He has shorn the
  sheep
  shearing

shearer
shears
sheath
shebang
shed
she'd
  = she had, she would
sheen
sheep
sheepish
sheepshank
sheepskin
sheer
  a sheer drop: sheer
  delight
  sheered
  The car sheered off
  the road
  sheering
sheet
sheikh
shekel
shelf
  a wooden shelf
  pl shelves
shell
she'll
  = she will
shellfish
shelter
  sheltered
  sheltering
shelve
  to shelve the problem:
  The cliff shelves
  slightly
shelving

shenanigans
shepherd
sherbet
sheriff
sherry
shiatsu
shied
  see shy
shield
shier, shiest
  see shy
shift
shiftily
shiftless
shifty
shilling
shimmer
  shimmered
  shimmering
shin
shindig
shine
  shone
  shining
shingles
Shinto
Shintoism
Shintoist
shinty
shiny
ship
  shipped
  shipping
shipment
shipwreck
shipyard

shire

shirk

shirker

shirt

shirty

shit
  shit, shitted, shat
  shitting

shitty

shiver
  shivered
  shivering

shivery

shoal

shock

shocking

shod
  see shoe

shoddily

shoddiness

shoddy

shoe
  to shoe a horse
  shod
  shoeing

shoelace

shoestring

shone
  see shine

shoo
  to shoo the birds away
  shooed
  shooing

shook
  see shake

shoot
  to shoot dead

shot

shooting

shop
  shopped
  shopping

shopkeeper

shoplift

shoplifter

shoplifting

shopper

shore

shorn
  see shear

short

shortage

shortbread

shortcoming

shorten
  shortened
  shortening

shortfall

shorthand

shortlist

shortly

shorts

short-sighted

short-tempered

short-term

shot
  see shoot

shotgun

should
  see shall

shoulder
  shouldered
  shouldering

shouldn't

  = should not

shout

shove
  shoved
  shoving

shovel
  shovelled
  shovelling

show
  showed
  He showed me the book
  shown
  He has shown me the book
  showing

showbiz

showcase

showdown

shower
  showered
  showering

showery

showily

showjumping

shown
  see show

showroom

showy

shrank
  see shrink

shrapnel

shred
  shredded
  shredding

shredder

shrew

shrewd

shrewish

shriek
shrieked
shrieking

shrift

shrill

shrilly

shrimp
shrimping

shrine

shrink
shrank
That dress shrank
shrunk
That dress has shrunk
shrinking

shrink-wrap

shrivel
shrivelled
shrivelling

shroud

shrub

shrubbery
pl shrubberies

shrug
shrugged
shrugging

shrunk
see shrink

shrunken

shudder
shuddered
shuddering

shuffle
shuffled
shuffling

shufti

shun
shunned
shunning

shunt

shut
shut
shutting

shutter

shuttle

shuttlecock

shy
compar shyer, shier
superl shyest, shiest

shyly

shy
shied
shying

shyness

sibilant

sibling

Sibyl

sick

sicken
sickened
sickening

sickle

sickly

sickness

side
sided
siding

sideboard

sideburn

sidekick

side-step
side-stepped
side-stepping

sidetrack

sidewalk

sideways

siding

sidle
sidled
sidling

siege

sienna

sierra

siesta

sieve
sieved
sieving

sift

sigh
sighed
sighing

sight
*What a sight he is in
that hat!: The sight of
him made her cry: to
sight land from the
ship*
sighted
sighting

sightless

sightseeing

sightseer

sign
signed
signing

signal
signalled
signalling

signalman

signatory

pl signatories
signature
signet
  a signet ring
significance
significant
signify
  signified
  signifying
signpost
Sikh
Sikhism
silage
silence
  silenced
  silencing
silencer
silent
silhouette
  silhouetted
  silhouetting
silicon
  Silicon is a common element
silicone
  silicone polish
silk
silken
silkworm
silky
sill
silly
silo
  pl silos
silt
silver
silverfish

silverside
silversmith
silvery
similar
similarity
  pl similarities
simile
simmer
  simmered
  simmering
simnel
simper
  simpered
  simpering
simple
simply
simpleton
simplicity
simplification
simplify
  simplified
  simplifying
simplistic
simply
simulate
  simulated
  simulating
simulation
simulator
simultaneous
sin
  sinned
  sinning
since
sincere
sincerely
sincerity

sine
sinecure
sinew
sinful
sinfully
sing
  sang
  He sang a song
  sung
  He has sung a song
  singing
  singing a song
singe
  singed
  singeing
  singeing the shirt with the iron
singer
single
  singled
  singling
single-handed
single-minded
singleness
singlet
singly
singular
singularity
sinister
sink
  sank
  The ship sank
  sunk
  The ship has sunk
  sinking
sinner
Sinn Fein

sinuous
sinuous curves

sinus
He has sinus trouble
pl sinuses

sinusitis

sip
sipped
sipping

siphon
siphoned
siphoning

sir

sire

siren

sirloin

sirocco

sisal

sissy

sister

sisterhood

sister-in-law
pl sisters-in-law

sisterly

sit
sat
sitting

sitar

sitcom

site
the site of the new
factory
sited
siting

sit-in

sitting-room

situate

situated

situation

six

sixpence

sixteen

sixteenth

sixth

sixtieth

sixty
pl sixties

size
sized
sizing

sizeable, sizable

sizzle
sizzled
sizzling

ska

skate
skated
skating

skateboard

skateboarding

skater

skein

skeletal

skeleton

sketch
pl sketches

sketchily

sketchy

skew

skewer
skewered
skewering

skew-whiff

ski
pl skis
He fastened on his skis
skied
skiing

skid
skidded
skidding

skier

skiff

skilful

skilfully

skill

skilled

skillet

skim
skimmed
skimming

skimp

skimpily

skimpy

skin
skinned
skinning

skinflint

skinful

skinhead

skinny

skint

skip
skipped
skipping

skipper

skirl

skirmish
pl skirmishes

skirt

skirting

skit

skittish

skittle

skive
skived
skiving

skiver

skivvy
pl skivvies

skulk

skull

skunk

sky
pl skies
blue skies

skylark

skylight

skyscraper

slab

slack

slacken
slackened
slackening

slacks

slag

slain
see **slay**

slake
slaked
slaking

slalom

slam
slammed
slamming

slander
slandered

slandering

slanderous

slang

slant

slanting

slap
slapped
slapping

slapdash

slapstick

slash
pl slashes

slat

slate
slated
The roof is slated. His book was slated by the critics
slating

slatted
a slatted wooden fence

slaughter
slaughtered
slaughtering

slaughterhouse

slave

slaver
slavered
slavering

slavery

slavish

slay
to slay the enemy
slew
He slew his enemy
slain
He has slain the

enemy
slaying

sleaze

sleazy

sled

sledge
sledged
sledging

sledgehammer

sleek

sleep
slept
sleeping

sleeper

sleepily

sleepless

sleepwalk

sleepwalking

sleepy

sleet

sleeve

sleeveless

sleigh
a sleigh in the snow

sleight-of-hand

slender

slept
see **sleep**

sleuth

slew
see **slay**

slew
The car began to slew round
slewed
slewing

slice

sliced
slicing
slicer
slick
slide
slid
sliding
slight
slightly
slightness
slim
slimmed
slimming
slime
slimy
sling
slung
slinging
slingback
slink
slunk
slinking
slinkily
slinky
slip
slipped
slipping
slip-on
slipper
slippery
slipshod
slipstream
slit
slit
slitting
slither
slithered

slithering
sliver
slob
slobber
slobbered
slobbering
slobbish
sloe
a ripe sloe
slog
slogged
slogging
slogan
sloop
slop
slopped
The water slopped in the pail
slopping
slope
sloped
The hill sloped down
sloping
slopped
see **slop**
sloppily
sloppy
slosh
slot
slotted
slotting
sloth
slothful
slothfully
slouch
slough [*slow*]
= a marsh
the slough of despond

slough [*sluf*]
to slough off skin
sloughed
sloughing
slovenly
slow
a slow train: to slow down
slowcoach
slow-worm
sludge
slug
sluggish
sluice
slum
slumber
slumbered
slumbering
slump
slung
see **sling**
slunk
see **slink**
slur
slurred
slurring
slurp
slurry
slush
slushy
slut
sluttish
sly
slyly
slyness
smack
smacker

small
smallholder
smallness
smallpox
smarmy
smart
smarten
smash
 pl smashes
smashing
smattering
smear
 smeared
 smearing
smell
 smelled, smelt
 They smelled smoke:
 It smelt of fish
 smelling
smelly
smelt
 see smell
smelt
 to smelt ore
 smelted
 smelting
smelter
smidgen
smile
 smiled
 smiling
smirch
smirk
smite
 smote
 smiting
 smitten

smithereens
smithy
smitten
smock
smocking
smog
smoke
 smoked
 smoking
smokeless
smoker
smokescreen
smoky
smooch
smooth
 smoothed
 smoothing
smoothie
smorgasbord
smother
 smothered
 smothering
smoulder
 smouldered
 smouldering
smudge
 smudged
 smudging
smug
smuggle
 smuggled
 smuggling
smuggler
smut
smutty
snack
snag

snagged
snagging
snail
snake
 snaked
 snaking
snakebite
snap
 snapped
 snapping
snapdragon
snapper
snappily
snappy
snapshot
snare
 snared
 snaring
snarl
snatch
 pl snatches
snazzy
sneak
sneakers
sneaky
sneer
 sneered
 sneering
sneeze
 sneezed
 sneezing
snide
sniff
sniffle
 sniffled
 sniffling
snifter

snigger
  sniggered
  sniggering
snip
  snipped
  She snipped the thread
  snipping
snipe
  sniped
  They sniped at the enemy
  sniping
sniper
snipped
  see snip
snippet
snitch
snivel
  snivelled
  snivelling
snob
snobbery
snobbish
snobby
snog
  snogged
  snogging
snood
snook
snooker
snoop
  snooped
  snooping
snooty
snooze
  snoozed
  snoozing

snore
  snored
  snoring
snorkel
snorkelling
snort
snot
snotty
snout
snow
  snowed
  snowing
snowball
snowboard
snowboarding
snowbound
snowdrift
snowdrop
snowfall
snowflake
snowman
snowplough
snowy
snub
  snubbed
  snubbing
snuff
snuffbox
snuffle
  snuffled
  snuffling
snug
snuggle
  snuggled
  snuggling
so
  so beautiful: *so much*

soak
so-and-so
soap
soapiness
soapstone
soapy
soar
  to soar high in the air
  soared
  soaring
sob
  sobbed
  sobbing
sober
  sobered
  sobering
soberness
sobriety
sobriquet
soca
soccer
sociability
sociable
  He is friendly and sociable
sociableness
sociably
social
  social history: *a social occasion*: *social class*
socialism
socialist
socialistic
socialite
socialize, -ise
  socialized
  socializing

socially

society

sociolinguistics

sociological

sociologist

sociology

sock

socket

sod

soda

sodden

sodium

sodomize

sodomy

sofa

soft

soften
  softened
  softening

softener

software

soggy

soil
  soiled
  soiling

sojourn
  sojourned
  sojourning

solace
  solaced
  solacing

solar

solarium
  pl solariums, solaria

sold
  see **sell**

solder
  to solder metal
  soldered
  soldering

soldier
  The soldier left the
  army
  soldiered
  soldiering

sole
  the sole of the foot:
  lemon sole: He is the
  sole survivor

solely

solecism

solemn

solemnly

solemnity

solenoid

sol-fa

solicit
  solicited
  soliciting

solicitor

solicitous

solid

solidarity

solidify
  solidified
  solidifying

solidity

soliloquy
  pl soliloquies

solitaire

solitary

solitude

solo

  pl solos

soloist

solstice

solubility

soluble

solution

solve
  solved
  solving

solvency

solvent

sombre

sombrely

sombreness

sombrero
  pl sombreros

some
  some people

somebody

somehow

someone

somersault

something

sometime

sometimes

somewhat

somewhere

somnambulist

somnolence

somnolent

son
  a son and a daughter

sonar

sonata

son-in-law
  pl sons-in-law

sonata

song

songster

songstress
pl songstresses

sonic

sonnet

sonny

sonority

sonorous

soon

sooner

soot
soot in the chimney

soothe
soothed
soothing

soothsayer

sooty

sop

sophism

sophist

sophisticated

sophistication

sophistry

sophomore

soporific

sopping

soppy

soprano
pl sopranos

sorbet

sorcerer

sorceress

sorcery

sordid

sore
a sore leg

sorely

soreness

sorghum

sorority

sorrel

sorrow

sorrowful

sorrowfully

sorry

sort

sortie

SOS

so-so

sotto voce

soufflé

sought
see **seek**

souk

soul
spirit and soul: the soul
of kindness: a dear old
soul: soul music

soulful

soulfully

soulless

sound

soundbite

soundtrack

soup

sour

source

sourpuss

souse
soused

sousing

south

southbound

south-east

south-easterly

south-eastern

southerly
a southerly wind

southern
the southern seas

southerner

south-west

south-westerly

south-western

souvenir

sou'wester

sovereign

sovereignty

sow [sow]
a sow in the pigsty

sow [sō]
to sow seeds
sowed
He sowed seeds
sown
He has sown seeds
sowing

sower
a sower of seeds

soy

soya

spa

space
spaced
spacing

spacecraft

spaceman

spacewoman
spacious
spaciousness
spade
spaghetti
spam
span
  spanned
  spanning
spangle
spaniel
spank
spanking
spanner
spar
  sparred
  He sparred with his opponent
  sparring
spare
  spared
  They spared his life
  sparing
sparing
sparingly
spark
sparkle
  sparkled
  sparkling
sparkler
sparred
  see **spar**
sparrow
sparse
sparsely
spartan
spasm

spasmodic
spasmodically
spastic
spat
  see **spit**
spate
spatial
spats
spatter
  spattered
  spattering
spatula
spawn
spay
speak
  spoke
  She spoke to me
  spoken
  He has spoken at last
  speaking
speaker
spear
spearhead
spearmint
special
specialist
speciality
  Cream cakes are their speciality
  pl specialities
specialization, -isation
specialize, -ise
  specialized
  specializing
specially
specialty

  Which medical specialty is he in?
  pl specialties
species
  pl species
  animals of different species
specific
specifically
specification
specify
  specified
  specifying
specimen
specious
  a specious argument
speck
speckled
spectacle
spectacles
spectacular
spectacularly
spectator
spectral
spectre
spectrum
  pl spectrums, spectra
speculate
  speculated
  speculating
speculation
speculative
speculatively
speculator
speculum
sped

see **speed**
speech
  pl speeches
speechless
speed
  speeded
  The driver always
  speeded
  sped
  They sped along the
  path
  speeding
speedboat
speedometer
speedwell
speedily
speedy
spell
  spelled, spelt
  spelling
spellbinding
spellbound
spelunking
spend
  spent
  spending
spendthrift
sperm
spermatozoon
  pl spermatozoa
spermicide
spew
sphagnum
sphere
spherical
sphincter
sphinx

spice
spiciness
spick-and-span
spicy
spider
spidery
spiel
spigot
spike
spiked
spiky
spill
  spilled, spilt
  spilling
spillage
spin
  spun
  spinning
spina bifida
spinach
spinal
spindle
spindly
spin-drier
spine
spine-chiller
spine-chilling
spineless
spinet
spinnaker
spinner
spinneret
spinney
  pl spinneys
spin-off
spinster

spiny
spiral
  spiralled
  spiralling
spire
spirit
  spirited
  spiriting
spiritual
spiritualism
spiritualist
spirituality
spiritually
spirogyra
spit
  spat
  spitting
spite
spiteful
spitefully
spittle
spittoon
splash
  pl splashes
splat
splatter
splay
splay-footed
spleen
splendid
splendour
splice
  spliced
  splicing
splint
splinter

splintered
splintering
split
split
splitting
splodge
splurge
splutter
spluttered
spluttering
spoil
spoilt, spoiled
spoiling
spoiler
spoilsport
spoke
see **speak**
spoke
spoken
see **speak**
spokesman
spokesperson
spokeswoman
sponge
sponged
sponging
sponger
spongy
sponsor
sponsored
sponsoring
sponsorship
spontaneity
spontaneous
spoof
spooky
spool

spoon
spooned
spooning
spoonbill
spoonerism
spoon-feed
spoon-fed
spoon-feeding
spoonful
pl spoonfuls
sporadic
sporadically
spore
sporran
sport
sporting
sportsman
pl sportsmen
sportsmanlike
sportsmanship
sportswoman
sporty
spot
spotted
spotting
spotless
spotlight
spot-on
spotty
spouse
spout
spouted
spouting
sprain
sprained
spraining
sprang

see **spring**
sprat
sprawl
spray
sprayed
spraying
spread
spread
spreading
spread-eagled
spreadsheet
spree
sprig
sprightliness
sprightly
spring
sprang
He sprang to his feet
sprung
He had sprung to his feet
springing
springboard
springbok
spring-clean
springer
springtime
springy
sprinkle
sprinkled
sprinkling
sprinkler
sprint
sprinter
sprite
spritzer
sprocket

sprout
 sprouted
 sprouting
spruce
sprucely
sprung
 see spring
spry
spryly
spud
spume
spun
 see spin
spunk
spunky
spur
 spurred
 spurring
spurious
spurn
spurt
sputter
 sputtered
 sputtering
sputum
spy
 pl spies
 spied
 spying
spyhole
squabble
 squabbled
 squabbling
squad
squaddy
squadron
squalid

squall
squally
squalor
squander
 squandered
 squandering
square
square-bashing
squarely
squash
 to squash under foot:
 to squash the fruit
squash (rackets)
squat
 squatted
 squatting
squatter
squaw
squawk
 squawked
 squawking
squeak
 squeaked
 squeaking
squeaky
squeal
 squealed
 squealing
squeamish
squeeze
 squeezed
 squeezing
squelch
squelchy
squib
squid

squiffy
squiggle
squiggly
squint
squire
squirm
squirrel
squirt
squishes
stab
 stabbed
 stabbing
stability
stabilize, -ise
 stabilized
 stabilizing
stabilizer, -iser
stable
staccato
stack
stadium
 pl stadiums
staff
 staffed
 staffing
stag
stage
 staged
 staging
stagecoach
stage-manage
stagger
 staggered
 staggering
stagnant
stagnate
 stagnated

stagnating

stagnation

staid
She is staid and respectable

stain
stained
staining

stainless

stair
a winding stair

staircase

stairway

stairwell

stake
a wooden stake: a stake in the firm: to stake a claim
staked
staking

stalactite

stalagmite

stale

stalemate

stalk
the stalk of the flower: to stalk off angrily: to stalk deer

stalker

stall

stallion

stalwart

stamen

stamina

stammer
stammered
stammering

stamp

stampede
stampeded
stampeding

stance

stanch, staunch
to stanch the blood

stand
stood
standing

standard

standardization, -isation

standardize, -ise
standardized
standardizing

standby

stand-in

stand-offish

standpipe

standpoint

standstill

stank
see **stink**

stanza

stapes

staple

stapler

star
starred
Who starred in that film?
starring

starboard

starch
pl starches

starchy

stardom

stare
a disapproving stare: to stare in amazement
stared
She stared in amazement at him
staring

starfish

stark

starkers

starlet

starling

starlit

starred
see **star**

starry

start

starter

startle
startled
startling

startling

starvation

starve
starved
starving

stash

state
stated
stating

stately

statement

state-of-the-art

statesman
pl statesmen

statesmanlike

statesmanship
stateswoman
static
station
stationary
  The car was stationary
stationer
stationery
  pens, pencils and
  other stationery
statistical
statistically
statistician
statistics
statue
  a statue of Nelson
statuesque
statuette
stature
status
status quo
statute
  by statute of
  Parliament
statutory
staunch
  a staunch supporter
staunch
  see **stanch**
stave
  staved, stove
  staving
stay
  stayed
  We stayed at that
  hotel: She stayed
  unmarried

staying
steadfast
steadiness
steadily
steadied
steadying
steady
steak
  steak and chips
steakhouse
steal
  Did he steal the
  jewels?
  stole
  He stole the ring
  stolen
  He has stolen the ring
  stealing
stealth
stealthily
stealthy
steam
  steamed
  steaming
steam-boat
steamer
steamroller
steamy
steed
steel
  iron and steel
steelworks
steely
steep
  steeped
  steeping
steeple

steeplechase
steeplejack
steer
  steered
  steering
steering-wheel
stellar
stem
  stemmed
  stemming
stench
stencil
  stencilled
  stencilling
stenographer
stenography
stentorian
step
  He climbed the
  wooden steps
  stepped
  stepping
stepbrother
stepchild
  pl stepchildren
stepdaughter
stepfather
stepladder
stepmother
steppe
  the steppes of Russia
stepson
stereo
stereophonic
stereotype
stereotyped
sterile

sterility

sterilization, -isation

sterilize, -ise
 sterilized
 sterilizing

sterling

stern

sternness

sternum
 pl sternums, sterna

steroid

stertorous

stet
 stetted
 stetting

stethoscope

stetson

stevedore

stew

steward

stewardess
 pl stewardesses

stick
 stuck
 sticking

stickiness

stickleback

stickler

sticky

stiff

stiffen
 stiffened
 stiffening

stiffness

stifle
 stifled
 stifling

stigma
 pl stigmata

stigmatize, -ise
 stigmatized
 stigmatizing

stile
 Climb over the stile
 into the other field

stiletto
 pl stilettos

still

stillborn

stillness

stilt

stilted

stilts

stimulant
 Is that drug a
 stimulant?

stimulate
 stimulated
 stimulating

stimulation

stimulus
 the stimulus provided
 by competing against
 others
 pl stimuli

sting
 stung
 stinging

stingray

stingy

stink
 stank
 The pigsty stank
 stunk
 It has stunk for days

stinking

stinkhorn

stint

stipend

stipendiary

stipple
 stippled
 stippling

stipulate
 stipulated
 stipulating

stipulation

stir
 stirred
 stirring

stir-fry
 stir-fried
 stir-frying

stirrup

stitch
 pl stitches

stitchwort

stoat

stock
 He comes of noble
 stock: a stock of tinned
 food: stocks and
 shares: Criminals
 used to be put in the
 stocks: We do not
 stock newspapers
 stocked
 He stocked many
 brands of whisky
 stocking

stockade

stockbroker

stockbroking

stocked
  see **stock**
stockily
  stockily-built
stockiness
stocking
stockinged
stockist
stockpile
  stockpiled
  stockpiling
stockroom
stocktaking
stocky
stodge
stodginess
stodgy
stoic
stoical
stoically
stoicism
stoke
  stoked
  He stoked the fire
  stoking
stoker
stole
  see **steal**
stolen
  see **steal**
stolid
stolidity
stomach
stomach-ache
stomp
stone

stonechat
stoned
stonemason
stonewall
stonewashed
stonily
stony
stood
  see **stand**
stooge
stool
stoop
  stooped
  stooping
stop
  stopped
  stopping
stopcock
stopgap
stop-over
stoppage
stopper
stopwatch
storage
store
  stored
  storing
storey
  a four-storey building
  pl storeys
stork
storm
stormily
stormtrooper
stormy
story
  a fairy story

pl stories
storyline
stout
stoutness
stove
  see **stave**
stove
stow
stowaway
strabismus
straddle
  straddled
  straddling
straggle
  straggled
  straggling
straggler
straggly
straight
  a straight line: a
  straight actor
straighten
  straightened
  The dentist
  straightened her teeth
  straightening
straightforward
straightness
strain
  strained
  straining
strainer
strait
  a strait between
  pieces of land
straitened
  in straitened
  circumstances

straitjacket
straitlaced
strand
strange
strangely
strangeness
stranger
strangle
 strangled
 strangling
stranglehold
strangler
strangulation
strap
 strapped
 strapping
strata
stratagem
strategic
strategically
strategist
strategy
 pl strategies
strathspey
stratification
stratified
stratosphere
stratum
 a stratum of rich ore: a
 stratum of society
 pl strata
stratus
 stratus clouds
straw
strawberry
 pl strawberries

stray
 strayed
 straying
streak
 streaked
streaker
streakiness
streaky
stream
 streamed
 streaming
streamer
streamline
 streamlined
 streamlining
street
streetwise
strength
strengthen
 strengthened
 strengthening
strenuous
streptococcus
 pl streptococci
stress
 pl stresses
 stressed
 stressing
stressful
stress-mark
stretch
 pl stretches
stretcher
stretchy
strew
 strewed
 They strewed the

 flowers
 strewn
 strewn with wild
 flowers
 strewing
stricken
strict
stricture
stride
 strode
 striding
stridency
strident
strife
 quarrelling and strife
strike
 struck
 striking
striker
string
 strung
 stringing
stringency
 pl stringencies
stringent
stringy
strip
 stripped
 He stripped the wood:
 They stripped the
 wallpaper off
 stripping
striped
 red and white striped
stripling
stripped
 see **strip**
stripper

striptease

stripy

strive
to strive to do better
strove
He strove to do well
striven
He has striven
striving

strobe

strode
see stride

stroke
stroked
stroking

stroll

strong

stronghold

strontium

stroppy

strove
see strive

struck
see strike

structural

structuralism

structuralist

structurally

structure

structured

strudel

struggle
struggled
struggling

strum
strummed
strumming

strung
see string

strut
strutted
strutting

strychnine

stub
stubbed
stubbing

stubble

stubbly

stubborn

stubbornness

stubby

stucco

stuck
see stick

stuck-up

stud
studded
studding

student

studio
pl studios

studious

studiousness

study
pl studies
studied
studying

stuff

stuffing

stuffy

stultify
stultified
stultifying

stumble

stumbled
stumbling

stumbling-block

stump

stumpy

stun
stunned
stunning

stung
see sting

stunk
see stink

stunner

stunning

stunt

stunted

stuntman

stuntwoman

stupefaction

stupefy
stupefied
stupefying

stupendous

stupid

stupidity

stupor

sturdily

sturdiness

sturdy

sturgeon

stutter
stuttered
stuttering

sty
a pig in a sty
pl sties

stye, sty

a stye on the eye
pl styes, sties

style
  style of dress: literary
  style
  styled
  styling

stylish

stylist

stylistic

stylistics

stylize, -ise
  stylized
  stylizing

stylus
  pl styluses

stymie
  stymied
  stymieing, stymying

styptic

suave

suavely

suavity

sub
  subbed
  subbing

subaltern

subaqua

subcommittee

subconscious

subcontinent

subcontract

subcontractor

subculture

subdirectory

subdivide
  subdivided

subdividing

subdivision

subdue
  subdued
  subduing

subject

subjection

subjective

subjectively

subjectiveness

subjectivity

subjugate
  subjugated
  subjugating

subjunctive

subjugation

sublet

sublieutenant

sublime

sublimely

subliminal

sublimity

submarine

submerge
  submerged
  submerging

submersion

submission

submissive

submissively

submit
  submitted
  submitting

subnormal

subordinate
  subordinated

subordinating

subordination

suborn
  suborned
  suborning

subplot

subpoena
  subpoenaed
  subpoenaing

subscribe
  subscribed
  subscribing

subscriber

subscription

subsequent

subservience

subservient

subset

subside
  subsided
  subsiding

subsidence

subsidiary
  pl subsidiaries

subsidize, -ise
  subsidized
  subsidizing

subsidy
  pl subsidies

subsist

subsistence

subsoil

substance

substandard

substantial

substantially

substantiate

substantiated
substantiating
substantiation
substantive
substitute
substituted
substituting
substitution
subsume
subsumed
subsuming
subterfuge
subterranean
subtext
subtitle
subtle
subtlety
pl subtleties
subtly
subtract
subtraction
subtropical
suburb
suburban
suburbia
subvention
subversion
subversive
subversively
subvert
subway
succeed
succeeded
succeeding
success
pl successes

successful
successfully
succession
successive
successively
successor
succinct
succinctly
succour
succoured
succouring
succulence
succulent
succumb
succumbed
succumbing
such
such-and-such
suchlike
suck
sucker
suckle
suckled
suckling
sucrose
suction
sudden
suddenly
suddenness
suds
sue
sued
suing
suede
a suede jacket
suet

suffer
suffered
suffering
sufferance
sufferer
suffice
sufficed
sufficing
sufficiency
sufficient
suffix
pl suffixes
suffocate
suffocated
suffocating
suffocation
suffrage
suffragette
suffuse
suffused
suffusing
suffusion
sugar
sugar-beet
sugared
sugary
suggest
suggestible
suggestion
suggestive
suggestively
suicidal
suicide
suit [soot]
a suit of clothes: This
will suit you
suited

suiting
suitability
suitable
suitably
suitcase
suite [*swēt*]
  a suite of rooms: a
  bedroom suite
suitor
sulk
sulkily
sulky
sullen
sullenness
sully
  sullied
  sullying
sulphate
sulphur
sulphuric
sulphurous
sultan
sultana
sultrily
sultry
sum
  a difficult sum
  summed
  summing
summarily
summarize, -ise
  summarized
  summarizing
summary
  a summary of our
  plans: a short
  summary of the plot of

  the play
  pl summaries
summation
summer
summerhouse
summertime
summery
  a summery day: a
  summery dress
summing-up
summit
summon
  summoned
  summoning
summons
  pl summonses
sumo
sumptuous
sun
  The sun shone brightly
  sunned
  sunning
sunbathe
  sunbathed
  sunbathing
sunbed
sunburn
sunburned,
  sunburnt
sundae
  an ice cream sundae
Sunday
  They went to church
  on Sunday
sundial
sundries
sundry

sunflower
sung
  see sing
sunglasses
sunk
  see sink
sunken
  sunken cheeks
sun-lamp
sunlight
sunlit
sunnily
sunny
sunrise
sunroof
sunset
sunshade
sunshine
sunspot
sunstroke
suntan
  suntanned
  suntanning
sup
  supped
  supping
super
  a super holiday
superannuated
superannuation
superb
supercilious
superego
superficial
superficiality
superficially

superfluity
superfluous
supergrass
superhuman
superimpose
 superimposed
 superimposing
superintend
superintendence
superintendent
superior
superiority
superlative
superlatively
superman
supermarket
supernatural
supernaturally
supernova
superpower
superscript
supersede
 superseded
 superseding
supersonic
superstar
superstition
superstitious
superstitiously
superstructure
supervise
 supervised
 supervising
supervision
supervisor

supervisory
supine
supper
 They had supper at 9 pm
supplant
supple
supply
supplement
supplementary
supplementation
suppleness
suppliant
supplicant
supplicate
 supplicated
 supplicating
supplication
supplier
supply
 pl supplies
 supplied
 supplying
support
supporter
supportive
suppose
 supposed
 supposing
supposedly
supposition
suppositional
suppository
suppress
suppression
suppurate
 suppurated

suppurating
supremacy
supreme
supremely
surcharge
sure
sure-fire
sure-footed
surely
surety
 pl sureties
surf
surface
 surfaced
 surfacing
surfboard
surfeit
surfer
surfing
surge
 surged
 surging
surgeon
surgery
 pl surgeries
surgical
surgically
surlily
surliness
surly
surmise
 surmised
 surmising
surmountable
surname
surpass

surplice
a priest's surplice

surplus
a surplus of butter

surprise
surprised
surprising

surreal

surrender
surrendered
surrendering

surreptitious

surrogacy

surrogate

surround

surroundings

surtax

surtitle

surveillance

survey
surveyed
surveying

surveyor

survival

survive
survived
surviving

survivor

susceptibility

susceptible

sushi

suspect

suspend

suspender

suspender-belt

suspenders

suspense

suspension

suspicion

suspicious

suss

sustain
sustained
sustaining

sustenance

suture

svelte

swab
swabbed
swabbing

swaddle
swaddled
swaddling

swag

swagger
swaggered
swaggering

swain

swallow

swallowtail

swam
see swim

swamp

swampy

swan

swank

swanky

swap, swop
swapped, swopped
swapping, swopping

swarm

swarthy

swashbuckling

swat
swatted
swatting

swatch

swathed

sway
swayed
swaying

swear
swore
He swore to be true
sworn
He has sworn to be true
swearing

swear-word

sweat
sweated
sweating

sweatband

sweater

sweatshirt

sweatshop

sweaty

swede
The farmer grows swedes

Swedish

sweep
swept
sweeping

sweeper

sweepstake

sweet
a sweet smile: a sweet orange: to suck a sweet

sweetbread

sweetcorn
sweeten
  sweetened
  sweetening
sweetener
sweetheart
sweetie
sweetmeat
sweet-talk
sweet-toothed
sweetness
swell
  swelled
  His leg swelled
  swollen
  His leg has swollen
  swelling
swelter
  sweltered
  sweltering
swept
  see **sweep**
swerve
  swerved
  swerving
swift
swiftness
swig
  swigged
  swigging
swill
swim
  swam
  She swam a length
  swum
  She has swum a
  length
  swimming

swimmer
swimming-bath
swimming-costume
swimmingly
swimming-pool
swimsuit
swindle
  swindled
  swindling
swindler
swine
swing
  swung
  swinging
  swinging on a gate
swingeing
  swingeing cuts
swinger
swinish
swipe
  swiped
  swiping
swirl
swish
switch
  pl switches
switchback
switchboard
swivel
  swivelled
  swivelling
swizz
swollen
  see **swell**
swoon
swoop
  swooped

swooping
swop
  see **swap**
sword
swordfish
swordsman
swordsmanship
swore, sworn
  see **swear**
swum
  see **swim**
swot
  swotted
  swotting
swung
  see **swing**
sycamore
sycophancy
sycophant
sycophantic
syllabary
syllabic
syllable
syllabub
syllabus
  pl syllabuses, syllabi
sylph
symbiosis
  pl symbioses
symbiotic
symbol
  a mathematical
  symbol: a symbol of
  the king's authority
symbolic
symbolically
symbolism

symbolize, -ise
  symbolized
  symbolizing
symmetrical
symmetrically
symmetry
sympathetic
sympathetically
sympathize, -ise
  sympathized
  sympathizing
sympathy
symphonic
symphony
  pl symphonies
symposium
  pl symposia,
  symposiums
symptom
symptomatic
synagogue
synapse
synapsis

synchronic
synchronization,
  -isation
synchronize, **-ise**
  synchronized
  synchronizing
syncopate
  syncopated
  syncopating
syncopation
syncope
syndicalism
syndicate
syndrome
synergy
synod
synonym
synonymous
synopsis
  pl synopses
syntactic
syntactical

syntax
synthesis
synthesize, -ise
  synthesized
  synthesizing
synthesizer, -iser
synthetic
synthetically
syphilis
syphilitic
syringe
syrup
syrupy
system
systematic
systematically
systematize, -ise
  systematized
  systematizing
systemic

t

If you can't find the word you're looking for under letter **T**, it could be that it starts with a different letter. Try looking under **PT** for words like *pterodactyl*. Also, don't forget **TH** for words like *thyme*.

ta
tab
tabard
tabbouleh
tabby
  pl tabbies
tabernacle
table
  tabled
  tabling
tableau
  pl tableaux
tablecloth
tablespoon
tablespoonful
  pl tablespoonfuls
tablet
tableware
tabloid
taboo
tabor
tabular
tabulate
  tabulated
  tabulating
tabulation
tacit
taciturn

taciturnity
tack
  pl tacks
  tin tacks: shoe tacks
tackle
  tackled
  tackling
tacky
taco
tact
tactful
tactfully
tactical
tactically
tactician
tactics
tactile
tactless
tadpole
taekwondo
taffeta
tag
  tagged
  tagging
tagliatelle
tahini
t'ai chi
tail

a dog's tail: the tail of his coat: Did the police tail him?
tailed
tailing
tailback
tailless
tailor
  tailored
  tailoring
tailor-made
taint
take
  took
  He took a book
  taken
  He has taken a book
  taking
takeaway
take-off
takeover
talc
talcum (powder)
tale
  a fairy tale
talent
talented
talisman
talk

talkative
tall
tallboy
tallness
tallow
tally
 pl tallies
 tallied
 tallying
tally-ho
talon
tamarind
tamarisk
tambourine
tame
tamely
 tamed
 taming
tamer
tamper
 tampered
 tampering
tampon
tam-tam
tan
 tanned
 tanning
tandem
tandoori
tang
tangent
tangential
tangerine
tangible
tangibly
tangle

tangled
tangling
tango
 pl tangos
 tangoed
 tangoing
tangy
tank
tankard
tanker
tanned
tannery
 pl tanneries
tannin
tantalize, -ise
 tantalized
 tantalizing
tantalus
tantamount to
tantrum
tap
 tapped
 The enemy tapped the telephone line: She tapped the table
 tapping
tapas
tape
 taped
 They taped the music
 taping
taper
 a lighted taper
 tapered
 tapering
tape recorder
tape-recording
tapestry

 pl tapestries
tapeworm
tapioca
tapir
 A tapir resembles a pig
tapped
 see tap
tappet
tar
 tarred
 tarring
taramasalata
tarantula
tardily
tardy
tare
 Tare is the weight of an empty truck: weeds and tares
target
 targeted
 targeting
tariff
tarmac
tarmacadam
tarn
tarnish
tarot
tarpaulin
tarragon
tarry
 tarried
 tarrying
tarsal
tart
tartan

tartar
task
task-force
tassel
tasselled
taste
  tasted
  tasting
tasteful
tastefully
tasteless
taster
tasty
tattered
tatters
tattle
tattoo
  tattooed
  tattooing
tattooist
tatty
taught
  see **teach**
taunt
taupe
Taurus
taut
  The string is taut
tauten
  tautened
  tautening
tautological
tautologically
tautologous
tautology
tavern

taverna
tawdry
tawny
tax
  income tax
taxable
taxation
taxi
  pl taxis
  taxied
  taxiing
taxicab
taxidermist
taxidermy
taxonomic
taxonomy
taxpayer
tea
  a cup of tea
teacake
teach
  taught
  She taught French
  teaching
teachable
teacher
tea-cosy
teacup
teak
teal
team
  football team
team (up) with
  teamed (up) with
  teaming (up) with
team-work
teapot

tear [*tēr*]
  a tear of grief
tear [*tār*]
  to tear one's coat
  tore
  She tore her coat
  torn
  She has torn her coat
  tearing
tearaway
teardrop
tearful
tear-jerker
tearoom
tease
  teased
  teasing
teasel
teaser
teaspoon
teaspoonful
  pl teaspoonfuls
teat
technical
technicality
  pl technicalities
technically
technician
technique
techno
technobabble
technocrat
technological
technologically
technologist
technology
  pl technologies

tectonics
teddy-bear
tedious
tedium
tee
  *a golf tee: to tee a
  golf-ball*
  teed
  teeing
teem
  *to teem with rain: to
  teem with fish*
  teemed
  teeming
teen
teenage
teenager
teens
teenybopper
teeny-weeny
teeter
teeth
  see tooth
teethe
  *When do babies
  teethe?*
  teethed
  teething
teetotal
teetotaller
telebanking
telecommunication
telecommuting
teleconferencing
telecottage
telegram
telegraph

telegraphese
telegraphic
telekinesis
telekinetic
telemarketing
telepathic
telepathically
telepathy
telephone
  telephoned
  telephoning
telephonist
telephoto lens
telesales
telescope
  telescoped
  telescoping
telescopic
telescopically
teletext
televise
  televised
  televising
television
televisual
teleworking
telex
tell
  told
  telling
teller
telly
temerity
temp
temper
  tempered

tempering
temperament
temperamental
temperamentally
temperance
temperate
temperature
tempest
tempestuous
template
temple
tempo
  pl tempos, tempi
temporal
  temporal, not spiritual
temporary
  a temporary job
temporize, -ise
  temporized
  temporizing
tempt
temptation
tempting
tempter
temptress
tempura
ten
tenable
tenacious
tenacity
tenancy
  pl tenancies
tenant
tenanted
tench
tend

tendency
pl tendencies

tendentious

tender
tendered
tendering

tenderize, -ise
tenderized
tenderizing

tenderizer, -iser

tenderloin

tendinitis,
tendonitis

tendon
a damaged tendon in his leg

tendril

tenement

tenet

tenner

tennis

tenon
mortise and tenon

tenor
a tenor and a soprano

tense

tensely

tensile

tension

tent

tentacle

tentacular

tentative

tentatively

tenterhooks

tenth

tenuous

tenure
land tenure

tepee

tepid

tequila

tercentenary

tergiversate
tergiversated
tergiversating

term

termagant

terminal

terminate
terminated
terminating

termination

terminology

terminus
pl terminuses, termini

termite

tern

terrace

terracing

terracotta

terra firma

terrain

terrapin

terrestrial

terrible

terribly

terrier

terrific

terrifically

terrify
terrified
terrifying

terrine

territorial

territory
pl territories

terror

terrorism

terrorist

terrorize, -ise
terrorized
terrorizing

terry

terse

tersely

terseness

tertiary

tessellate
tessellated
tessellating

test

testament

test-drive
test-drove
test-driving
test-driven

tester

testes

testicle

testicular

testify
testified
testifying

testily

testimonial
Did her previous

employer give her a testimonial?

testimony
the testimony of the witness
pl testimonies

testing

testosterone

testy

tetanus

tetchy

tête-à-tête

tether
tethered
tethering

text

textbook

textile

textual

texture

Thailand

thalassotherapy

thalidomide

than

thank

thankful

thankfully

thankless

thanksgiving

that

thatch
thatched
thatching

thaw

the

theatre

theatrical

theatrically

thee

theft

their
They lost their gloves

theirs

theism

theist

them

theme

themselves

then

thence

thenceforth

theocracy

theodolite

theologian

theological

theology

theorem

theoretic, theoretical

theoretically

theorist

theorize, -ise
theorized
theorizing

theory
pl theories

therapeutic

therapist

therapy

there
There is no-one there: I saw it there

thereabouts

thereafter

thereby

therefore

therein

thereof

thereto

thereunder

thereupon

therm

thermal

thermometer

Thermos® (flask)

thermostat

thesaurus

these

thesis
pl theses

they

they'd
= they had, they would

they'll
= they will

they're
= they are
They're coming today

they've
= they have

thiamine

thick

thicken
thickened
thickening

thicket

thickhead

thick-headed
thickness
  pl thicknesses
thickset
thick-skinned
thief
  pl thieves
thievish
thigh
thimble
thin
  compar thinner
  superl thinnest
  thinned
  thinning
thine
thing
thingummy
thingummybob
thingummyjig
think
  thought
  thinking
thinness
third
third-rate
thirst
thirstily
thirsty
thirteen
thirteenth
thirtieth
thirty
this
thistle
thong

thoracic
thorax
thorn
thorny
thorough
  a thorough search
thoroughbred
thoroughfare
thoroughgoing
those
thou
though
thought
thought
  see **think**
thoughtful
thoughtfully
thoughtfulness
thoughtless
thousand
thousandth
thrall
thrash
  *Did he thrash that
  child?: to thrash out
  the problem*
thread
threadbare
threadworn
threat
threaten
  threatened
  threatening
three
threepence
threepenny

thresh
  to thresh corn
thresher
threshold
threw
  see **throw**
thrice
thrift
thriftily
thrifty
thrill
thriller
thrilling
thrive
  thrived
  thriving
throat
throaty
throb
  throbbed
  throbbing
throes
  *in the throes of moving
  house*
thrombosis
throne
  the king's throne
throng
throttle
  throttled
  throttling
through
  through the door
throughout
throw
  pl throws
  three throws of the

dice
threw
He threw a stone
thrown
He has thrown a stone
throwing

throwaway

throwback

thrush
pl thrushes

thrust
thrust
thrusting

thud
thudded
thudding

thug

thuggery

thuggish

thumb

thumbscrew

thumbtack

thump

thunder
thundered
thundering

thunderbolt

thunderclap

thunderous

thunderstorm

thunderstruck

thundery

Thursday

thus

thwack

thwart
thwarted
thwarting

thy

thyme
to season the sauce with thyme

thyroid

thyroxine

ti

tiara

tibia
pl tibias, tibiae

tic
a nervous tic

tick
in a tick: a dog tick: a tick at each answer: the tick of a clock

ticker

ticker-tape

ticking-off

ticket

tickle
tickled
tickling

ticklish

tickly

tidal

tiddler

tiddlywinks

tide

tidemark

tidily

tidiness

tidings

tidy

compar tidier
superl tidiest
tidied
tidying

tie
tied
tying

tie-dyed

tie-pin

tier
two tiers of the wedding cake

tiff

tiffin

tiger

tight

tighten
tightened
tightening

tight-fisted

tight-lipped

tightness

tightrope

tights

tigress
pl tigresses

tike

tikka

tilde

tile
tiled
He tiled the floor
tiling

tiler

till
tilled
He tilled the land
tilling

tiller

tilt

timber
The timber is rotting

timbre
the timbre of his voice

time
What time is it?: to time a race
timed
timing

timekeeper

timeless

timely

timepiece

timer

timetable
timetabled
timetabling

timid

timidity

timorous

timpani, tympani

timpanist, tympanist

tin
tinned
tinning

tincture

tinder

tine

tinfoil

tinge
tinged
tinging

tingle
tingled

tingling

tingly

tinker
tinkered
tinkering

tinkle
tinkled
tinkling

tinned

tinnitus

tinny

tin-opener

tinsel

tint

tiny

tip
tipped
tipping

tip-off

tippet

Tipp-Ex®

tipple

tippler

tipsy

tiptoe
tiptoed
tiptoeing

tiptop

tirade

tire
The runner began to tire: Did the journey tire you?
tired
tiring

tiredness

tireless

tiresome

tissue

tit

titanium

titbit

tithe

titillate
titillated
titillating

titillation

titivate
titivated
titivating

title

titled

titrate
titrated
titrating

titration

titter
tittered
tittering

tittle-tattle

titular

tizzy

to
to go to town

toad

toadflax

toad-in-the-hole

toadstool

toady
toadied
toadying

toast

toasted

toaster

tobacco

tobacconist

Tobago

toboggan
  tobogganed
  tobogganing

toccata

today

toddle
  toddled
  toddling

toddler

toddy

to-do

toe
  the toe of her shoe

toenail

toerag

toff

toffee

tofu

toga

together

togetherness

toggle
  toggled
  toggling

togs

toil
  toiled
  toiling

toilet

toiletries

token

tokenism

tolbooth

told
  see **tell**

tolerable

tolerably

tolerance

tolerant

tolerate
  tolerated
  tolerating

toleration

toll

tollgate

tomahawk

tomato
  pl tomatoes

tomb
  the tomb of the late king

tombola

tomboy

tombstone

tomcat

tome
  a learned Latin tome

tomfoolery

tommy-rot

tomorrow

tomtom

ton
  a ton of coal

tonal

tone
  toned
  toning

tone-deaf

tongs

tongue

tongue-tied

tongue-twister

tonic

tonight

tonnage

tonne
  a tonne is 1000 kilogrammes

tonsil

tonsillectomy

tonsillitis

tonsorial

tonsure

too
  I am going too

took
  see **take**

tool

toolbox

toolkit

toot
  tooted
  tooting

tooth
  pl teeth
  She had two teeth filled

toothache

toothbrush

toothless

toothpaste

toothpick

toothy

tootle
  tootled
  tootling

top
  topped
  topping

topaz

toper

top-heavy

topi, topee
  A topi is a sun-helmet

topiary

topic

topical

topically

topless

topmost

top-notch

topography

topological

topology

topping

topple
  toppled
  toppling

topside

topsoil

topspin

topsyturvy

toque

torch
  pl torches

torchlight

tore
  see **tear**

toreador

torment

tormentor

torn

  see **tear**

tornado
  pl tornadoes

torpedo
  pl torpedoes
  torpedoed
  torpedoing

torpid

torpidity

torpor

torrent

torrential

torrid

torso
  pl torsos

tortilla

tortoise

tortoiseshell

tortuous
  a tortuous road

torture
  tortured
  torturing

torturous
  a torturous task

Tory
  pl tories

toss

toss-up

tot

total
  totalled
  totalling

totalitarian

totality

totally

tote

totem pole

totter
  tottered
  tottering

tot up
  totted up
  totting up

toucan

touch

touchdown

touche

touched

touchily

touchiness

touching

touchline

touchpaper

touch-type
  touch-typed
  touch-typing

touchy

tough

toughen
  toughened
  toughening

toughness

toupee
  toupees and wigs

tour
  toured
  touring

tourism

tourist

touristy

tournament

tourniquet

tousled
tout
  touted
  touting
tow
  to tow a car
  towed
  towing
toward
towards
towbar
towel
  towelled
  towelling
tower
  towered
  towering
town
township
towpath
towrope
toxic
toxicity
toxicologist
toxicology
toxin
toy
trace
  traced
  tracing
traceable
tracery
trachea
tracheotomy
trachoma
track
tracksuit

tract
traction
tractor
trade
  traded
  trading
trademark
tradename
trade-off
trader
tradesman
trade union
trade unionist
tradition
traditional
traditionalism
traditionalist
traditionally
traffic
  trafficked
  trafficking
trafficker
tragedian
tragedy
  pl tragedies
tragic
tragically
tragicomedy
trail
  trailed
  trailing
trailblazer
trailer
train
  trained
  training

trainee
trainer
train-spotter
train-spotting
traipse
  traipsed
  traipsing
trait
  *Patience is not one of
  his traits*
traitor
traitorous
trajectory
tram
tramcar
tramline
trammel
  trammelled
  trammelling
tramp
trample
  trampled
  trampling
trampoline
tramway
trance
tranquil
tranquillity
tranquillize, -ise
  tranquillized, -ised
  tranquillizing, -ising
tranquillizer, -iser
tranquilly
transaction
transatlantic

transcend
transcended
transcending
transcendence
transcendent
transcendental
transept
transfer
transferred
transferring
transferable
transference
transfiguration
transfix
transform
transformation
transformational
transformer
transfuse
transfusion
transgress
transgression
transgressor
transhumance
transience
transient
transistor
transit
transition
transitional
transitive

transitorily
transitory
translate
translated
translating
translation
translator
transliterate
transliterated
transliterating
transliteration
translucence
translucent
transmissible
transmission
transmit
transmitted
transmitting
transmitter
transmutable
transmute
transmuted
transmuting
transparency
  pl transparencies
transparent
transpire
transpired
transpiring
transplant
transport
transportation
transporter
transpose
transposed
transposing
transposition

transsexual
transverse
transvestism
transvestite
trap
trapped
trapping
trapdoor
trapeze
trapezium
  pl trapeziums,
  trapezia
trapezoid
trapper
trappings
trash
trashcan
trashy
trauma
traumatic
traumatize, -ise
traumatized
traumatizing
travel
travelled
travelling
traveller
travelogue
traverse
traversed
traversing
travesty
trawl
trawled
trawling
trawler
tray

cups and saucers on a tray

treacherous

treachery

treacle

tread
trod
He trod on her toe
trodden
He has trodden on it

treadle

treadmill

treason

treasonable

treasure

treasurer

treasury
pl treasuries

treat

treatise
a philosophical treatise

treatment

treaty
pl treaties
treaties signed after the war

treble

tree

trefoil

trek
trekked
trekking

trellis
pl trellises

tremble
trembled

trembling

tremendous

tremolo

tremor

tremulous

trench
pl trenches

trenchant

trencherman

trend

trendsetter

trendy

trepidation

trespass
pl trespasses

trespasser

tress
pl tresses

trestle

trews

triad

trial

triangle

triangular

triangulate
triangulated
triangulating

triangulation

triathlete

triathlon

tribal

tribalism

tribe

tribesman

tribeswoman

tribulation

tribunal

tribune

tributary
pl tributaries

tribute

trice

triceps

trick

trickery

trickle
trickled
trickling

trickster

tricky

tricolour

tricycle

trident

tried
see try

triennial

trier

tries
see try

trifle
trifled
trifling

trifling

trigger
triggered
triggering

trigger-happy

trigonometry

trike

trilby

trilingual

trill

trillion

trilogy
  pl trilogies

trim
  trimmed
  trimming

trimmer

Trinity

trinket

trio
  pl trios

trip
  tripped
  tripping

tripartite

tripe

triple

triplet

triplicate

tripod

tripper

triptych

trip-wire

trite

triumph
  triumphed
  triumphing

triumphal

triumphant

trivet

trivia

trivial

triviality
  pl trivialities

trivialize, -ise
  trivialized

trivializing

trod, trodden
  see **tread**

troglodyte

troll

trolley
  pl trolleys

trollop

trombone

trombonist

troop
  a troop of soldiers: a
  cavalry troop: to troop
  out of the hall
  trooped
  trooping

trooper

trophy
  pl trophies

tropic

tropical

trot
  trotted
  trotting

trotters

troubadour

trouble
  troubled
  troubling

troublemaker

troubleshooter

troubleshooting

troublesome

trough

trounce
  trounced
  trouncing

troupe
  a troupe of actors

trousers

trousseau
  pl trousseaux, trous-
  seaus

trout

trove

trowel

truancy

truant

truce

truck

trucker

truckle

truculence

truculent

trudge
  trudged
  trudging

true

truffle

trug

truism

truly

trump

trumpet
  trumpeted
  trumpeting

truncated

truncheon

trundle
  trundled
  trundling

trunk

truss

pl trusses
trussed
trussing
trust
trustee
trustful
trustfully
trusting
trustworthy
trusty
truth
truthful
truthfully
truthfulness
try
  pl tries
  tried
  trying
tryst
tsar, tzar, czar
tsarina
tsetse
T-shirt
T-square
tsunami
tub
tuba
tubby
tube
tuber
tuberculin
tuberculosis
tubing
tubular
tuck
Tuesday

tuffet
tuft
tug
  tugged
  tugging
tug-of-war
tuition
tulip
tulle
tumble
  tumbled
  tumbling
tumbledown
tumble-drier
tumble-dryer
tumbler
tumbleweed
tumbrel, tumbril
tummy
  pl tummies
tummy-button
tumour
tumult
tumultuous
tumulus
  pl tumuli
tun
  A tun is a large cask
tuna
tundra
tune
  tuned
  tuning
tuneful
tunefully
tuneless

tuner
tungsten
tunic
tunnel
  tunnelled
  tunnelling
tunny
tuppence
turban
  He wore a turban on
  his head
turbid
turbine
  a turbine engine
turbojet
turbot
turbulence
turbulent
turd
tureen
turf
turgid
turkey
  pl turkeys
Turkish
turmeric
turmoil
turn
turnaround
turncoat
turning
turning-point
turnip
turnoff
turn-on
turn-out

turnover
turnpike
turnstile
turntable
turpentine
turpitude
turquoise
turret
turreted
turtle
turtledove
turtleneck
tusk
tussle
tut
 tutted
 tutting
tutelage
tutor
tutorial
tutu
tuxedo
twaddle
twang
twat
tweak
twee
tweed
tweedy
tweet
tweezers
twelfth
twelve
twentieth
twenty

 pl twenties
twerp
twice
twiddle
 twiddled
 twiddling
twig
twilight
twill
twin
 twinned
 twinning
twine
 twined
 twining
twinge
twinkle
 twinkled
 twinkling
twinset
twirl
twist
twisted
twister
twit
twitch
 pl twitches
twitchy
twitter
 twittered
 twittering
twittery
two
 two apples
two-edged
two-faced
twofold

twopence
twopenny
twosome
two-step
two-time
 two-timed
 two-timing
two-timer
two-way
tycoon
 a business
 tycoon
tympani
 see **timpani**
type
 typed
 typing
typecast
 typecast
 typecasting
typeface
typescript
typeset
 typeset
 typesetting
typesetter
typewriter
typhoon
 The ship was sunk in a
 typhoon
typhus
typical
typically
typify
 typified
 typifying

typing
typist
typo
typographer
typographic
typography
tyrannical

tyrannically
tyrannize, -ise
tyrannized
tyrannizing
tyrannosaurus
tyranny
tyrant

tyre
a tyre for the car
tzar
see **tsar**
tzatziki
tzigane

u

ubiquitous
ubiquity
ufology
udder
ugh
ugli
pl uglis, uglies
ugliness
ugly
compar uglier
superl ugliest
ukelele, ukulele
ulcer
ulcerate
ulceration
ulcerous
ulna
pl ulnae, ulnas
ulnar
ulterior
ultimate

ultimately
ultimatum
pl ultimatums,
ultimata
ultramarine
ultrasonic
ultrasound
ultraviolet
ululate
ululated
ululating
ululation
umbilical
umbrage
umbrella
umlaut
umpire
umpired
umpiring
umpteen
umpteenth

unable
unaccountable
unaccountably
unaccustomed
unadulterated
unaffected
unalienable
unanimity
unanimous
unapproachable
unarmed
unassuming
unattached
unattended
unaware
*I was unaware of his
presence*
unawares
*The blow took him
unawares*
unbalanced

unbearable
unbeknownst
unbelievable
unbelieving
unbend
 unbent
 unbending
unblock
unborn
unbounded
unbridled
unburden
 unburdened
 unburdening
uncalled for
uncannily
uncanniness
uncanny
uncared for
unceremonious
unceremoniously
uncertain
uncertainty
uncharted
unclasp
uncle
unclean
unclear
unclothed
uncoil
 uncoiled
 uncoiling
uncomfortable
uncommon
uncompromising
unconcern

unconditional
unconscionable
 He has been an
 unconscionable time
 doing that job
unconscious
 He was knocked un-
 conscious: He was
 unconscious of the
 trouble
unconsciously
unconstitutional
uncork
uncouth
unction
unctuous
undaunted
undecided
undeniable
undeniably
under
underachieve
underachiever
under-age
underarm
underbelly
undercarriage
underclothes
undercover
undercurrent
undercut
 undercut
 undercutting
underdeveloped
underdog
underdone

underestimate
 underestimated
 underestimating
underfoot
undergarment
undergo
 underwent
 undergone
 undergoing
undergraduate
underground
undergrowth
underhand
underlay
underline
 underlined
 underlining
underling
underlying
undermine
 undermined
 undermining
underneath
underpants
underpass
underpin
 underpinned
 underpinning
underprivileged
underrate
 underrated
 underrating
underside
undersigned
undersized
underskirt
understaffed

understand
understood
understanding
understandable
understandably
understate
understated
understating
understatement
understood
see **understand**
understudy
understudied
understudying
undertake
undertook
undertaken
undertaking
undertaker
undertone
undertook
see **undertake**
undervalue
undervalued
undervaluing
underwater
underwear
underwent
see **undergo**
underworld
underwrite
underwrote
underwritten
underwriting
underwriter
undesirable
undies
undo

undid
He undid his coat
undone
His coat is undone
undoing
undoubted
undress
undue
undulate
undulated
undulating
unduly
undying
unearth
unearthly
unease
uneasily
uneasiness
uneasy
uneconomical
unemployed
unemployment
unequal
unequalled
unequivocal
unequivocally
unerring
uneven
uneventful
unexceptional
unexpected
unfailing
unfair
unfaithful
unfasten
unfastened

unfastening
unfathomable
unfavourable
unfeeling
unfit
unfitted
unflagging
unflappable
unflinching
unfold
unforgettable
unforgettably
unfortunate
unfortunately
unfounded
unfunny
unfurl
ungainly
ungracious
ungrateful
ungratefully
unguarded
unguent
ungulate
unhand
unhappily
unhappiness
unhappy
unhealthily
unhealthy
unheard-of
unhelpful
unhinge
unhinged
unhinging

unholy
unicorn
unicycle
unidentified
unification
uniform
uniformed
uniformity
unify
  unified
  unifying
unilateral
uninspired
uninspiring
uninterested
uninterrupted
union
unionist
unique
uniquely
uniqueness
unisex
unison
unit
unitary
unite
  united
  uniting
unity
universal
universally
universe
university
  pl universities
unkempt
unkind

unknown
unleaded
unleash
unleavened
unless
unlike
unlikely
unlimited
unlit
unload
  unloaded
  unloading
unlock
unlooked for
unloose
  unloosed
  unloosing
unloved
unluckily
unlucky
unmade
unmanly
unmarried
unmask
unmentionable
unmistakable
unmistakably
unmitigated
unmoved
unnamed
unnatural
unnecessarily
unnecessary
unnerve
  unnerved
  unnerving

unobtrusive
unobtrusively
unpack
unpaid
unpalatable
unparalleled
unpick
unpleasant
unpleasantness
unplug
  unplugged
  unplugging
unpopular
unpractical
unpractised
unprecedented
unpremeditated
unprepossessing
unpretentious
unprincipled
unprintable
unprofessional
unqualified
unquestioning
unravel
  unravelled
  unravelling
unreal
unrelenting
unremitting
unrequited
unrest
unrivalled
unruffled
unruliness

unruly
unsafe
unsavoury
unscathed
unscrew
unscrupulous
unseasonable
unseen
unselfish
unsettled
unsightly
unskilled
unsociable
unsophisticated
unsound
unspeakable
unspeakably
unstable
unstoppable
unstudied
unsung
unsure
unsuspecting
unswerving
unthinkable
unthinking
until
untidy
untie
until
untimely
unto
untold
untouchable
untoward

untrue
untruth
untruthful
untruthfully
unusual
unusually
unvarnished
unveil
  unveiled
  unveiling
unvoiced
unwaged
unwanted
  unwanted children
unwell
unwieldy
unwilling
unwillingness
unwind
  unwound
  unwinding
unwise
unwitting
unwittingly
unwonted
  = not usual
  unwonted generosity
unworthy
unwritten
unzip
  unzipped
  unzipping
up
up-and-coming
upbeat
upbraid

upbraided
upbraiding
upbringing
update
  updated
  updating
upfront
upgrade
  upgraded
  upgrading
upheaval
uphill
uphold
  upheld
  upholding
upholder
upholster
  upholstered
  upholstering
upholsterer
upholstery
upkeep
upland
uplifting
up-market
upmost
upon
upper
uppercut
uppermost
uppity
upright
uprising
uproar
uproarious
uproot

uprooted
uprooting
upset
 upset
 upsetting
upshot
upside-down
upstage
 upstaged
 upstaging
upstairs
upstanding
upstart
upstream
upsurge
uptake
uptight
upward
up-to-date
uranium
urban
 an urban motorway
urbane
 an urbane young man
urbanities
urbanization,
 -isation
urchin
Urdu
ureter
urethra
urge

urged
urging
urgency
urgent
urinal
urinary
urinate
 urinated
 urinating
urine
urn
ursine
Uruguay
us
usable
usage
use
 used
 using
useful
usefully
usefulness
useless
uselessness
user
user-friendly
usher
 ushered
 ushering
usherette
usual

usually
usurer
usurious
usurp
usurper
usury
utensil
uterus
utilitarian
utilitarianism
utility
 pl utilities
utilization, -isation
utilize, -ise
 utilized
 utilizing
utmost
utopia
utopian
utter
 uttered
 uttering
utterance
utterly
U-turn
uvula
 pl uvulas, uvulae
uvular
uxorious

V

vacancy
 pl vacancies

vacant

vacate
 vacated
 vacating

vacation
 a summer vacation in Spain

vaccinate
 vaccinated
 vaccinating

vaccination

vaccine

vacillate
 vacillated
 vacillating

vacuous

vacuum

vacuum-packed

vade-mecum

vagabond

vagary
 pl vagaries

vagina

vaginal

vagrancy

vagrant

vague

vaguely

vagueness

vain

conceited and vain

vainglorious

valance

vale
 the Vale of Evesham

valency
 pl valencies

valentine

valet

valiant

valid

validate
 validated
 validating

validation

validity

valley
 pl valleys

valorous

valour

valuable

valuation

valuator

value
 valued
 valuing

valuer

valve

vamp

vampire

van

vandal

vandalism

vandalize, -ise
 vandalized
 vandalizing

vane
 a weather vane

vanguard

vanilla

vanish

vanity
 pl vanities

vanquish

vantage

vapid

vaporize, -ise
 vaporized
 vaporizing

vaporizer, -iser

vapour

variability

variable

variably

variance

variant

variation

varicose

varied

variegated

variety
 pl varieties

various

varnish

pl varnishes
varsity
vary
 varied
 varying
vase
vasectomy
Vaseline®
vassal
vast
vat
vaudeville
vault
vaunt
veal
vector
veer
 veered
 veering
vegan
veganism
vegeburger
vegetable
vegetarian
vegetarianism
vegetate
 vegetated
 vegetating
vegetation
vegetative
veggie
vehemence
vehement
vehicle
vehicular
veil

*a bride's veil: to veil in
mystery*
veiled
veiling
vein
*a clot of blood in a
vein: a vein of
cheerfulness*
veined
veld
vellum
velocity
 pl velocities
velour
velvet
velveteen
velvety
venal
*corrupt and venal
lawyers*
vend
vendetta
vending
vendor
veneer
venerable
venerate
 venerated
 venerating
veneration
venereal disease
Venetian blind
vengeance
vengeful
venial
venial sins
venison

venom
venomous
vent
ventilate
 ventilated
 ventilating
ventilation
ventilator
ventricle
ventriloquism
ventriloquist
venture
 ventured
 venturing
venue
veracity
*They doubted the
veracity of his
statement*
verandah, veranda
verb
verbal
verbalize, -ise
 verbalized
 verbalizing
verbally
verbatim
verbena
verbose
verbosity
verdant
verdict
verdigris
verdure
verge
 verged
 verging

verger
verification
verify
 verified
 verifying
verily
verisimilitude
veritable
veritably
verity
vermicelli
vermilion
vermin
verminous
vermouth
vernacular
vernal
verruca
versatile
versatility
verse
versification
versify
 versified
 versifying
version
verso
versus
vertebra
 pl vertebrae
vertebral
vertebrate
vertex
 the vertex of a cone
 pl vertices
vertical

vertically
vertiginous
vertigo
verve
very
vespers
vessel
vest
vestibule
vestige
vestigial
vestment
vestry
 pl vestries
vet
 vetted
 vetting
vetch
veteran
veterinarian
veterinary surgeon
veto
 pl vetoes
 vetoed
 vetoing
vex
 vexed
 vexing
vexation
vexatious
via
viable
viaduct
viands
vibes

vibrant
vibraphone
vibrate
 vibrated
 vibrating
vibration
vibrato
vibrator
vicar
vicarage
vicarious
vice
viceroy
vice versa
vicinity
vicious
vicissitude
victim
victimization, -isation
victimize, -ise
 victimized
 victimizing
victor
victorious
victory
 pl victories
victuals
video
 pl videos
 videoed
 videoing
videocassette
videotape
videotext
vie

vied
vying
view
viewer
viewfinder
viewpoint
vigil
vigilance
vigilant
  to keep a vigilant watch
vigilante
  The vigilantes helped the police
vignette
vigorous
vigour
Viking
vile
vilification
vilify
  vilified
  vilifying
villa
village
villager
villain
villainous
villainy
  pl villainies
villus
vinaigrette
vindicate
  vindicated
  vindicating
vindictive

vindictively
vindictiveness
vine
vinegar
vinegary
vineyard
viniculture
viniculturist
vintage
vintner
vinyl
viol
viola
violate
  violated
  violating
violation
violence
violent
violet
violin
violinist
violoncello
viper
virago
  pl viragos
viral
virgin
virginal
virginity
virile
virility
virtual
virtually
virtue

virtuosity
virtuoso
  pl virtuosos
virtuous
virulence
virulent
virus
  pl viruses
visa
  pl visas
visage
vis-à-vis
viscera
visceral
viscid
viscose
viscosity
viscount
viscountess
  pl viscountesses
viscountship
viscous
visibility
visible
visibly
vision
visionary
  pl visionaries
visit
  visited
  visiting
visitation
visitor
visor
vista
  pl vistas

visual
visualize, -ise
  visualized
  visualizing
visually
vital
vitality
vitally
vitamins
viticulture
vitreous
vitrification
vitrified
vitrify
  vitrified
  vitrifying
vitriol
vitriolic
vituperation
vituperative
vivacious
vivacity
viva voce
vivid
vividness
vivisection
vivisectionist
vixen
viz
vizier
vocabulary
  pl vocabularies
vocal
vocalist
vocalize, -ise
  vocalized

vocalizing
vocally
vocation
  a vocation to be a
  priest
vocational
vocative
vociferous
vodka
vogue
voice
  voiced
  voicing
voice-box
voiceless
voice-over
void
volatile
vol-au-vent
volcanic
volcano
  pl volcanoes
vole
volition
volley
  pl volleys
volleyball
volt
voltage
volte-face
voltmeter
volubility
voluble
volubly
volume
voluminous

voluntarily
voluntary
volunteer
  volunteered
  volunteering
voluptuous
vomit
  vomited
  vomiting
voodoo
voracious
voracity
  the voracity of his
  appetite
vortex
  the vortex of a
  whirlpool
  pl vortices, vortexes
vortical
vote
  voted
  voting
voter
vouch
voucher
vouchsafe
  vouchsafed
  vouchsafing
vow
  vowed
  vowing
vowel
voyage
  voyaged
  voyaging
voyager
voyeur

voyeurism
voyeuristic
vulcanize, -ise
vulcanized
vulcanizing
vulgar

vulgarity
vulgarize, -ise
vulgarized
vulgarizing
vulgarization,
-isation

vulnerability
vulnerable
vulture
vulva

W

If the word you're looking for sounds as if it begins with a
straightforward **W** but you can't find it, try looking under **WH**
for words like *when* and *whether*.

wacky
wad
wadding
waddle
waddled
waddling
wade
waded
wading
wader
wafer
an ice cream wafer
waffle
waffled
waffling
waffler
waft
wag
wagged
The dog wagged his

tail
wagging
wage
waged
He waged war
waging
wager
wagged
see **wag**
waggish
waggle
waggled
waggling
waggon
waif
a poor little waif
wail
wailed
wailing
wainscoting
waist

She has a tiny waist
waistband
waistcoat
wait
waiter
waiting-room
waitress
waive
*to waive the right to the
throne*
waived
waiving
waiver
wake
woke, waked
*He woke up in the
night*
woken, wakened
You've woken him
waking
wakeful

waken
  wakened
  wakening
walk
walkabout
walker
walkie-talkie
walkout
walkover
walkway
wall
wallaby
  pl wallabies
wallet
wallflower
wallop
  walloped
  walloping
wallow
wallpaper
wally
walnut
walrus
  pl walruses
waltz
  pl waltzes
wampum
wan
wand
wander
  wandered
  wandering
wanderer
wanderlust
wane
  waned

waning
wangle
  wangled
  wangling
wank
wanker
wannabe
wanness
want
  dying of want: for want
  of money: They want
  money
wanting
wanton
wantonness
war
  warred
  warring
warble
  warbled
  warbling
warbler
ward
  warded
  warding
warden
  warden of the hostel
warder
  a prison warder
wardrobe
ware
  earthenware,
  stoneware
warehouse
wares
  He sold his wares at
  the fair
warfare

warfarin
warhead
warily
wariness
warlike
warlock
warlord
warm
warmly
warmonger
warmth
warn
warning
warp
warpaint
warpath
warrant
warranty
warren
warrior
warship
wart
warthog
wartime
wary
was
  see be
wash
washable
washbasin
washcloth
washer
wash-hand basin
washhouse
washing

washing-machine
washing-up
washout
washroom
washstand
wasp
waspish
wastage
waste
a waste of food: to waste food
wasted
wasting
wasteful
wastefully
wasteland
waster
wastrel
wastepaper basket
watch
pl watches
watchdog
watchful
watchfully
watchman
pl watchmen
watchword
water
watered
watering
waterborne
watercolour
watercress
waterfall
waterfront
waterhole

waterlogged
watermark
watermill
waterproof
watershed
water-ski
water-skied,
water-ski'd
water-skiing
watertight
waterway
waterwheel
waterworks
watery
watt
wattage
wattle
wave
He gave a friendly wave: a heat wave: Did he wave to you?
waved
waving
waveband
wavelength
waver
to waver and hesitate
wavered
wavering
wavy
wax
waxen
waxwork
waxy
way
the way home: the way she wears her hair

wayfarer
waylay
waylaid
waylaying
wayside
wayward
we
weak
a weak child
weaken
weakened
weakening
weakling
weakly
a sick and weakly child
weakness
weal
wealth
wealthy
compar wealthier
superl wealthiest
wean
weaned
weaning
weapon
weaponry
wear
She often wears an apron
wore
She wore the dress
worn
She's worn that before
wearing
wearable
wearer
wearily
wearisome

weary
  wearied
  wearying

weasel

weather
  weathered
  weathering

weatherbeaten

weatherboard

weathercock

weatherman

weatherproof

weathervane

weave
  wove
  She wove cloth
  woven
  She has woven a rug
  weaving

weaver

web

webbed

webbing

web-footed

wed
  wedded
  wedding

we'd
  = we had, we would

wedding

wedge
  wedged
  wedging

wedlock

Wednesday

wee
  weed

  weeing

weed

weedkiller

weedy

week
  two days a week

weekday

weekend

weekly
  a weekly paper. He
  visits his mother
  weekly

weep
  wept
  weeping

weepy

weevil

wee-wee
  wee-weed
  wee-weeing

weft

weigh
  to weigh the potatoes
  weighed
  weighing

weight

weightless

weightlifter

weightlifting

weighty

weir

weird

weirdness

weirdo

welcome
  welcomed
  welcoming

weld

welder

welfare

well
  compar better
  superl best

we'll
  = we shall, we will

wellbeing

wellingtons

well-known

well-off

well-to-do

well up
  welled up
  welling up

well-wisher

welly

Welsh rarebit

welt

welter

welterweight

wench
  pl wenches

wend

went
  see go

wept
  see weep

were
  see be

we're
  = we are

weren't
  = were not

werewolf

west

westbound

westerly
a westerly wind

western
western ideas

westerner

westward

westwards

wet
a wet day: to wet the carpet
compar wetter
superl wettest
wet
wetting

wetness

we've
= we have

whack

whale

whalebone

whaler

whaling

wharf
pl wharves, wharfs

what

whatever

whatnot

whatsit

whatsoever

wheat

wheaten

wheatmeal

wheatsheaf

wheedle
wheedled
wheedling

wheedler

wheel
wheeled
wheeling

wheelbarrow

wheelchair

wheeler-dealer

wheeler-dealing

wheelie

wheelwright

wheeze
wheezed
wheezing

wheezy

whelk

whelp

when

whence

whenever

where

whereabouts

whereas

whereby

wherefore

wherein

wheresoever

whereupon

wherever

wherewithal

whet
to whet the appetite
whetted
whetting

whether

whetstone

whey

which

whichever

whiff

while

while away
whiled away
whiling away

whilst

whim

whimper
whimpered
whimpering

whimsical

whimsically

whimsy
pl whimsies

whine
whined
whining

whinge
whinged
whingeing

whinny
pl whinnies
whinnied
whinnying

whip
whipped
whipping

whiplash

whipper-snapper

whippet

whirl

whirlpool

whirlwind

whirr

whisk

whisker

whisky
 pl whiskies

whisper
 whispered
 whispering

whist

whistle
 whistled
 whistling

whistle-stop

whit
 not a whit

white

whitebait

whiten
 whitened
 whitening

whitener

whiteness

whitewash

whither

whiting

Whitsun, Whit

whittle
 whittled
 whittling

whizz

who

whoa

whodunnit

whoever

whole
 a whole orange: the whole household

wholehearted

wholemeal

wholesale

wholesaler

wholesome

who'll
 = who will

wholly

whom

whoop
 She gave a whoop of joy: to whoop with joy
 whooped
 whooping

whoopee

whooping-cough

whoops

whopper

whopping

whore
 the whore of Babylon

whorehouse

who's
 = who is, who has

whose

whosoever

why

wick

wicked

wickedness

wicker

wickerwork

wicket

wide

widely

widen
 widened
 widening

widespread

widget

widow

widower

width

wield
 wielded
 wielding

wife
 pl wives

wig

wiggle
 wiggled
 wiggling

wiggly

wigwam

wild

wildcat

wildebeest

wilderness

wildfire

wildfowl

wildlife

wildness

wile

wilful

wilfully

will
 would
 I would go if I could

will
 willed
 She willed him to win: He willed her all his money

willing

willingness

will-o'-the-wisp
willow
willpower
willowy
willynilly
wilt
wily
wimp
win
  won
  winning
wince
  winced
  wincing
winch
  pl winches
wind [*wind*]
  winded
  The blow winded him
  winding
wind [*wīnd*]
  wound
  He wound the
  bandage round her
  arm
  winding
windbag
windbreak
windcheater
windchill
windfall
windlass
windmill
window
windowsill
windpipe
windscreen

windshield
windsock
windsurfing
windswept
windy
wine
wing
winged
wingspan
wink
winkle
winner
winnings
winsome
winter
  wintered
  wintering
wintry
wipe
  wiped
  wiping
wiper
wire
  wired
  wiring
wireless
wiry
wisdom
wise
wisely
wish
  pl wishes
wishbone
wishful
wishywashy
wisp

wispy
wisteria
wistful
wistfully
wistfulness
wit
  cleverness and wit
witch
  pl witches
witchcraft
witchery
with
withdraw
  withdrew
  He withdrew his
  application
  withdrawn
  He has withdrawn his
  application
  withdrawing
withdrawal
wither
  withered
  withering
withhold
  withheld
  withholding
within
without
withstand
  withstood
  withstanding
witless
witness
  pl witnesses
witticism
wittily

He spoke wittily and interestingly

wittingly
He did not wittingly deceive her

witty

wizard

wizened

woad

wobble
wobbled
wobbling

wobbly

wodge

woe
sadness and woe

woebegone

woeful

woefully

wok

woke, woken
see **wake**

wolf
pl wolves
wolfed
wolfing

wolfcub

wolfish

wolfsbane

woman
pl women

womanhood

womanish

womanize, -ise
womanized
womanizing

womanizer

womanly

womb

wombat

womenfolk

won
see **win**

wonder
wondered
wondering

wonderful

wonderfully

wonderland

wonderment

wondrous

wonky

wont
as he was wont to do

won't
= will not

woo
to woo a girl and marry her
wooed
He wooed her ardently
wooing

wood
a beech wood: wood for the fire

woodbine

woodcock

woodcut

woodcutter

wooded

wooden

woodenness

woodland

woodlouse

pl woodlice

woodpecker

woodwind

woodwork

woodworm

woody

wooed
see **woo**

wooer

woof

woofer

wool

woollen

woolly

woozy

word

wording

word-perfect

word-processing

wordy

wore
see **wear**

work

workable

workaday

workaholic

worker

workforce

workhouse

workload

workman
pl workmen

workmanship

workout

workplace

workshop
workshy
worktop
world
world-class
worldliness
worldly
worldwide
worm
wormcast
worn
  see **wear**
worrier
worry
  pl worries
  worried
  worrying
worse
worsen
  worsened
  worsening
worship
  worshipped
  worshipping
worshipful
worshipfully
worshipper
worst
worsted
worth
worthily
worthiness
worthless
worthwhile
worthy
would

see **will**
would-be
wouldn't
  = would not
wound [wōōnd]
  a bullet wound
wound [wownd]
  see **wind**
wove, woven
  see **weave**
wow
wrack
wraith
wrangle
  wrangled
  wrangling
wrap
  to wrap in paper
  wrapped
  *The book was
  wrapped in brown
  paper*
  wrapping
wraparound
wrapround
wrapper
wrath
  wrathful
  wrathfully
wreak
  *to wreak vengeance:
  to wreak havoc*
  wreaked
  wreaking
wreath
  a wreath of flowers
wreathe

*to wreathe in flowers:
to wreathe in smiles*
wreathed
wreathing
wreck
  *a wreck on the
  sea-bed: to wreck the
  car*
  wrecked
  wrecking
wreckage
wren
wrench
  pl wrenches
wrest
  *to wrest it from his
  grasp*
wrestle
  wrestled
  wrestling
wrestler
wrestling
wretch
  a poor wretch
  pl wretches
wretched
wretchedness
wriggle
  wriggled
  wriggling
wriggly
wright
wring
  *to wring the clothes: to
  wring a promise from
  her*
  wrung
  She wrung the clothes
  wringing

wringer
wrinkle
 wrinkled
 wrinkling
wrinkly
wrist
wristwatch
writ
write
 to write neatly
 wrote

He wrote a letter
written
He has written a letter
writing
writer
writhe
 writhed
 writhing
wrong
wrongdoer
 wrongdoing

wrongfoot
wrongful
wrongfully
wrote
 see write
wrought-iron
wrung
 see wring
wry
 *a wry smile: a wry
 neck*

X

xenon
xenophobe
xenophobia
xenophobic
Xerox®

xerox
 xeroxed
 xeroxing
Xmas
X-ray

X-rayed
X-raying

xylophone

xylophonist

y

If you can't find the word you're looking for under letter **Y**, it could be that it starts with a different letter. Try looking under **EU** for words like *euphemism*, **EW** for words like *ewe*, and **U** for words like *use* and *usual*.

yacht
yachting
yachtsman
yachtswoman
yack
yahoo
yam
yak
yank
yap
  yapped
  yapping
yappy
yard
yardstick
yarn
yashmak
yawn
yeah
year
yearling
yearly
yearn
yeast
yeasty
yell
yellow

yellowhammer
yellowish
yellowness
yelp
yen
yeoman
yes
yesterday
yesteryear
yet
Yeti
yew
  a yew tree
Y-fronts
yield
yippee
ylang-ylang
yob
yobbo
yodel
  yodelled
  yodelling
yodeller
yoga
yoghurt
yogi
yoke
  the yoke of a plough;

  the yoke of a dress
yokel
yolk
  the yolk of an egg
yonder
yore
  days of yore
you
  you and I
you'd
  = you had, you
  would
you'll
  = you will
young
youngster
your
  your house
you're
  = you are
yours
yourselves
youth
youthful
youthfully
you've
  = you have
Yo-Yo®
yucca

yucky	yummy	yuppie
Yule	yum-yum	

Z

If you can't find the word you're looking for under letter **Z**, it could be that it starts with a different letter. Try looking under **X** for words like *xylophone* and *Xerox*.

zabaglione
Zaire
zany
zap
  zapped
  zapping
zapper
zeal
zealot
zealous
zebra
zenith
zephyr
zero
  zeroed
  zeroing
zest
zestful

zestfully
zeugma
zigzag
  zigzagged
  zigzagging
zilch
zillion
Zimmer frame
zinc
zing
zinnia
zip
  zipped
  zipping
zipper
zippy
zither
zodiac

zombie
zonal
zone
zonked
zoo
zoological
zoologist
zoology
zoom
  zoomed
  zooming
zouk
zucchini
  pl zucchini,
  zucchinis
zygote

Appendices

Spelling rules

VERBS

In most cases, you can add **-ing** and **-ed** without changing the spelling of the first part of the verb:

walk	walk*ing*	walk*ed*
stay	stay*ing*	stay*ed*
pick	pick*ing*	pick*ed*

But if a verb consists of only one syllable, with a single short vowel, and ends in a consonant, double this final letter before adding **-ing** and **-ed**:

stop	stop*ping*	stop*ped*
grin	grin*ning*	grin*ned*
hum	hum*ming*	hum*med*

If a verb has two or more syllables, and the last one contains a single short vowel and ends in a consonant, double this final letter, but only if the stress comes on the last syllable:

pre'fer	pre'fer*ring*	pre'fer*red*
ad'mit	ad'mit*ting*	ad'mit*ted*
e'quip	e'quip*ping*	e'quip*ped*

But if the stress is *not* on the last syllable, the final letter is not doubled:

'enter	'enter*ing*	'enter*ed*
'gossip	'gossip*ing*	'gossip*ed*

If the last syllable has a short vowel and ends in **-l**, double the **l**, regardless of where the stress comes:

'equal	'equal*ling*	'equal*led*
re'pel	re'pel*ling*	re'pel*led*

If the verb ends in **-c**, add a **k** before adding **-ing** or **-ed**:

picnic	picnic*king*	picnic*ked*
panic	panic*king*	panic*ked*

If the verb ends in **-e**, you remove the **e** before adding **-ing**. Instead of adding **-ed**, just add **-d**:

stare	staring	stared
bake	baking	baked
issue	issuing	issued
refine	refining	refined

But notice that verbs ending in **-oe**, **-ee** and **-ye** are exceptions to this rule:

agree	agreeing	agreed
dye	dyeing	dyed
hoe	hoeing	hoed
eye	eyeing	eyed

If the verb ends in **-y**, and there is no vowel before the **y**, change the **y** to **i** before adding **-es** or **-ed**:

cry	crying	cries	cried
hurry	hurrying	hurries	hurried

But if a verb has a vowel before the **y**, keep the **y** when you add **-es** and **-ed**:

stay	staying	stays	stayed
play	playing	plays	played

but watch out for these:

lay	laying	laid
pay	paying	paid
say	saying	said

If the verb ends in **-ie**, you change **ie** to **y** before adding **-ing**:

tie	tying	tied
die	dying	died

ADJECTIVES

In general, **-er** and **-est** are added to adjectives to form comparatives and superlatives. There are, however, rules to be observed in certain cases as follows:

If an adjective ends in **-e**, just add **-r** for the comparative and **-st** for the superlative:

white	whiter	whitest
simple	simpler	simplest
free	freer	freest

If the adjective is only one syllable long, with a single short vowel, and ends in a consonant, double this final letter before adding **-er** and **-est**.

| red | red*d*er | red*d*est |
| big | big*g*er | big*g*est |

If an adjective has two syllables and ends in **-y**, you change the **y** to **i** before adding **-er** or **-est**:

| angry | angr*i*er | angr*i*est |
| funny | funn*i*er | funn*i*est |

But note these one-syllable adjectives ending in **-y**:

dry	dr*i*er	dr*i*est
sly	sly*er	sly*est
shy	sh*i*er or shy*er	sh*i*est or shy*est

ADVERBS

Most adverbs are formed by adding **-ly** to the adjective:

foolish	foolish*ly*
strange	strange*ly*
initial	initial*ly*

Note that adjectives ending in **-e** keep the **e** before adding **-ly**, but in the following four cases, it is removed:

true	tru*ly*
due	du*ly*
whole	whol*ly*
eerie	eeri*ly*

If the adjective ends in **-ic**, you add **-ally** to form the adverb:

| basic | basic*ally* |
| economic | economic*ally* |

An exception to this rule is:

| public | public*ly* |

If the adjective ends in **-y**, you change the **y** to **i** before adding **-ly**:

| happy | happi*ly* |
| hungry | hungri*ly* |

If the adjective ends in **-le**, you remove the **e** and add **-y**:

| simple | simply |
| double | doubly |

Adjectives ending in a **-y** that is pronounced [ī], often have two possible adverb forms:

| dry | drily or dryly |
| shy | shily or shyly |

IE OR EI?

A well-known and useful way of remembering this rule is the rhyme *i before e, except after c.*

This means that the order is **ie** except when a **c** comes first – then the order is **ei**. Have a look at these words:

chief	brief	conceit
siege	grief	deceive
achieve	thief	deceit
belief	ceiling	receive
relieve	conceive	receipt

A few common words pronounced with an [ē] sound have *ei* where *ie* would be expected:

seize	neither
weird	protein
either	caffeine
counterfeit	heinous

SINGULAR AND PLURAL

To form a plural noun, it is usually sufficient to add **-s** to the singular noun:

car	cars
house	houses
monkey	monkeys

If the singular form of the noun ends in **-s**, **-ss**, **-x**, **-z**, **-sh**, or **-ch** (when it is pronounced **ch** and not **k**) you form the plural by adding **-es**:

| gas | gases |
| kiss | kisses |

box	boxes
waltz	waltzes
bush	bushes
church	churches

But notice the plural if **-ch** is pronounced **k**. You add only **-s** to form the plural:

| stomach | stomachs |
| monarch | monarchs |

Words ending in a consonant followed by a **-y** usually take **-es** as their plural form, the **y** being changed to **i**.

fly	flies
ally	allies
fairy	fairies
butterfly	butterflies

The plural of nouns that have a vowel before the **y** are simply formed with **-s**.

| boy | boys |
| day | days |

For some nouns ending in **-f** and **-fe** the plurals are formed by changing **-f** or **-fe** to **-ves**:

calf	calves
knife	knives
loaf	loaves
thief	thieves

But there are some exceptions which add only **-s** to form the plural.

belief	beliefs
chief	chiefs
proof	proofs
roof	roofs
safe	safes

For most nouns ending in **-o**, you just add **-s** to form the plural.

piano	pianos
radio	radios
yoyo	yoyos
zoo	zoos

But certain nouns have plurals ending in **-oes**.

potato*es*	hero*es*
tomato*es*	veto*es*
echo*es*	Negro*es*
domino*es*	embargo*es*

Some nouns change their vowels to form the plural.

foot	f*ee*t
goose	g*ee*se
tooth	t*ee*th
man	m*e*n
mouse	m*i*ce

There is also a plural formed by adding **-en**

child	childr*en*
ox	ox*en*

American spelling

Below are some of the common differences between British and American spelling:

British English	American English
-our as in **colour, humour**	**-or** as in **color, humor**
-re as in **centre, theatre, metre**	**-er** as in **center, theater, meter**
-ae- as in **haemoglobin, anaemia**	**-e-** as in **hemoglobin, anemia**
NOTE: There is a growing tendency in British English for the **ae** in such words to become **e** as in **medieval, encyclop(a)edia**.	
-ogue as in **catalogue**	**-og** as in **catalog**
NOTE: Many words of this type can be spelt either **-ogue** or **-og** in American English as in **prologue / prolog, dialogue / dialog**.	
-ll- as in **travelling, equalled**	**-l-** as in **traveling, equaled**
-pp- as in **kidnapped, worshipping**	**-p-** as in **kidnaped, worshiping**
-l- as in **skilful, wilful**	**-ll-** as in **skillful, willful**

Words which may be confused

a
an
aboard
abroad
accept
except
access
excess
acme
acne
ad
add
adapter
adaptor
addition
edition
adverse
averse
advice
advise
aesthetic
ascetic
affect
effect
affluent
effluent
ail
ale
air
heir
aisle
isle
ale
ail
all
awl
allay

alley
allegory
allergy
alley
allay
alliterate
illiterate
allude
elude
allusion
delusion
illusion
altar
alter
alteration
altercation
alternately
alternatively
amateur
amateurish
amend
emend
amiable
amicable
among
between
amoral
immoral
immortal
an
a
angel
angle
annals
annuals
annex
annexe

annuals
annals
ant
aunt
antiquated
antique
arc
ark
arisen
arose
arose
arisen
artist
artiste
ascent
assent
ascetic
aesthetic
assay
essay
assent
ascent
astrology
astronomy
ate
eaten
aunt
ant
aural
oral
averse
adverse
awl
all
axes
axis
bad

bade
bade
bid
bail
bale
bale out
baited
bated
bale
bale out
bail
ball
bawl
ballet
ballot
banns
bans
bare
bear
barn
baron
barren
base
bass
bass
(pl)basses
bated
baited
bath
bathe
baton
batten
bawl
ball
bazaar
bizarre
be

bee
beach
beech
bean
been
being
bear
bare
beat
beaten
beat
beet
beau
bow
became
become
bee
be
beech
beach
been
bean
being
beer
bier
beet
beat
befallen
befell
began
begun
being
bean
been
belief
believe
bell

belle	boast	breach	calve	cereal
bellow	boost	breech	calf	serial
below	bonny	bread	came	chafe
beret	bony	bred	come	chaff
berry	bookie	break	canned	charted
bury	bouquet	brake	could	chartered
berth	boor	breath	cannon	chased
birth	boar	breathe	canon	chaste
beside	bore	bred	can't	cheap
besides	boost	bread	cant	cheep
between	boast	breech	canvas	check
among	bootee	breach	canvass	cheque
bid	booty	bridal	carat	checked
bade	bore	bridle	carrot	chequered
bier	boar	broach	carpal	cheep
beer	boor	brooch	carpel	cheap
bight	bore	broke	cart	cheque
bite	born	broken	kart	check
birth	borne	brooch	cartilage	chilli
berth	borough	broach	cartridge	chilly
bit	burgh	buffet ['bufit]	carton	choir
bitten	bough	buffet	cartoon	quire
bite	bow	['boofā]	cartridge	choose
bight	bound	buoy	cartilage	chose
bizarre	bounded	boy	cash	chosen
bazaar	bouquet	burgh	cache	chord
blew	bookie	borough	cast	cord
blown	bow	bury	caste	chose
blew	beau	beret	cavalier	choose
blue	bow	berry	cavalry	chosen
bloc	bough	but	ceiling	chute
block	boy	butt	sealing	shoot
blond	buoy	buy	cell	cite
blonde	brae	by	sell	sight
blown	bray	bye	cellular	site
blew	brake	cache	cellulose	clothes
blue	break	cash	censor	cloths
blew	brassière	caddie	censure	coarse
boar	brazier	caddy	cent	course
boor	bray	calf	scent	collage
bore	brae	calve	sent	college
board	brazier	callous	centenarian	coma
bored	brassière	callus	centenary	comma

come	correspondent	dear	dough	earthy
came	co-respondent	deer	doily	easterly
comma	cost	decry	dolly	eastern
coma	costed	descry	done	eaten
commissionaire	could	deer	did	ate
commissioner	canned	dear	dough	eclipse
complement	council	delusion	doe	ellipse
compliment	counsel	allusion	draft	economic
complementary	consul	illusion	draught	economical
complimentary				
concert	councillor	dependant	dragon	edition
consort	counsellor	dependent	dragoon	addition
confidant	coup	deprecate	draught	eerie
confidante	coop	depreciate	draft	eyrie
confident	course	descendant	drawn	effect
conscience	coarse	descendent	drew	affect
conscientious	courtesy	descry	drank	effluent
conscious	curtsy	decry	drunk	affluent
consort	creak	desert	drew	elder
concert	creek	dessert	drawn	eldest
consul	crevasse	device	driven	elicit
council	crevice	devise	drove	illicit
counsel	crochet	devolution	drunk	eligible
continual	crotchet	evolution	drank	legible
continuous	cue	dew	dual	ellipse
coop	queue	due	duel	eclipse
coup	curb	Jew	dudgeon	elude
coral	kerb	diary	dungeon	allude
corral	currant	dairy	due	emend
cord	current	did	dew	amend
chord	curtsy	done	Jew	emigrant
co-respondent	courtesy	die	duel	immigrant
correspondent	cygnet	dye	dual	emigration
cornet	signet	died	dully	immigration
coronet	cymbal	dyed	duly	emission
cornflour	symbol	dinghy	dungeon	omission
cornflower	dairy	dingy	dudgeon	emphasis
coronet	diary	disbelief	dye	emphasize
cornet	dam	disbelieve	die	employee
corps	damn	discreet	dyed	employer
corpse	dammed	discrete	died	ensure
corral	damned	discus	dyeing	insure
coral	damn	discuss	dying	entomologist
	dam	doe	earthly	etymologist

envelop	expatiate	fir	four	franc
envelope	extant	fur	foregone	frank
epigram	extinct	fission	forgone	freeze
epitaph	eyrie	fissure	foresaw	frieze
epithet	eerie	flair	foreseen	froze
ere	faerie	flare	foreword	frozen
err	fairy	flammable	forward	funeral
erotic	fain	inflammable	forgave	funereal
erratic	feign	flare	forgiven	fur
err	faint	flair	forgone	fir
ere	feint	flea	foregone	
erratic	fair	flee	forgone	gabble
erotic	fare	flew	forwent	gable
escapement	fairy	flu	forgot	gaff
escarpment	faerie	flue	forgotten	gaffe
essay	fallen	flew	forsaken	gait
assay	fell	flown	forsook	gate
etymologist	felled	flocks	forswore	galleon
entomologist	fare	phlox	forsworn	gallon
evolution	fair	floe	fort	gamble
devolution	fate	flow	forte	gambol
ewe	fête	flour	forty	gaol
yew	faun	flower	forth	goal
you	fawn	floury	fourth	gate
except	feat	flowery	forty	gait
accept	feet	flow	fort	gave
excess	feign	floe	forte	given
access	fain	flower	forward	genie
executioner	feint	flour	foreword	genius
executor	faint	flowery	forwent	genus
exercise	fell	floury	forgone	genteel
exorcise	fallen	flown	foul	gentile
expand	felled	flew	fowl	gentle
expend	ferment	flu	found	genus
expansive	foment	flue	founded	genie
expensive	fête	flew	fount	genius
expatiate	fate	foment	font	gild
expiate	fiancé	ferment	four	guild
expend	fiancée	font	fore	gilt
expand	filed	fount	fourth	guilt
expensive	filled	forbade	forth	given
expansive	final	forbidden	fowl	gave
expiate	finale	fore	foul	glacier
				glazier

goal	halo	hoarse	immortality	due
gaol	halve	horse	impetuous	jib
gone	half	hole	impetus	jibe
went	hangar	whole	impracticable	judicial
gorilla	hanger	honorary	impractical	judicious
guerrilla	hanged	honourable	in	junction
gourmand	hung	hoop	inn	juncture
gourmet	hanger	whoop	inapt	kart
gradation	hangar	hoped	inept	cart
graduation	hare	hopped	incredible	kerb
grate	hair	horde	incredulous	curb
great	hart	hoard	indigenous	key
grew	heart	horse	indigent	quay
grown	heal	hoarse	industrial	knave
grief	heel	hue	industrious	nave
grieve	hear	hew	ineligible	knead
grill	here	human	illegible	kneed
grille	heart	humane	inept	need
griped	hart	humiliation	inapt	knew
gripped	heel	humility	inflammable	known
grisly	heal	hung	flammable	knew
gristly	heir	hanged	ingenious	new
grizzly	air	hymn	ingenuous	knight
grope	here	him	inhuman	night
group	hear	idle	inhumane	knightly
ground	heron	idol	inn	nightly
grounded	herring	illegible	in	knit
grown	hew	ineligible	insure	nit
grew	hue	illicit	ensure	knot
guerrilla	hewed	elicit	intelligent	not
gorilla	hewn	illiterate	intelligible	knotty
guild	hid	alliterate	interment	naughty
gild	hidden	illusion	internment	know
guilt	higher	allusion	invertebrate	no
gilt	hire	delusion	inveterate	known
hail	him	immigrant	isle	knew
hale	hymn	emigrant	aisle	lade
hair	hire	immigration	it's	laid
hare	higher	emigration	its	lay
half	hoar	immoral	jam	lied
halve	whore	amoral	jamb	lain
hallo	hoard	immortal	Jew	lane
hallow	horde	immorality	dew	lair

layer	licence	lumbar	matt	might
lama	license	lumber	mayor	moat
llama	lied	lute	mare	mote
lane	lade	loot	maze	modal
lain	laid	lyre	maize	model
laterally	lay	liar	mean	module
latterly	lightening	macaroni	mien	momentary
lath	lightning	macaroon	meat	momentous
lathe	lineament	made	meet	momentum
latterly	liniment	maid	mete out	moose
laterally	liqueur	magnate	medal	mouse
lay	liquor	magnet	meddle	mousse
lade	literal	maid	mediate	moped
laid	literary	made	meditate	mopped
lied	literate	mail	meet	moral
layer	llama	male	meat	morale
lair	lama	main	mete out	morality
lea	load	mane	merino	mortality
lee	lode	maize	marina	mote
lead	loan	maze	metal	moat
led	lone	male	mettle	motif
leak	loath	mail	mete out	motive
leek	loathe	mane	meat	mouse
led	local	main	meet	moose
lead	locale	maniac	meter	mousse
lee	lode	manic	metre	mucous
lea	load	manner	mettle	mucus
leek	lone	manor	metal	multiple
leak	loan	mare	mews	multiply
legible	looped	mayor	muse	muscle
eligible	loped	marina	mien	mussel
lemming	lopped	merino	mean	muse
lemon	loose	marshal	might	mews
leopard	lose	martial	mite	mussel
leper	loot	marten	miner	muscle
lessen	lute	martin	minor	mystic
lesson	loped	martial	minister	mystique
liable	lopped	marshal	minster	naught
libel	looped	martin	missal	nought
liar	lose	marten	missile	naughty
lyre	loose	mask	mistaken	knotty
libel	loth	masque	mistook	naval
liable	loathe	mat	mite	navel

nave	official	pare	personal	poplar
knave	officious	pear	personnel	popular
navel	omission	pair	petrel	pore
naval	emission	parr	petrol	pour
navvy	oral	par	pheasant	pored
navy	aural	passed	peasant	poured
nay	ore	past	phlox	poser
née	oar	pastel	flocks	poseur
neigh	organism	pastille	piazza	pour
need	orgasm	pate	pizza	pore
knead	outdid	pâté	piece	poured
kneed	outdone	patty	peace	pored
negligent	overcame	peace	pier	practicable
negligible	overcome	piece	peer	practical
neigh	overdid	peak	pined	practice
nay	overdone	peek	pinned	practise
née	overran	pique	piped	pray
net	overrun	peal	pipped	prey
nett	overtaken	peel	pique	precede
new	overtook	pear	peak	proceed
knew	overthrew	pair	peek	premier
night	overthrown	pare	pistil	première
knight	packed	pearl	pistol	prerequisite
nightly	pact	purl	pizza	perquisite
knightly	pail	peasant	piazza	prey
nit	pale	pheasant	place	pray
knit	pain	pedal	plaice	price
no	pane	peddle	plain	prise
know	pair	peek	plane	prize
northerly	pare	peak	plaintiff	principal
northern	pear	pique	plaintive	principle
not	palate	peel	plait	prise
knot	palette	peal	plate	price
nougat	pallet	peer	plane	prize
nugget	pale	pier	plain	private
nought	pail	pence	plate	privet
naught	palette	pennies	plait	prize
nugget	palate	pendant	plum	prise
nougat	pallet	pendent	plumb	price
oar	pane	pennies	politic	proceed
ore	pain	pence	political	precede
of	par	perquisite	pool	profit
off	parr	prerequisite	pull	prophet

program	reign	reproof	ruff	sculpture
programme	rein	reprove	rout	sea
proof	raise	respectful	route	see
prove	raze	respective	row	
property	rampant	rest	roe	sealing
propriety	rampart	wrest	rowed	ceiling
prophecy	ran	retch	road	seam
prophesy	run	wretch	rode	seem
prophet	rang	review	ruff	sear
profit	ringed	revue	rough	seer
propriety	rung	rhyme	run	sere
property	rap	rime	ran	
prostate	wrap	ridden	rung	secret
prostrate	raped	rode	wrung	secrete
prove	rapped	right	rye	see
proof	rapped	rite	wry	sea
pull	rapt	write	sail	seem
pool	wrapped	rime	sale	seam
purl	rated	rhyme	salon	seen
pearl	ratted	ring	saloon	scene
put	raze	wring	sang	seer
putt	raise	ringed	sung	sear
quash	read	rang	sank	sere
squash	red	rung	sunk	sell
quay	read	risen	sunken	cell
key	reed	rose	saviour	
queue	real	rite	savour	sensual
cue	reel	right	saw	sensuous
quiet	red	write	seen	
quite	read	road	sawed	sent
quire	reed	rode	sawn	cent
choir	read	rowed	scared	scent
quite	reel	rode	scarred	septic
quiet	real	ridden	scene	sceptic
racket	refuge	roe	seen	sere
racquet	refugee	row	scent	sear
radar	regal	rôle	cent	seer
raider	regale	roll	sent	serial
raged	reign	rose	sceptic	cereal
ragged	rain	risen	septic	series
raider	rein	rote	scraped	serious
radar	relief	wrote	scrapped	sew
rain	relieve	rough	sculptor	so
				sow
				sewed

sewn	cite	southerly	statue	stile
sewer	sight	southern	statute	
sower			staunch	suede
	skies	sow	stanch	swede
sewn	skis	sew		
sewed		so	stayed	suit
sewn	slain		staid	soot
sown	slew	sowed		
		sown	steak	suite
sextant	slated		stake	sweet
sexton	slatted	sower		
		sewer	steal	sum
shaken	slay		steel	some
shook	sleigh	sown		
	slew	sewn	step	summary
shear	slain		steppe	summery
sheer	sloe	spared		
	slow	sparred	stile	sun
sheared			style	son
sheered	sloped	speciality		
shorn	slopped	specialty	stimulant	sundae
	slow		stimulus	Sunday
shelf	sloe	species		
shelve		specious	stock	sung
	smelled		stalk	sang
shoe	smelt	sped		
shoo		speeded	stocked	sunk
	sniped		stoked	sank
shook	snipped	spoke		
shaken		spoken	storey	sunken
	so		story	
shoot	sew	sprang		super
chute	sow	sprung	straight	supper
			strait	
shorn	soar	squash		surplice
sheared	sore	quash	straightened	surplus
sheered			straitened	
	sociable	staid		swam
showed	social	stayed	stratum	swum
shown			stratus	
	solder	stair		swede
shrank	soldier	stare	strewed	suede
shrunk		stake	strewn	
	sole	steak		sweet
sight	soul		strife	suite
cite		stalk	strive	
site	some	stock		swelled
	sum	stanch	striped	swollen
signet		staunch	stripped	
cygnet	son			swingeing
	sun	stank	strive	swinging
silicon		stunk	strife	
silicone	soot			swollen
	suit	stare	striven	swelled
singeing		stair	strove	
singing	sore			swore
	soar	stared	stunk	sworn
sinuous		starred	stank	
sinus	soul			swum
	sole	stationary	sty	swam
site		stationery	stye	
			style	symbol
				cymbal
				tacks

tax	they're	tome	unwanted	waif
tail	thorough	ton	unwonted	waive
tale	through	tonne	urban	waver
taken	thrash	tun	urbane	wafer
took	thresh	too	vacation	way
tale	threw	to	vocation	weigh
tail	through	two	vain	weak
taped	threw	took	vane	week
tapped	thrown	taken	vein	wear
taper	throes	topi	vale	ware
tapir	throws	toupee	veil	weekly
tapped	throne	tore	venal	weakly
taped	thrown	torn	venial	weigh
tare	through	tortuous	veracity	way
tear	thorough	torturous	voracity	went
taught	through	tow	vertex	gone
taut	threw	toe	vortex	westerly
tax	thrown	trait	vigilant	western
tacks	threw	tray	vigilante	wet
tea	thrown	treaties	vocation	whet
tee	throne	treatise	vacation	whit
team	throws	trod	voracity	wit
teem	throes	trodden	veracity	whole
tear	thyme	troop	vortex	hole
tare	time	troupe	vertex	whoop
tear	tic	tun	wafer	hoop
tier	tick	ton	waver	whore
tee	tier	tonne	waged	hoar
tea	tear	turban	wagged	willed
teem	tiled	turbine	waif	would
team	tilled	two	waive	winded
teeth	timber	to	wave	wound
teethe	timbre	too	waist	wit
temporal	time	tycoon	waste	whit
temporary	thyme	typhoon	want	withdrawn
tendon	tire	tyre	wont	withdrew
tenon	tyre	tire	warden	wittily
tenor	to	unaware	warder	wittingly
tenure	too	unawares	ware	woe
testimonial	two	unconscionable	wear	woo
testimony	toe	unconscious	waste	woke
their	tow	undid	waist	woken
there	tomb	undone	wave	wont

want	wooed	wreck	write	wry
woo	wove	wreath	right	rye
woe	woven	wreathe	rite	
wore	wrap	wrest		yew
worn	rap	rest	wrote	ewe
would	wrapped		rote	you
willed	rapped	wretch		
would	rapt	retch	wrote	yoke
wood	wreak		written	yolk
		wring	wrung	yore
		ring	rung	your